DUMBARTON CASTLE

DUMBARTON CASTLE

I. M. M. MacPhail

JOHN DONALD PUBLISHERS LTD.
EDINBURGH

To Edith

Printed in Great Britain by Bell & Bain Ltd., Glasgow.
Phototypesetting by Burns & Harris Ltd., Dundee

Acknowledgements

I have been indebted to a great many people in the production of this book and it is a pleasure to express my gratitude to them all, in particular to Admiral Sir Angus Cunninghame Graham for his constant encouragement over the years; to Sir Iain Moncreiffe of that Ilk for making available the papers of the late Harry Pirie-Gordon; to Sir Marc Noble for permission to peruse the papers of his ancestor, Captain John Noble; to the staffs of the Scottish Record Office, the National Library of Scotland, the Public Record Office, the House of Lords Record Office, the Scottish United Services Museum, the Strathclyde Regional Archives, Glasgow University Library, and Strathclyde University Library for facilitating my researches; to Mr Arthur F. Jones for the maps; to Mr Michael Taylor, librarian, Dumbarton Public Library, for dealing so competently and cheerfully with my numerous requests; to Mrs Grace Lawrie for typing from a difficult manuscript; and to Messrs Hiram Walker & Sons (Scotland) Limited for a generous grant towards publication.

Acknowledgements are due to the following for permission to reproduce illustrations:- Professor Leslie Alcock (no. 1); the Scottish National Portrait Gallery (nos. 2, 3, 4, 7, 8, 9); the Scottish United Services Museum, Edinburgh Castle (nos. 16, 17, 18, 19); the Trustees of the National Library of Scotland (no. 15); the Controller of H.M. Stationery Office (no. 14, crown copyright, S.R.O., E 28/276/4, and no. 14, crown copyright, P.R.O., MPF 244); the *Glasgow Herald* (nos. 24, 25); and Owenslaw, Dumbarton (no. 36).

I. M. M. MacPhail, 1979.

Contents

1

Earliest Times

Prehistory

Dumbarton Rock stands at the confluence of the river Leven and the river Clyde and rises steeply, in some places precipitously, from the surrounding alluvial plain. It is a rock divided into two by a large central gully running roughly north and south, with a rugged western peak and an eastern peak with a broad, fairly level summit. The story of Dumbarton Rock goes back a long way, long before human occupation. Geologists tell us that millions of years ago there was a great deal of volcanic activity in the area and that when the volcanoes became extinct, the vents filled up with molten rock basalt, which during the Ice Ages that followed proved more resistant to erosion than the surrounding rocks. A bore-hole made at Dumbarton Distillery, half a mile from the Castle Rock, showed that the sediment of clay, sands and gravel left by the glaciers of about 40,000 years ago was 243 feet thick, which means that Dumbarton Rock, now about 240 feet high, stood at one time nearly 500 feet above the valley floor. Its appearance today resembles that of the other Scottish royal fortresses, Edinburgh and Stirling, with the difference that Dumbarton Rock rises more precipitously from a flat alluvial plain.[1]

When Dumbarton Rock was first occupied no one can tell. Not very far distant from it are hill-forts which have been reckoned by archaeologists to have been occupied before the Christian era, one of them only a mile away at Dumbuie, also a volcanic plug. Others, situated within two or three miles from Dumbarton Rock and occupied during what is known as the Iron Age, are Sheep Hill near Bowling and Carman Hill above Renton. The latter hill-fort was discovered by aerial photography and has not yet been made the subject of excavation but its features conform to a type found in the Iron Age. Unlike Dumbuie, Sheep Hill and Carman Hill, Dumbarton Rock was occupied continuously as a fortress for hundreds of years and traces of earlier, prehistoric settlements have been all but obliterated by building activities of the Middle Ages and modern times. Excavations in recent years have been attempted, however, and have revealed some interesting relics from the Dark Age.[2]

Dark Age Legends

The first written records of Scotland's past are connected with the Roman occupation of the first and second centuries A.D. Supplemented by the results of archaeological research, these writings often provide us with more factual information than is to be gained about the centuries succeeding the Roman withdrawal, the Dark Age. Much of the history of Dumbarton Castle Rock in older accounts of the Dark Age may be described as myth or legend; but myths and legends are often based on actual events and it would be wrong to dismiss them out of hand. Joseph Irving, the first county historian, writing over a hundred years ago, like most other contemporary historians, included many of them, sometimes with a word of caution, sometimes with picturesque details added from his imagination.

The Antonine Wall, which the Roman soldiers built from the Forth to the Clyde in 142-143 A.D., had as its western terminal a fort at Kilpatrick, five miles from Dumbarton. It is not surprising that experts on the history of Roman Britain have considered it possible that the military way, which ran parallel with the rampart of the Antonine Wall, was continued to Dumbarton. The main reason for assuming such an extension was that the river Clyde was then so shallow at Dumbuck, a mile upstream from Dumbarton Rock, that it could be forded at low tide, and thus navigation of the Clyde by Roman ships conveying supplies to the garrisons on the Antonine Wall would be difficult, if not impossible. Although the author of the most recent book on the Antonine Wall considers that the military way was continued beyond Kilpatrick, 'probably to a harbour at or below Dumbarton', there has not yet been any confirmation of her theory from archaeological research.[3] The statement by Joseph Irving and older historians that there was a Roman naval station called Theodosia at Dumbarton in the latter part of the fourth century, however, is one which has no archaeological evidence to support it, for it is derived not from any genuine source but from the fertile imagination of Charles Bertram, the literary forger. Bertram, an English teacher in Copenhagen, produced in 1758 a forged history of Britain in Roman and post-Roman times, which was accepted by all historians for a century. The forgery was exposed independently by two scholars in the late 1860's; but the errors of Bertram continued to be found in many histories down to this century.[4]

Writing about the same time as Charles Bertram was a Scotsman whose work was denounced as a forgery during his own lifetime. He was James MacPherson, who published what he claimed to be trans-lations from ancient Gaelic poems composed by a bard, Ossian, in the heroic age of Irish legend. One of MacPherson's Ossianic poems is a lament by the mighty Irish hero, Fingal, about Dumbarton Rock, which MacPherson christened 'Balclutha'. 'I have seen the walls of Balclutha but they were desolate. . . The thistle shook its lonely head; the moss whistled to the wind.' Although his critics were able to expose MacPherson's claim that his poems were genuine translations, Celtic scholars since his time have been able to show that there existed a considerable corpus of Ossianic or ancient Gaelic poems, which had been preserved by oral tradition through the centuries, but none has been found which could be connected with Dumbarton Rock.[5]

The much celebrated British hero of the Dark Age, Arthur, has also been associated with Dumbarton Rock, as with many other places in the west of Britain. Arthur (or the historical person whom we today call Arthur) fought many battles in different parts of Britain, and it is possible that at least one of them was fought not far from Dumbarton, in Glen Douglas on Lochlomondside. On the basis of a mis-reading of a medieval exchequer roll, George Chalmers, whose *Caledonia* was published in 1807, suggested that Dumbarton Castle was also known as 'Arthur's Castle' in the Middle Ages, a claim that has been repeated by many writers since 1807. In a seventeenth-century account, based on centuries-old tradition, of the genealogy of the Campbells, the author traces their descent from 'King Arthur of the round table', whose son, Smerevie Mor, was born in Dumbarton, 'on the south side thereof, in a place called the redd hall or in Irish Tour in Talla Dherig, that is, the tower of the redd hall'. The name, 'the Red Hall', occurs in other Gaelic folk tales as that of Arthur's residence. Although there is no possibility of proving the truth or falsity of the Campbell claim (similar claims of royal or mythical descent are not uncommon in the genealogies of clans and noble families), 'the Tower of the Red Hall' has a historical connection with Dumbarton Rock. One of the buildings of the medieval castle in Dumbarton Rock was the Red Tower, which was repaired in 1460. An old rhyme about the Galbraiths, one of the oldest British names in south-west Scotland, also mentions the Red Hall:

> Bhreatunnach o'n Talla Dhearg
> Uaisle 'shliochd Albainn do shloinne.

(Briton of the Red Hall, your name's the noblest race in Scotland.)
Perhaps all that we can accept with any confidence from these scraps of information is the existence of a red hall or tower at Dumbarton Rock in the early Middle Ages.[6]

Another legend associated with Dumbarton Castle Rock relates to the patron saint of Ireland, Patrick, who was said to have been born there. The earliest reference to Dumbarton as St Patrick's birthplace dates only from the eleventh century and is contained in a marginal gloss on a manuscript copy of a hymn to St Patrick. The medieval chapel in Dumbarton Castle was actually dedicated to St Patrick; and of the five medieval parish churches in Scotland with a similar dedication, the one nearest Dumbarton, at Kilpatrick, attracted a steady stream of pilgrims to the shrine of St Patrick from the twelfth century. By the sixteenth century, the tradition that St Patrick was born at Dumbarton Rock was commonly accepted.[7] The question of the location of *Bannavem taburniae* (the name which St Patrick himself gave to his birthplace in his *Confession*) has been debated by Dark Age specialists for almost a century but none has considered Dumbarton as even a remote possibility. St Patrick, in his *Confession*, stated that his father, a decurion (a Romano-British official) owned a *villa* or estate on which several workers were employed and that his father was a deacon and his grandfather a priest in the Christian church. As St Patrick's most recent biographer has pointed out, there is no evidence whatever that Roman villas ever existed in the area which later became the kingdom of Strathclyde, of which Dumbarton was the 'capital'. Most authorities have favoured regions much farther south for the saint's birthplace — Cumbria, South Wales, or south-west England.[8]

Rock of the Clyde

As has already been mentioned, the castle rock of Dumbarton was the seat of the British kings whose realm in course of time extended from the north end of Loch Lomond as far south as Morecambe Bay, north of Lancaster. Before 872, when mention is first made of Strathclyde, the kings were known as the kings of Alocluade, Alochluaithe, Ailecluithe, Altclut, Alclut, a British name meaning 'rock of the Clyde'. The last two forms are from Welsh sources and are presumably closer to the original, as the language of the Britons of Strathclyde was similar to that spoken in Wales.[9] The first king of Alclut of whom we have any detailed information was Riderch, who lived in the time of St Columba and St Kentigern at the end of the sixth century. In Adamnan's life of St Columba, written c. 700, Riderch is named as the king of *Petra Cloithe*, a Latin form of Alclut, 'the rock of the Clyde'. In a much later life of St. Kentigern, who was the patron saint of Glasgow, there are many references to Riderch, who was said to have lived sometimes at Partick, twelve miles up the river Clyde from Dumbarton and now part of Glasgow.[10]

North of the kingdom of Britons in Strathclyde was the kingdom of Dál Riata, peopled by the Gaelic-speaking Scots, who had come over from Ireland. It was these Scots who were later to christen the castle rock on the Clyde 'Dun Breatann', 'the fortress of the Britons', a name which in time became Dumbarton. Away to the north of Loch Lomond in Glen Falloch is a rock still known as Clach nam Breatuinn, 'the stone of the Britons', which presumably marked the boundary between the Britons and the Scots.[11] Wars between the Scots and their southern neighbours, the Britons, were intermittent for centuries. In 704 there was a great slaughter of the Britons by the Scots at a place in the Vale of Leven between Alclut and Loch Lomond; and seven years later the tables were turned at a place called Lorg-eclet, hitherto unidentified. In 717, the two armies met again, this time 'at the stone called Minuirc' and once again the Britons met with defeat.[12]

To the north-east of Strathclyde lay the kingdom of the Picts, for long the most powerful race in North Britain. In the middle of the eighth century, Oengus or Angus Mac Fergus, who has been called a 'Pictish Napoleon', overthrew his rivals within Pictland and then turned on his neighbours, the Scots of Dál Riata, defeating them in 741, and the Britons of Strathclyde, whom he met in battle in 744. Fighting between the Picts and Britons occurred again in 750, when the Britons were victorious at Mugdock (near the modern Milngavie), the brother of the Pictish king being among the slain. During all this warring between the Britons and their neighbours, there is no mention of Alclut; but in 756, Angus, thirsting to avenge the defeat at Mugdock and accompanied by a force of Angles from Northumbria, led his army to the town of Alclut and forced the Britons to accept terms. This happened on the first day of August but nine days later, on the homeward journey from Alclut, the Anglian army was overwhelmed at a place called Ovania.[13]

During the century which followed, the annals and chronicles do not mention battles between the Britons and their neighbours, but in 780 the Annals of Ulster record 'combustio Alocluade' (the burning of Alclut) on the first day of January. There is no reference to an enemy having destroyed the fortress by fire and it may be assumed that the fire was accidental. When Professor Alcock of Glasgow University was carrying out excavation of the eastern peak of the castle rock in 1975, he came upon evidence of a tremendous conflagration having occurred. Parts of the rock, where a timber-and-rubble rampart had been built, were found to have been subjected to such intense heat that they were vitrified. The possibility of the vitrification having taken place at the time of the great fire of 780 is obvious; but Professor Alcock, because of certain finds among the debris, considers that a more probable occasion was when Norsemen from Dublin and York captured the castle rock almost a century later.[14]

It was in the year 870 that the Norse king of Dublin, Olaf the White, who had established himself there in 853, decided on an expedition to plunder the kingdom of the Britons in Strathclyde. He set off with a large fleet from Dublin and, sailing up the Firth of Clyde, laid siege to Alclut. He was joined by another Viking ruler, Ivar Beinlaus ('cripple' or 'one-legged'), who came north from York, which he had seized in 867. The garrison of Alclut held out for four months but at length was compelled to surrender, as the well on the rock had dried up ('miraculously', according to one annal, or by the Norsemen 'wonderfully' drawing off the water, according to another). The citadel was destroyed and the kingdom of the Britons lay prostrate before the invaders, who remained in Strathclyde over the winter, sailing back to Dublin with a fleet of two hundred ships laden with slaves and booty. The king of Strathclyde was killed shortly afterwards and the kingdom for a time passed under the control of neighbouring kings. After these disasters, Alclut disappears from the annals and chronicles and when it reappears in the thirteenth century it is with a new name, Dunbritan, which is a form of the Gaelic *Dun Breatann*, 'the fortress of the Britons'.[15]

In 1018, the king of Strathclyde was Owen the Bald, who was the ally of Malcolm II, ruler of the united kingdom of Scots and Picts, at the battle of Carham-on-Tweed, where they defeated a Northumbrian army. Owen seems to have been the last king of an independent Strathclyde. Some time after the battle of Carham-on-Tweed, Duncan, grandson of Malcolm II, became king of the Cumbrians (another name for the Britons) of Strathclyde; and when in 1034 Duncan succeeded his grandfather as king of Scotland, Strathclyde became merged in the united kingdom of the Scots.

Excavations

About the appearance of Alclut in the Dark Age we know very little. In the eighth century Bede, the English historian, described it as *civitas Brettonum munitissima*, 'the very well fortified city of the Britons'. The natural features of Alclut were similar to those of other Dark Age strongholds — Dunadd in Dál Riata, Dundurn in Pictland, Bamburgh in Northumbria. Nature had endowed the 'Rock of the Clyde' with a strength probably unmatched elsewhere; but Bede's word, *munitissima*, would indicate that to the natural defences provided by precipitous cliffs the hand of man had added fortifications. When a planned programme was begun by Professor Alcock in 1974, the broad summit of the eastern peak was the first object of investigation. It bore a striking resemblance to what is known as the citadel of Dunadd, the fortress of the Scottish kings of Dál Riata. But painstaking excavation revealed that the summit had been artificially levelled, probably in the seventeenth century, and the prospect of establishing the outline of a Dark Age or prehistoric fort on the eastern summit seemed hopeless.

The excavations of the following year, 1975, were more rewarding. It was decided to concentrate on a part of the rock unlikely to have been interfered with by building activities in medieval or modern times — a terrace outside the modern castle rampart, overlooking an almost sheer precipice on the eastern or landward side. Under debris of the last war, when the eastern summit was occupied by an anti-aircraft battery, the young archaeologists assisting Professor Alcock began to find relics of medieval warfare — spearheads, arrows, fragments of a coat of mail, and, in addition, a hoard of silver pennies of Edward I and Edward II of England, that is, of the period of the War of Independence in the early fourteenth century. Lower down, in what was really a rubbish heap, were sherds of pottery and glass dating from

the fifth to the eighth centuries. They also found pieces of amphorae —
wine jars from the eastern Mediterranean — of the same period.

All these finds merely confirmed what was already known from
literary sources — that the rock was the seat of kings in the Dark Age
and later. But there was a more important discovery still to be made.
As the digging went deeper, fire-reddened stones, some of them
vitrified, were found and gradually it became obvious that what
Professor Alcock and his team had uncovered was a timber-and-rubble
rampart which had gone on fire and had burned so fiercely that the
stones and the rock itself had been vitrified. This rampart, which,
according to radio-carbon dating, was probably constructed not earlier
than 600 A.D., had been strategically sited so as to command the only
approach by land to the rock fortress. It has been mentioned earlier
that the great conflagration which caused the vitrification may have
occurred in the year 780. But Professor Alcock has suggested as a more
likely occasion the end of the successful siege by the Norsemen in 870,
for in the debris were found a sword pommel of a type similar to that
used in western Ireland at that period and fragments of a glass bangle
set in a lead matrix, similar to a type used by the Vikings.[16]

The sum total of information gathered from the excavations of 1974
and 1975 at Dumbarton Rock may not seem very impressive in
comparison with that gained by excavations of sites unoccupied for
over a thousand years, but it supplements in a fascinating way the
meagre details provided by the Dark Age annals and chronicles.

2

The Middle Ages

The 'New Castle' of Dumbarton

The first reference to Dumbarton Castle in the Middle Ages is contained in the charter of Alexander II, founding a burgh 'at my new castle at Dumbarton' in July, 1222.[1] A month earlier, Alexander had led an expedition against the men of Argyll, and the creation of a new burgh at Dumbarton was designed to encourage trading and peaceful ways of living on the borders of the unruly Highland zone, a policy which he also pursued in founding a burgh at Dingwall a few years later in 1227. The association of the king's castle and the king's burgh was not unusual in Scotland, e.g. at Edinburgh, Stirling, Berwick, Inverness, Banff, Forres and other places, and in the case of Dumbarton Castle and the burgh of Dumbarton, it was part of a deliberate policy of extending royal control in the west of Scotland.[2]

Dumbarton Rock was situated in the middle of the earldom of Lennox and was considered as part of the earldom until Alexander II's reign. It is significant that in Alexander's charter of 1238 to Maldouen, third Earl of Lennox, the latter was confirmed in possession of all the lands held by his father except for the castle of Dumbarton and the lands granted to the burgh of Dumbarton since its foundation in 1222.[3] The acquisition or annexation of the Castle Rock by the king was almost certainly connected with the setting up of the office of sheriff of Dumbarton, through which control over the district could be exercised by the central government. The sheriffs were the king's administrative officers, representing and responsible to the king and his council, in the various parts of the kingdom; and the extent and number of sheriffdoms, which first came into existence in the eastern lowlands in the twelfth century, marked the extent of the king's power.[4] From the king's castle, the sheriff (*vicecomes*) controlled the area of the sheriffdom (*vicecomitatus*), being responsible for military, financial, administrative and judicial functions of government in the sheriffdom. Although we have no mention of Dumbarton Castle at the time of the expedition of King Haakon of Norway to Scotland in 1263, we know that in that year the sheriff of Inverness strengthened the fortifications of Inverness Castle, the sheriff of Dumfries carried out repairs on Dumfries Castle, and the sheriffs of Stirling and Ayr both increased the garrisons of their castles.[5] The sheriffs were also responsible for collecting the king's revenues such as rents, feudal dues and customs, rendering their accounts personally or by a deputy at the royal exchequer, and they also officiated in cases which came before the sheriff's court. Today, the Scottish sheriff's duties are restricted to judicial and minor administrative functions.

We know little of the early history of the medieval burgh and castle. To encourage merchants to settle in the newly-created burghs, the Scottish kings made provision in their charters for newcomers to enjoy a rent-free period, generally one year, but in the case of the burgh of Dumbarton the period was extended to five years as a special incentive. (In Dingwall, founded soon after Dumbarton and also on the verge of the Highlands, the rent-free period was ten years.)[6] Much of the trade in Scotland in the thirteenth century was in the hands of foreign immigrants — Flemish, English, Norman. None of the first Dumbarton burgesses of whom we have record — Warin, Baldric, Clement, William Fleming — bore a Scottish or even an English name.[7] The burgesses were given the right to hold a weekly market on Wednesdays and a monopoly of trade over a wide area. This trade-precinct was more or less equivalent to the area of the sheriffdom but extended farther to the west, where no other burgh existed, and not so far to the east, where there were three other burghs, Glasgow, Rutherglen and Kirkintilloch. The burgesses' rents were at first collected by the sheriff, but later the bailies paid the rents or ferme of the burgh direct to the royal exchequer.

The sheriffdom of Dumbarton in the early Middle Ages was of much greater extent than the modern Dumbartonshire, as it contained all the area of the modern shire less the detached portion but, in addition, several parishes of the modern Stirlingshire. In the fourteenth century, the barony of Kirkintilloch, which was in the sheriffdom of Stirling, belonged to the Flemings of Biggar, two of whom held the office of sheriff of Dumbarton; and an exchange was effected with the sheriff of

Stirling whereby Kirkintilloch became part of the sheriffdom of Dumbarton and in return six parishes — Fintry, Campsie, Drymen, Balfron, Buchanan (then called Inchcaillioch) and Strathblane — became part of the sheriffdom of Stirling. Despite attempts in the sixteenth and seventeenth century to revert to the old boundaries, the parishes still remain in Stirlingshire.[8]

Early Keepers

The early sheriffs of Dumbarton were important magnates, many of them English or Anglo-French in origin. The first sheriff of Dumbarton known to us was William Bisset, whose family, of English descent, was one of the most powerful in Scotland in the early thirteenth century but whose ambitions led to its downfall in Alexander III's reign. William Bisset is on record as sheriff in 1237, when a royal precept was issued for the construction of a lade to the mill-dam of Dumbarton.[9] Earlier, in 1224, he had witnessed a charter of confirmation of the grant of half a fish-yair in the river Leven to the monks of Paisley Abbey, but whether he was then sheriff of Dumbarton is unknown.[10]

In 1264-65 the sheriff of Dumbarton was William, Earl of Mar.[11] Mar, who was of the old Celtic family of Mar, was one of the most important men in the kingdom, holding the office of royal chamberlain at different times. In May, 1264, he led a punitive expedition against the islands of the west, whose lords such as Angus MacDonald of Islay and Murchadh of Kintyre had taken part in the Norse raid in 1263, when they dragged some of their galleys from Loch Long across the narrow isthmus at Arrochar over to Loch Lomond, spreading devastation around Loch Lomond and penetrating far into the surrounding countryside in their plundering. It is unlikely that the Islesmen and the Norsemen sailed down the Leven, as some historians have suggested. For one thing, Dumbarton Castle guarded the outlet to the Clyde, and for another, according to the saga, their galleys were delayed by storms in Loch Long for some days before re-joining Haakon's fleet. Mar's western expedition of 1264 was successful: Angus of Islay made submission, his son being brought back with his nurse to Ayr as a hostage, and other chiefs followed suit by submitting.[12]

Other early sheriffs of Dumbarton and keepers of Dumbarton Castle were Walter, Earl of Menteith, on record as sheriff in 1271; Duncan, Earl of Fife, sheriff in 1288; and Sir James the Steward, sheriff in

1291.[13] It was hardly to be expected that these nobles resided for more than brief periods at the castles of their sheriffdoms. Indeed, in 1291, twenty-two royal castles were in the hands of fourteen nobles, Sir James the Steward holding both Dumbarton and Ayr castles, and the Earl of Buchan having charge of four.[14] Important magnates such as these appointed deputies to perform the duties of sheriff and keeper of the king's castle. In 1288, the account of the sheriff of Dumbarton, the Earl of Fife, was rendered at the royal exchequer by his deputy, William Fleming, constable of the castle.[15] It is worthy of notice that none of the sheriffs of Dumbarton recorded in this early period was an Earl of Lennox. It was not until the next century that Robert Bruce, in return for the loyal support he had received from Malcolm, Earl of Lennox, during the darkest days of his struggle against the English, granted to the Earl and his successors the hereditary sheriffship of Dumbarton and the keepership of Dumbarton Castle, having already given to him the hereditary sheriffship of Clackmannan some years before.

We have no detailed record of the castle garrison at this period but a Henry of Liberton, clerk to the constable of Dumbarton (un-named), acted as assessor at an inquiry held by the sheriff of Dumbarton in 1263; and Adam, chaplain of the castle of Dumbarton, was witness to the assessor's findings at another inquiry in 1271.[16] Garrison duty or ward at the royal castles was a duty imposed on military tenants of the king and presumably it was from the baronies of the Lennox that most of the garrison of Dumbarton Castle were drawn.[17]

Edward I of England

The death in 1290 of Margaret, Maid of Norway, left the succession to the Scottish throne uncertain, and Edward I of England was not slow to avail himself of the opportunity to establish his claim to be overlord of Scotland. For the next fifteen years and more, as the English control over Scotland increased or diminished, there were frequent changes in the keepership of Dumbarton Castle. Invited to arbitrate between the rival claimants for the Scottish crown, Edward first extracted from them in 1291 an acknowledgement of his overlordship and demanded the surrender of all the royal castles, to be delivered in due course to the person adjudicated the rightful king. The fourteen Scottish nobles, holding between them twenty-two royal castles, made formal protest before submitting to the English king's demands.[18] In place of James the Steward, who held both Dumbarton and Ayr castles at the time, Edward appointed an English nobleman, Sir Nicholas de Segrave, to the keepership of both.[19]

After John Balliol had been enthroned as King of Scotland on St. Andrew's Day, 1292, the royal castles were restored to him by their English keepers, the new custodian of Dumbarton Castle being Sir Ingram de Umfraville, who was to hold the castle from 1292 to 1296. The Umfravilles were of Norman origin, related to the Balliols, and, like many other Scottish noble families, owned lands on both sides of the Border. Sir Ingram was one of the twelve commissioners sent to France in July, 1295, by King John to negotiate the Franco-Scottish treaty, which was aimed against the English king.[20] On March 26th, 1296, partly in consequence of this treaty, Edward invaded Scotland and in a matter of weeks overwhelmed the Scottish forces opposed to him. Among the first castles to be surrendered was Dumbarton; on June 28th, 1296, Sir Ingram delivered custody of it to James the Steward, acting on behalf of the English king. Sir Ingram was later confirmed by Edward I in the possession of all his lands and chattels in consideration of his prompt surrender of the castle.[21]

James the Steward, who had himself been deprived of the keepership five years before, was not to be entrusted for long with responsibility for the castle; on October 5th, 1296, he was commanded by Edward to put a Yorkshire knight, Sir Alexander de Ledes, in possession of the castle.[22] The Steward had supported the Bruce claim to the succession in 1290-92 but had accepted John Balliol as king, and only the outbreak of war in 1296 prevented him becoming Balliol's sheriff in a new sheriffdom of Kintyre.[23] In the year after his surrender of Dumbarton Castle, William Wallace, whose family occupied lands in the very heart of the Steward's domains, emerged as leader of a national rising against the English, and among the few nobles supporting him was James the Steward, who was actually suspected by the English of having encouraged Wallace in resorting to what they termed rebellion.[24]

Sir William Wallace

The national rising led by Wallace was quickly crowned with success at the battle of Stirling Brig on September 11th, 1297. Stirling Castle was held for a few days after the battle by the English garrison under

William Fitzwarin, Sir Marmaduke Tweng and William de Ros.[25] The English knights were taken to Dumbarton Castle, which had been evacuated by the English garrison soon after the battle, and there they lay for months, in irons and half-starved. It was not until April, 1299, that Edward I, in response to the petition of the wife of Fitzwarin and some of his friends, empowered the Bishop of Durham and two others to enter into negotiations for the exchange 'body for body' of Fitzwarin and Tweng for Henry de Sinclair and John de Mowbray, Scottish knights in English captivity.[26] The other prisoner in Dumbarton Castle, Sir William de Ros, may have arranged for his own ransom. Sir William was a brother of Sir Robert de Ros of Wark-on-Tweed, who had joined the Scots in 1296 and had intended to hand over Wark Castle to them. But William had ousted his brother and secured the castle for the English until the arrival of Edward I, who made it his headquarters for the invasion of Scotland. William de Ros, years later, in 1307, reminded Edward I of his services in taking Wark Castle and his imprisonment in Dumbarton Castle, in his petition to the English king for the grant of his mother's lands.[27] The English knights, Ros, Tweng and Fitzwarin, were the first recorded prisoners in Dumbarton Castle, which over the centuries was to hold many notable Scotsmen.

Wallace's triumph was short-lived. In 1298, the year after his victory at Stirling Brig, Edward I again invaded Scotland with a large army, and Wallace and the Scots suffered a crushing defeat at Falkirk. It was not, however, until 1304 that Edward, freed from troubles at home and abroad, was able to impose his rule on Scotland after another campaign in Scotland. Almost all the Scottish leaders made submission once again to the English king. Stirling Castle was gallantly defended by Sir William Oliphant until August, 1304; but four months earlier, Edward I had already appointed Sir John Menteith sheriff of Dumbarton and keeper of Dumbarton Castle.[28] Among the Scots who refused to submit was Wallace, whose dauntless and incessant opposition to English domination had aroused the implacable hatred of Edward. Orders were issued, inducements offered, to hunt down and capture Wallace, who with a small band of faithful followers kept on the move, aware that Scots as well as English were on his trail.

The name of Wallace is enshrined in Scottish folklore and even by the fifteenth century, when Henry the Minstrel ('Blind Harry') composed his poem in honour of the Scottish hero, there had accumulated around it a wealth of tradition. Almost every county in the south-west of Scotland has place-names associated with Wallace's exploits, actual or fictional. Not far from Dumbarton, at Havock on Clyde shore, is Wallace's Cave, where Wallace and his men, according to tradition, sought shelter, and at Rosneath, ten miles down the Clyde, is Wallace's Leap, where he is said to have escaped from English soldiers by leaping on horseback into the Gareloch.[29] According to 'Blind Harry's' poem, which consists of tales and traditions current two hundred years after the hero's death, Wallace and his men arrived one winter's night at the town of Dumbarton, then occupied by the English. The fugitives made their way to the house of a friendly Scot and received hospitality, 'baith meit and drynk', as well as a gift of a hundred pounds from the woman of the house. The next night, the houses occupied by the English were set on fire, Wallace and his men dealing with those who attempted to escape. Thereafter, the Scottish leader went with his companions to the cave of Dumbarton, where they spent the day until darkness fell and then proceeded to Rosneath on the Gareloch. The cave in the red sandstone cliff at Havock (one mile west of the town of Dumbarton) is now known as Wallace's Cave but in the seventeenth century was known simply as the Hole of Havock or Havock's Hole; and it may be that the present name was applied after 'Blind Harry's' poem became popular, although this does not necessarily mean that Wallace did not shelter there.

There is no definite evidence connecting him with the castle itself. The weapon known as Wallace's sword, which was kept for centuries in the castle until its removal to Stirling in 1888, was, according to experts, of much later date than the time of Wallace. The Wallace Tower, which guarded the old, northern entrance to the castle, has no other connection with Wallace than his name, which was probably bestowed in his honour. The tower was built in the late fifteenth or early sixteenth century; and to the sixteenth century also belongs the guard-house between the peaks, despite the name, 'Wallace's prison', which used to be applied to it. This last name is linked with the tradition that Wallace, after his capture near Glasgow in 1305, was brought to Dumbarton Castle, then in the charge of Sir John Menteith, and lodged there before being taken to London for trial and execution. Dumbarton children for generations have been pointed out a leering stone face on a skewput as that of the 'fause Menteith', as if in confirmation of that tradition. Although there is no record of Wallace's confinement in the castle after his capture, this was most likely to have happened as Sir John Menteith, who was sheriff of Dumbarton and keeper of the castle, was responsible for having him transported to

London; but it could only have been for a day or so, as Wallace was brought to trial in Westminster Hall a little over three weeks from the date of his capture.

Sir John Menteith

Sir John Menteith was a cousin of James the Steward, who had been keeper of Dumbarton Castle in 1291 and 1296. Sir John's father, Walter *Ballach* (freckled), son of the High Steward of Scotland, had acquired the title of Earl of Menteith in right of his wife, heiress to the earldom, and Sir John, a younger son, came to be known as Sir John of Menteith or, simply, Sir John Menteith. He held the lands of Rusky in Menteith, a day's journey from Dumbarton; through the marriage of one of his descendants, Robert Menteith of Rusky, with the daughter of the eighth Earl of Lennox, the Haldanes of Gleneagles and the Napiers of Merchiston came to share in the partition of the Lennox in the fifteenth century.[30] Sir John had been captured by the English at Dunbar in April, 1296 and in June of the same year entered the peace of King Edward, to whom (apart from a brief period after 1300) he remained loyal until the English king's death in 1307. He was almost the only Scot entrusted with the keepership of a castle after Edward established his supremacy over Scotland in 1304.

Some documents recently examined in the Public Record Office in London, containing the accounts of the Chamberlain of Scotland for the period 1305-1307, reveal details of the garrisons of the castles in the hands of the English king. For example, Sir Peter Lubaud, constable of Linlithgow, had a garrison of 15 esquires, 5 hobelars, 8 balisters and 20 archers; William Bisset, who was constable of Stirling and the only Scottish keeper other than Menteith, had a garrison of 1 knight, 12 esquires, 3 hobelars, 17 balisters and 12 archers; Sir Robert Leyburn, constable of Ayr, had a smaller garrison — 7 esquires, 4 balisters and 7 archers. (A hobelar was a light-armed horseman, mounted on a 'hobby' or pony; a balister fired an arbalest or cross-bow.) The omission of Sir John Menteith's garrison in Dumbarton Castle may or may not be significant; and his own account as sheriff of Dumbarton may one day come to light.[31]

Menteith's name is invariably associated with the capture of Sir William Wallace in 1305. Contemporary and near-contemporary English chronicles definitely state that Wallace was captured by

Menteith, one of the chronicles, that of Peter Langtoft, adding that he took Wallace one night when he was with his 'leman' (sweetheart), through the treachery of one of Wallace's men, Jack Short, whose brother had been killed by Wallace.[32] Andrew Wyntoun, the Scottish cleric, whose rhyming chronicle dates from about a century after Wallace's death, merely stated that Menteith captured Wallace; but a rubric in a later hand added that Menteith 'deceived' Wallace.[33] Henry the Minstrel ('Blind Harry'), whose poem on Wallace was composed almost two centuries after his hero's death, gives a most circumstantial account of Wallace's arrest at a place near Glasgow, which has been identified as Robroyston. According to 'Blind Harry', Wallace was sleeping in a house there and Menteith's nephew, who had joined Wallace's band at the instigation of Menteith, led his uncle with 60 men to the house after midnight. Wallace, weaponless, surrendered only on a promise from Menteith that his life would be spared:

> To Dunbertane ye sall furth pass with me;
> At your awn hous ye may in saifte be.

He was however (perhaps after a day or so in Dumbarton Castle) led south, handed over to Lord Clifford and de Valence at the Solway, and taken to London, where he was tried and put to death after terrible torture and mutilation.[34]

Contemporary official records preserved in London throw a little more light on the affair. In what seems to be a list of memoranda of business to be brought before the English Parliament or Privy Council, there are three items: —

(1) Cause to remember the 40 marks which should be given to a valet who spied out William le Waleys.

(2) Of the 60 marks that ought to be given to the others, the King wills that these . . . 60 . . . who were at the taking of the said Waleys to be divided among them.

(3) Of the land valued at £100 for John of Menteith.[35]

Whether the 'valet who spied out Wallace' was the Jack Short of Langtoft's chronicle or Menteith's nephew or one of his pages will probably never be known. As for the item relating to land worth £100 for Menteith, the meaning is unclear but is usually taken to refer to a reward for Menteith's part in Wallace's capture.

As one might expect, there is no evidence in these English official records of 'treachery' on the part of Menteith. Nevertheless, as the historian of the Menteith family wrote:

'Whether he was a prime mover or only an abettor in the execution of his duty, Sir John Menteith has not escaped the execration of posterity for his alleged share in the death of Scotland's best patriot.'[36]

Robert Bruce

Wallace's death once again roused the national spirit in Scotland and brought to the forefront two young nobles, rivals for the succession to the Scottish crown, Sir John Comyn, Lord of Badenoch, and Robert Bruce, Earl of Carrick. Their meeting in the Greyfriars Church, Dumfries, on February 10th, 1306, ended in a tragic quarrel in which Bruce murdered Comyn. By this murder, Bruce made himself the sworn enemy of Comyn's relatives and friends, who were numerous and powerful in Scotland. Indeed, most of Bruce's early troubles after he was crowned at Scone on March 25th, 1306, were due to the enmity of Comyn's friends and supporters.

On his way from Dumfries to Scone, Bruce and his friends seized a number of castles in the south-west and arrived at Glasgow, where Bishop Robert Wishart gave him full absolution for his crime. They had a meal together and then Bruce and his small band set off for Dumbarton Castle. There he sent two of his knights, Alexander Lindsay and Walter Logan, to demand the surrender of the castle from Sir John Menteith, asking him to come out of the castle, under a truce, for a parley. Menteith, however, declined, saying he would surrender only if Bruce brought a letter from King Edward, signed with the king's great seal.[37] It was not long after this that Menteith's loyalty to the English king was rewarded with the gift of the earldom of Lennox (presumed to be forfeited by the rightful owner, who supported Bruce) as well as the sheriffship of Dumbarton and the keepership of Dumbarton Castle for life.[38] Bruce, on the run after his defeat at Methven on June 19th, 1306, fled to the west and for a few days after crossing Loch Lomond sojourned in the Lennox. From the Lennox, Bruce passed into Kintyre and the Hebrides, where he was hunted by English and Scots, among them Menteith. On October 3rd, 1306, Robert de Farnham was paid 20 shillings for carrying a letter from King Edward to Menteith in Kintyre; and on February 9th, 1307, Menteith was paid £20 for 'keeping the sea with Sir Simon Montague, admiral at Ayr', for the wages of himself and his men, the money being paid to him by Andrew de Fullarton, his valet, at Ayr.[39]

Edward I, on his way north to deal with the 'upstart' Scottish king, died at Burgh-by-Sands within sight of Scotland on July 7th, 1307, and was succeeded by his son, the ineffectual Edward II. From then onwards, Bruce was gradually able to gain mastery over most of Scotland, capturing one castle after another. When Dumbarton Castle came into Bruce's possession is uncertain but Menteith, who was freed of his oath of allegiance to Edward I by the English king's death in 1307, must have surrendered it some time before March, 1309, when he was one of the nobles who made the declaration at a parliament in St. Andrews that Robert Bruce was the true heir of Alexander III.[40] In August, 1309, Menteith and Sir Neil Campbell, one of Bruce's most loyal supporters, were given safe-conducts from Edward II as ambassadors of Bruce to negotiate with Richard de Burgh, Earl of Ulster and Bruce's father-in-law, as commissioner of the English king.[41]

There is, in some of the older Scottish chronicles, the story of an attempt by Menteith to seize Robert Bruce at Dumbarton Castle, a story which has been generally discredited as romantic fiction and incompatible with the relations that existed between the two men from at least 1309 onwards. It appeared first in the continuation of Fordun's *Scotichronicon* by Walter Bower, who wrote about a hundred years after Bruce's death. According to Bower, Menteith had offered to surrender the castle in return for the earldom of Lennox, which the English king before his death had granted to him, and Bruce was invited to the castle in order to negotiate terms. On the way to the castle, Bruce was stopped in the wood of Colquhoun (about a mile or so from the castle) by 'a certain carpenter called Roland' who informed him that Menteith had concealed some of his men in a 'hole-cellar' and that these would, at a given signal, spring out and capture Bruce and his men. Armed with this information, Bruce proceeded to the castle and forced Menteith to show him the cellar, where the hidden band of armed men was revealed. Menteith was pardoned and submitted to Bruce, to whom he was to remain loyal for the rest of his life. Bower's account adds that the carpenter, Roland, was rewarded with the grant of the lands of Eddlewood, near Hamilton.[42]

However improbable this story may appear, the inclusion of the place-name, Colquhoun, and the fact that a charter of David II confirmed the grant by his father, Robert I, of the lands of Eddlewood to Oliver Carpenter point to some basis of truth. George Buchanan, in his history of Scotland, suggests that Menteith's life was spared as Bruce was loth to offend his kindred, Menteith's daughters being married to men whose support was important to Bruce — Malise, Earl of Strathearn, Sir Archibald Campbell of Lochow and Maurice Buchanan of Buchanan.[43] Although George Buchanan is not a very reliable authority, this may have been true; but there were positive advantages for Bruce in having Menteith as an ally rather than as the object of revenge.

After Bannockburn

After the battle of Bannockburn in 1314, there were still many forays south of the border until the English at last acknowledged Scottish independence in 1328. Even before Bruce's active campaigning was over, he decided to settle down in retirement in the Lennox at Cardross, not where the present village of that name is situated but on the opposite side of the river Leven from the burgh of Dumbarton, about a mile upstream from the Castle Rock. In 1326 he acquired two plough-gates (over two hundred acres) of land there from the Earl of Lennox in return for the lands of Leckie in Stirlingshire and a larger portion from Sir David Graham of Kincardine, who received instead Old Montrose (the place from which a later Graham took his title). The house Bruce built for himself was not a castle but a manor-house (*manerium*) with a hall and a chapel. It was comfortably furnished, the walls were plastered and painted, the roof was thatched, and the windows were glazed. Near the house the king had a garden and a park for hunting, and there was a special building, surrounded by a hedge, for the king's falcons.[44]

The location of the manor-house has been debated for over a century. Previously it was thought to be at Castlehill, almost half a mile west of the river Leven, because of the name Castlehill and the existence of a mound nearby, which was considered to be a medieval motte. There is little doubt, however, that Bruce's manor-house was much nearer the river Leven, at the Mains of Cardross, a name which is the equivalent of the Latin *manerium de Cardross*.[45] Bruce was seriously ill for the last two years of his life but whether with leprosy, as English chronicles declared, or some other disease is uncertain. At any rate, it was at his manor of Cardross that the warrior-king died on June 7th, 1329, in his fifty-third year.

Before Bruce came to reside near Dumbarton, he had, according to Sir Thomas Grey, an English chronicler, caused all the castles in

Scotland to be dismantled except Dumbarton Castle.[46] Bruce's policy of demolishing the castles dated back to the period of English occupation and was intended to prevent the English at any time in the future lording it over the land by holding the castles.[47] He made an exception of Dumbarton, which was centrally situated in Scotland but far from the border and not so accessible to the English as the castles in eastern Scotland. (Berwick, too, was an exception; it was not re-captured from the English until 1318 but then had its fortifications strengthened because it lay on the border.)[48] It was in Dumbarton Castle that Sir William de Soules was imprisoned for life after the discovery in 1320 of the conspiracy to kill Bruce and place de Soules on the throne.[49]

In 1321 Bruce rewarded Malcolm, Earl of Lennox, who had given him staunch support throughout the long struggle to win the crown and achieve Scottish independence, with the grant of the hereditary sheriffship of Dumbarton and keepership of Dumbarton Castle. He had already in 1309 granted to Lennox the hereditary sheriffship of Clackmannan. The king in the charter of 1321 bound himself and his heirs to pay the earl and his heirs 500 marks annually from the royal customs, should the sheriffship or the castle be retained in the king's hands. In effect, the appointment of acting keepers and acting sheriffs remained in royal control except during periods of weak monarchy; and sheriffs made their returns, when required, to the royal exchequer, while there is no evidence of the annual payments of the 500 marks payable to the earls of Lennox. The claims of the earls to be owners and keepers of the castle were, however, revived in later centuries on the basis of this charter.[50]

The first keeper of Dumbarton Castle of whom we have record after Bannockburn was a Robert Wallace, constable from 1325 until 1330. The designation of constable would imply the office of a deputy, presumably in deference to the hereditary keeper, the Earl of Lennox. If, as has been suggested, Wallace belonged to the family of Auchincruive, there was a relationship by marriage with Bruce, which may indicate that the appointment was made either by the king or at his instigation. Wallace was in 1329 and 1330 paid for works carried out at Bruce's manor of Cardross and at Dumbarton Castle.[51] These were continued by his successor, Sir Malcolm Fleming, who contracted with John Carpenter of the Order of Friars Minor for work both inside and outside the castle.[52]

David II's Minority

David II was only a boy of five years of age when his father, Robert
Bruce, died in 1329; and unfortunately for Scotland Thomas Randolph,
Earl of Moray, the guardian who ruled for the young king, died in
1332, just on the eve of an attempt to restore the Balliol line to the
Scottish throne. Edward Balliol, son of John Balliol, who had been
deposed by Edward I in 1296, was accompanied in his enterprise by a
band of 'disinherited' knights and barons, whose lands had been
forfeited during the reign of Robert Bruce. Balliol won a surprising
victory at Dupplin Moor near Perth in August, 1332, and was crowned
King of Scotland at Scone a few weeks later. He was far from secure on
the throne, and one morning in December at Annan he narrowly
escaped capture and had to ride 'with one leg booted, the other naked',
over the border. In 1333, however, with massive aid from the English
king, Edward III, whose archers mowed down the Scots at Halidon
Hill, near Berwick, Balliol gained control over most of Scotland. The
Scots, who a few years before had extracted an acknowledgement of
their independence from the English, now suffered the humiliation of
having a king who not only recognised Edward III as his lord
paramount but surrendered to him all the southern counties from
Haddington in the east to Dumfries in the west.[53] There were only five
castles in Scotland not occupied by Balliol's supporters or by English
forces — Dumbarton, Kildrummy in Strathdon, Urquhart on Loch
Ness, Lochleven, and the peel of Lochdoon.[54] It was to Dumbarton
Castle that the young king, David, now aged nine, and his child-wife,
Queen Joanna, four years his senior, were brought for safety and it was
Dumbarton Castle, strategically the most important of the five castles,
which became the base for the recovery of Scottish power.

The keeper of Dumbarton Castle in this critical period was Sir
Malcolm Fleming, who held the barony of Kirkintilloch, formerly
possessed by the Comyns but bestowed by Bruce on Sir Malcolm's
father, one of Bruce's staunchest supporters, in recognition of his
services. In addition, Sir Malcolm was given by Bruce a life-grant of
the barony of Kilmaronock on the south-east side of Loch Lomond, a
grant which was extended to his heirs; and on the other side of Loch
Lomond, Auchendennan, which formerly belonged to Malcolm
Drummond, was also given to him by Bruce.[55] The charter which Sir
Malcolm received of the lands of Kirkintilloch, which lay in the
sheriffdom of Stirling, contained a clause which obliged him to render

suit at the sheriff's court in Dumbarton. Sir Malcolm himself became sheriff of Dumbarton sometime before 1330 and consequently it was to his benefit to effect the exchange, already mentioned, with the sheriff of Stirling, by which the sheriffdom of Dumbarton gained a detached portion, then consisting of one parish but later divided into two parishes, Lenzie and Cumbernauld, and lost six parishes to the sheriffdom of Stirling. During the winter of 1333-34, Sir Malcolm Fleming was guardian of the young King David and his queen in Dumbarton Castle. Dumbarton, as was so often the case in later times, was used as the gateway to France, Scotland's ally. In March, 1334, the royal couple were taken by Sir Malcolm to France, to the castle of Richard Coeur-de-Lion, Château Gaillard, on the river Seine, and there they remained until 1341. On his return from exile, David, now seventeen years of age, created a new earldom of Wigton for Sir Malcolm, who had borne himself 'faithfully and laudably towards us in times both good and bad'.[56]

Bruce's grandson, Robert the Steward, the future Robert II, was one of the few Scottish nobles who had escaped death or capture at Halidon Hill in 1333. As the nearest heir to the throne, he was under constant threat from the forces of Balliol. All his lands were given to one of the 'disinherited' nobles, David of Strathbogie, who was recognised by Edward Balliol as Earl of Atholl and was appointed Steward of Scotland. Robert, the rightful Steward, a youth of only seventeen years, could find no place of safety in his own lands of Renfrew; and even in his island of Bute, to which he fled, his enemies held Rothesay Castle. One night he crossed over the Firth of Clyde from Bute to Inverkip, where horses had been kept ready for him. From there he rode up Clydeside and then in a small coble and with only three servants as companions, carrying the family charters, he crossed over to Dumbarton Castle, where he received a warm welcome from Sir Malcolm Fleming. Keen to recover his lands, Robert the Steward planned a raid on Cowal from Dumbarton. With Dougal Campbell of Lochow and a small force of 400 men, he sailed down the Clyde and captured the castle of Dunoon by surprise. The next success for the Steward was in Bute, where the people, still loyal to the Steward, overwhelmed the garrison in Rothesay Castle with volleys of stones. This victory of the 'Brandanes' of Bute gave the Steward control of the Firth of Clyde and helped to keep open the sea-route to France; but it was still a long time before David II could return to his throne.[57]

By the autumn of 1334 Edward Balliol, deserted by some of the 'disinherited' who resented his distribution of lands, was again forced to flee over the border; and Richard Talbot, who had been created Earl of Mar by Balliol, was captured by some of his companions-in-arms and imprisoned, along with six of his knights, in Dumbarton Castle to await ransom.[58] In the following year, Edward III of England prepared a great offensive, involving a land force under Balliol based on Perth and a naval expedition of some fifty vessels from Ireland to the Clyde. But although some Scottish nobles, including even Robert the Steward, submitted to Edward III, Scotland, fortunate to have Sir Andrew de Moray of Bothwell as guardian, still continued in resi⁺ance; and Edward was finally compelled to abandon his attempt to dominate Scotland when he put forward his claim to the throne of France.

The Dennistoun Keepers

In the second half of the fourteenth century the custody of Dumbarton Castle was for most of the time in the hands of members of the Dennistoun family, originally known as Danzielstoun from their lands of Danzielstoun in the parish of Kilmacolm in Renfrewshire. Sir John Dennistoun, keeper from 1359 to 1363 and from 1371 to 1376, was son-in-law of Sir Malcolm Fleming, formerly sheriff of Dumbarton and keeper of the castle, who had been created Earl of Wigton in 1341. This connection with the Earl of Wigton probably explains in part Dennistoun's appointment as keeper; but he was also related to the family of the Steward, his niece, Elizabeth Mure of Rowallan, having married Robert the Steward, later Robert II — a marriage which gave the Dennistouns cause to boast: 'Kings have come of us, not we of kings.'[59] One of the first duties assigned to Sir John Dennistoun was the charge of the Earl of Angus, who was accused of having instigated the murder of Katherine Mortimer, David II's mistress, at Soutra in 1360. The Earl of Angus was imprisoned in Dumbarton Castle, where he died a short while afterwards of the plague.[60]

Sir John may have been absent from Scotland during the period 1364-76, as two other keepers are recorded — Sir Malcolm Fleming of Biggar and Cumbernauld, nephew of the Earl of Wigton, and Sir Robert Erskine. Sir Robert's lands of Erskine on the Clyde were adjacent to those of Robert the Steward; and when David II died child-less in 1371, Sir Robert Erskine was one of those instrumental in vindi-cating the claim of Robert the Steward, David's nephew, to the throne

Plate 1. Excavations, 1975: silver pennies and cut half-penny of
Edward I and Edward II

IACOBVS · I · D · GRATIA ·
REX · SCOTORVM

Plate 2.   James I

Plate 3. James IV

Plate 4.   Mary, Queen of Scots

Plate 5.   Matthew, Earl of Lennox

Plate 6.   Esmé, Duke of Lennox

Plate 7.   James VI

Plate 8.   Archibald, Marquis of Argyll

Plate 9. John, 10th Earl of Glencairn

Plate 10. View of Dumbarton Castle from south-west, c. 1690 (John Slezer)

Plate 11. View of Dumbarton Castle from north-west, *c.* 1680 (John Slezer)

Plate 12.   View of Dumbarton Castle from west, *c.* 1745 (Paul Sandby)

Accompt of Money disbursed be Major George
Arnot, deputy Governour of Dumbarton Castle
for Necessars & reparationes therat. And to
Robert Marshall Slaiter for Slaitwork
at the same as follows, viz.

Imprimis to Major George Arnot for the
change of 75 bolls of oat meall being as provision for the Garison for the year 1682
p Contract betwixt Sr Wm Sharp & him & anent   } 100:00:00

Item for Glasing of the Windowes of the said Castle
after they were broken down, by firing of the Guns
when his Royall Highnes was there   } 32:00:00

Item for 2000 Sclaites for theeking the said
Castle the most part whereof are yet undisposed of
& keept for that same us   } 32:00:00

Item for building the Chimney of the Hall which
has fallen down   } 100:00:00
                                                 _____
                          Suma is   #2 64:00:00

Item to Robert Marshall Slaiter for Slait
work he has furnished from May 1681 to May
1682 being 1500 Sclait at 16 lib dozr 1000   } 24:00:00

Item for 2000 forking & Slaitnailles, at 10s froth
dozr 100   } 10:00:00

Item for 15 dailles for forking & pinns, at
10s the peece   } 7:10:00

Item for half a Chalder of Lyme this yeir twelf
ysrs at 9s p boll   } 3:12:00

Item for Sand to mix the Lyme, & carrying
thereof to the Top of the Rock   } 3:00:00

Item for six Loads of Flag for flagging & laying
of the Sclaits for gathering & carrying thereof
at 8s ilk Load   } 2:08:00

Item for Sclaiting a rude of Newwork in the
Nether Bailie & for furnishing therto, Sclait
dailles, Nailles & workmanship is in all   } 22:00:00

Item for Maintaining & theeting the Roof of
the said Castle from May 1681 to May 1682
pr Contract betwixt Sr Wm Sharp his M hesplat
Castlekeeper & R bot Marshall the same
(the materialls therby being to be payed a part) } 33:06:00
                                                 _____
                          Suma totalis # 3 69:16:00

E 28
276/4

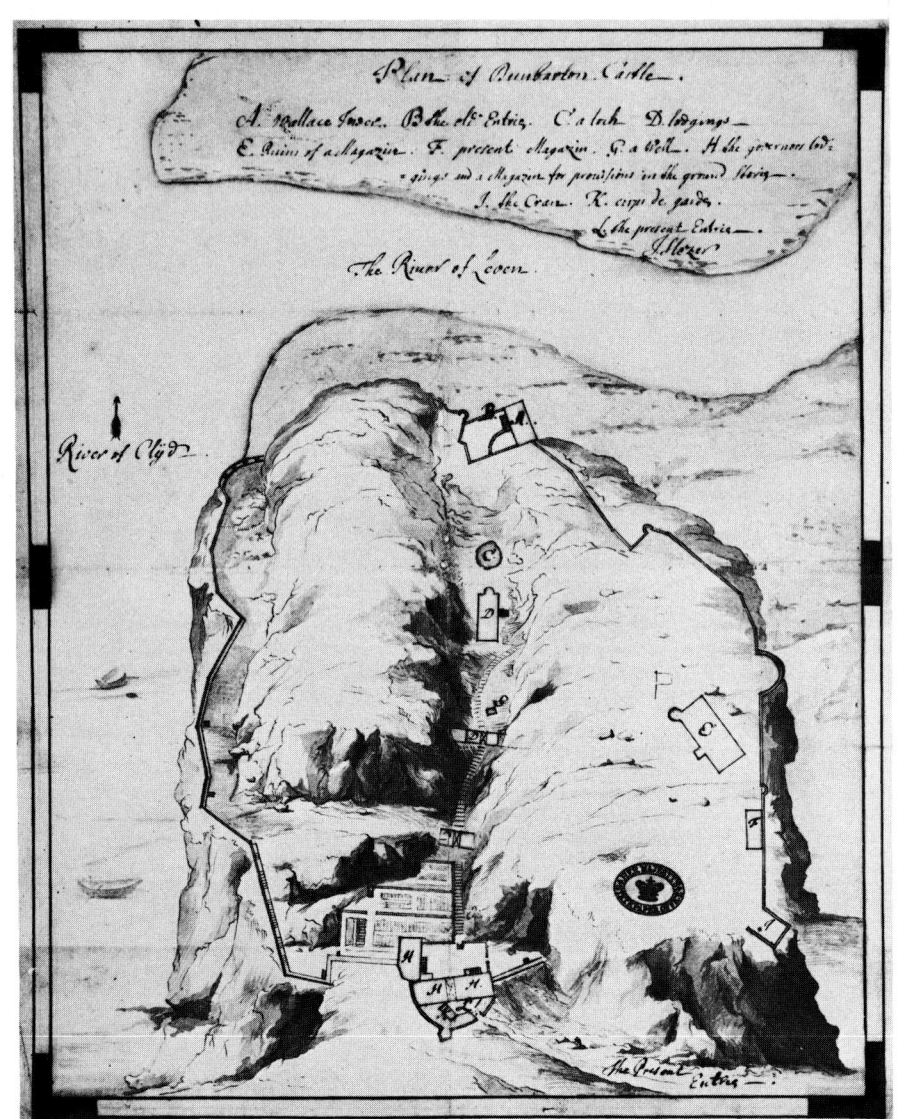

Plate 14.   Plan of Dumbarton Castle, 1696 (John Slezer)

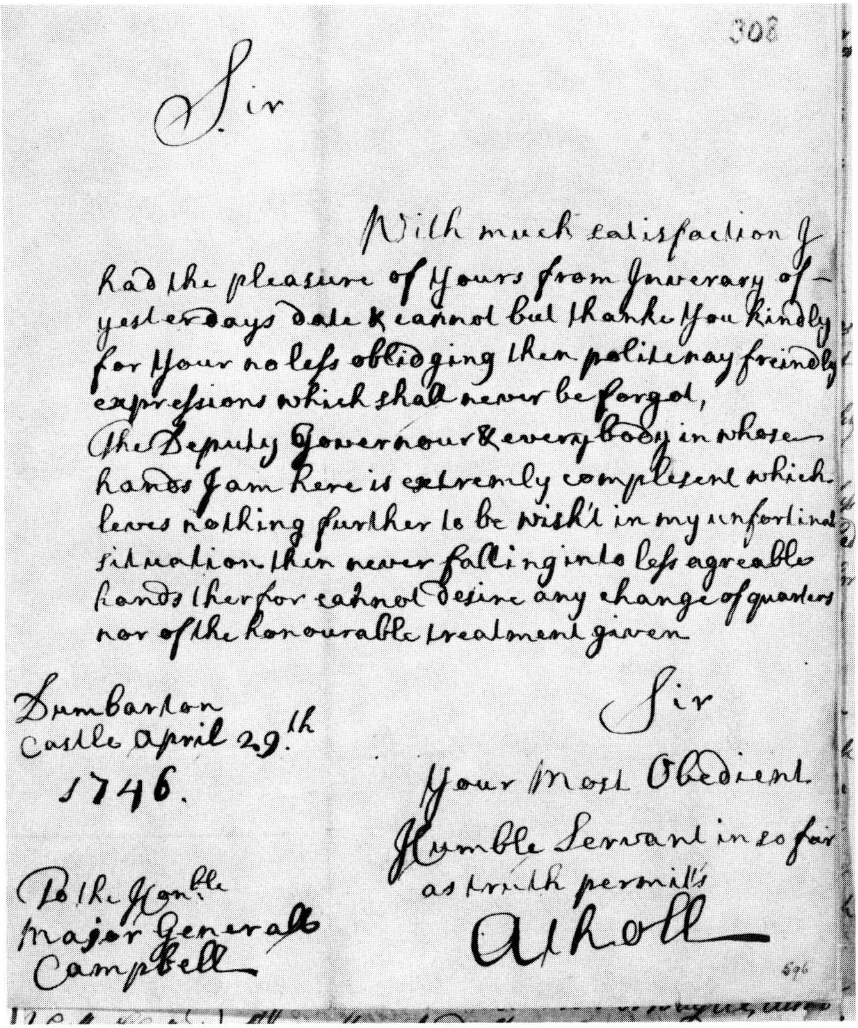

Sir

With much satisfaction I
had the pleasure of Yours from Inverary of
yesterdays date & cannot but thanke You kindly
for Your no less obliging then politenay freindly
expressions which shall never be forgot,
The Deputy Governour & every body in whose
hands I am here is extremly complesent which
leaves nothing further to be wish't in my unfortinat
situation then never falling into less agreeable
hands I therfor cannot desire any change of quarters
nor of the honourable treatment given

Dumbarton
Castle April 29th
1746.

Sir

Your Most Obedient
Humble Servant in so far
as truth permitts

Atholl

To the Hon:ble
Major Generall
Campbell

676

Plate 15.   Letter of Marquis of Tullibardine (Duke of Atholl), 1746

Plate 16.   Gunner, 18th century

of Scotland.[61]

Sir John Dennistoun was succeeded in 1376 by his son, Sir Robert, who was keeper of the castle until his death in 1397. He inherited his father's vast possessions, which were divided on his death between his two daughters and their husbands. Margaret, the elder daughter, who was married to Sir William Cunningham of Kilmaurs, succeeded to Kilmaronock in Dumbartonshire, Dennistoun and Finlayston in Renfrewshire, and Glencairn in Dumfries-shire. The Cunninghams, one of whom became the Earl of Glencairn a century later, were to hold Kilmaronock down to the seventeenth century and to have a long and at times an active association with Dumbartonshire and Dumbarton Castle. Sir Robert Dennistoun had two brothers, Sir William, who founded the family of Dennistoun of Colgrain near the modern Helensburgh (the Glasgow suburb of Dennistoun is called after one of them) and the other brother, Walter, who succeeded as keeper of Dumbarton Castle.

Master Walter Dennistoun (or Danzielstoun, as he is also designated) was a churchman, the parson of Kincardine O'Neil on Deeside, one who had studied in France as well as in Scotland and who aspired to a high position in the church. He might be thought the last person to be keeper of a royal castle but, maintaining that the Dennistouns had a hereditary claim to the keepership of the castle, he seized it on his brother's death. Certainly, his brother, Sir Robert, his father, Sir John, and his grandfather, Sir Malcolm Fleming, had all been keepers of the castle; but his action was only made possible by the lack of firm government in Scotland at the time. When Bishop Trail of St. Andrews died in July 1401, Walter Dennistoun's ambitions were turned to the lucrative bishopric of St. Andrews. There was however another candidate in this field, Thomas Stewart, a half-brother of the king, Robert III, and of the Duke of Albany, the most powerful man in Scotland. Stewart was elected bishop but his election awaited confirmation by Pope Benedict in Avignon. In the interval, the king's brother, the Duke of Albany, had imprisoned his nephew, the Duke of Rothesay, the heir to the throne, in the bishop's castle of St. Andrews (which the prince had taken over during the vacancy in the see) and then at Falkland, where he died in March, 1402. The Duke of Albany, now without a rival, made himself guardian of Scotland and, in order to secure Dumbarton Castle, persuaded his half-brother, Thomas Stewart, to renounce his claim to the bishopric of St. Andrews in favour of Walter Dennistoun.[62] Bishop Walter was not destined

c

however to enjoy the revenues of the see of St. Andrews for long, as he died a few months after his election:

> Sone efftyre at the Yule deit he;
> Swa litill mare than a halff yere
> Lestyt he in his powere.[63]

James I and the Lennox

When James I returned to Scotland in 1424 after nineteen years of captivity in England, he rapidly established his control over his kingdom and in the process brought about the destruction of the Albany family, which had so misgoverned Scotland during his absence that lawlessness and disorder prevailed everywhere. In so doing, he was inspired partly by motives of revenge for the neglect of his uncle, Duke Robert of Albany, and his cousin, Duke Murdoch of Albany, to procure his release from captivity in England and partly by the desire to rid himself and Scotland of a family which had become more powerful than the Crown. As Duke Murdoch was married to Isabella, daughter of the Earl of Lennox, James's policy of liquidation involved also the Lennox family.

Among those first arrested in May, 1424, by James's orders was Duke Murdoch's son, Sir Walter Stewart, who held, among other appointments, the keepership of Dumbarton Castle. Headstrong and wilful, he possessed all the qualities of the medieval robber baron. On one occasion when, as was not unusual, there was a delay in the payment of his fees for the custody of Dumbarton Castle, he imprisoned in the castle the custumars of Linlithgow, from whose revenues the fees were payable, and extracted from them the fees for the following year as well as the year just ended.[64] His misdeeds and lawlessness merited some form of punishment, but James was not finished with the Albany family: in less than a year James had brought about the arrest of Murdoch, Duke of Albany, his wife, Isabella, their son, Alexander Stewart, and the duke's father-in-law, Duncan, Earl of Lennox, then in his eightieth year. Albany's son, James Stewart, known as James *Mór* (Big James), in retaliation for the vindictive measures taken by the king, raided the town of Dumbarton in May, 1425, along with a relative, Finlay of Albany, who was Bishop of Argyll. They burned the houses in the town and killed Sir John Stewart of Dundonald (a natural son of Robert II known as the 'Red Stewart') and a force of thirty-two men sent to reinforce the garrison of the castle.[65] James *Mór* did not tarry long in Dumbarton but escaped along with the warrior-bishop to Ireland. Five of their accomplices who were arrested met a horrible death later at Stirling.[66]

James *Mór* (from whom the Stewarts of Ardvorlich are descended) was the only son of the Duke of Albany to escape execution. Not only Duke Murdoch himself and his two sons, Walter and Alexander, but also the duke's father-in-law, the aged Earl of Lennox, were all beheaded at Stirling in the last week of May, 1425.[67] With the destruction of the house of Albany disaster also befell that of Lennox; the earldom of Lennox passed into the hands of the king, and the title was in abeyance for half a century.

Before the overthrow of the Albany and Lennox families, James I had appointed John Colquhoun as keeper of Dumbarton Castle in place of Sir Walter Stewart, the first of the Albany family to be arrested. Colquhoun held lands in the Lennox on Lochlomondside and on Clydeside. The Colquhouns, originally, it would seem, a Norman family, had held from the early thirteenth century the lands of Colquhoun, which lay near Dumbarton Castle and from which they took their name.[68] Milton, two miles east of Dumbarton, was formerly known as Milton of Colquhoun, and near Milton was the Colquhouns' castle of Dunglass overlooking the river Clyde. In the fourteenth century Robert Colquhoun had married the heiress of one of the most ancient families of the Lennox, that of Luss on the west side of Loch Lomond, and their descendants came to be known as the Colquhouns of Luss. In or about 1411, John Colquhoun had entered into a contract with the Earl of Lennox, whereby he bound himself to marry the earl's daughter, Margaret, who had been left a widow by the death of her husband, Robert Menteith of Rusky. The marriage, however, did not take place and instead Colquhoun married Jean, daughter of Sir Robert Erskine, whose lands of Erskine lay on the opposite side of the Clyde from the Colquhoun castle of Dunglass.[69]

The Colquhouns' motto, '*Si je puis*', and their crest of a stag's head with two greyhounds as supporters have, like many heraldic devices, a story or legend attached to them; and this legend, which may have some foundation in fact, has been associated with the appointment of John Colquhoun as keeper of Dumbarton Castle. James I, keen to secure possession of Dumbarton Castle, asked Colquhoun to recover it from the king's enemies (presumably the followers of Albany's son); and to the king's command Colquhoun replied: '*Si je puis* (If I can)'. A stag captured by his men was brought near the castle and then liberated. Hounds were sent to chase the stag, and the sentinels of the castle garrison, who found the sight a relief from the boredom of guard duty, sallied forth to join in the chase, whereupon Colquhoun's men rushed through the open gate and captured the castle.[70]

Princess Margaret and the Dauphin

Before James I returned from England in 1424, many of his Scottish subjects had gone to help the French in their struggle against the English. The defeat of the English at the battle of Baugé in 1421 had been largely due to the Scots fighting in the French army. In the years following Baugé, the Scots bore the brunt of the defeats inflicted by the English at Cravant and Verneuil, and the uncrowned French king, Charles VII, could look for help only from Scotland. In 1428, he arranged with James I a marriage-contract, whereby Charles's son, Louis, then aged five, would marry James's daughter, Margaret, aged three. Margaret was to be sent to France with a French fleet which would also carry 6,000 Scots to fight against the English.[71] James was reluctant to implement the contract: he was chary about the possibility of a war with England and he feared for his daughter being subjected to the rigours of a voyage to France. Fortunately for Charles VII, Joan of Arc came to his rescue at the siege of Orleans in 1429. It was only after protracted negotiations that the marriage eventually took place, and during this period Dumbarton for the first time achieved importance as the gateway to France.

In November 1434, King Charles sent a mission to Scotland, headed by Girard, master of the royal household, and accompanied by the son of Sir Gilbert Kennedy of Dunure, Hugh Kennedy, who also had spent many years in France and had been one of Joan of Arc's companions-in-arms. Two ships left La Rochelle for Scotland and arrived, after a stormy passage of 56 days, off Galloway and, three days later, at Dumbarton on January 13, 1435.[72]

At Dumbarton, the French learned that an English mission, led by a brother of James's queen, Joan, had preceded them in order to prevent the proposed French marriage. Hugh Kennedy, fearing that the French mission, which was small in numbers, might fail to make as good an impression in Edinburgh as the English, mustered at Dumbarton his kinsmen and friends from his native Ayrshire; and eventually a company of at least 60 knights and esquires escorted Girard and the French mission from Dumbarton to Edinburgh, where they made a stately entry on January 25th. James was requested to send his daughter, Margaret, to La Rochelle at an early date, and on February 26th a provisional arrangement was made whereby Princess Margaret would sail from Dumbarton at the end of May with an escort of 2,000 Scottish troops, in ships provided by Charles. Things moved slowly, however, in those days and in such affairs, and it was not until September that a French squadron of eleven ships arrived in the Clyde off Dumbarton. James and his queen still made difficulties, reluctant to allow their daughter to sail during the stormy winter period and probably hoping to procure better terms for implementing the contract.

When the spring came, James at last travelled to Dumbarton and reviewed the French squadron lying in the Clyde. Part of the king's inspection of the ships involved races in the Firth of Clyde to choose the fastest ship in place of the galley which had been promised by the French king but which had not arrived. The French captains were displeased when a Spanish-built ship proved the fastest; and some of them even threatened to attack it when they left Scotland. The princess, only eleven years of age, parted tearfully from her father at Dumbarton on the 27th March, 1436, and sailed for France with a splendidly equipped escort said to number over a thousand, led by the admiral of Scotland, the Earl of Orkney. Her marriage to the dauphin, Louis, was celebrated on the 25th of June, but it proved an unhappy match. The young Princess Margaret, delicate in health, was neglected by her youthful husband. She pined for Scotland and died in 1445 in her twenty-first year. Just over a century later, the five-year-old Mary, Queen of Scots, was to depart for France from Dumbarton. She also married a dauphin, and her marriage also proved short-lived.[73]

Minority Troubles

When James I was murdered at Perth in 1437, his successor, James II, was a child of only six years of age, and Scotland was then subjected to the troubles and lawlessness associated with a king's minority. The Lennox, which lay on the border of the Highlands, was invaded in 1439 by marauding bands from the islands of Mull and Islay, who ravaged the countryside 'without respect for God or man'. John Colquhoun, keeper of Dumbarton Castle and sheriff of Dumbarton, met his death

not far from his own castle of Rossdhu on the isle of Inchmurrin in
Loch Lomond where he had gone, along with some of his men, on
September 24th, 1439, 'under an assurance' to meet two of the chiefs of
the Islesmen, Lachlan MacLean and Murdoch MacDonald.[74]

Colquhoun's father-in-law, Sir Robert Erskine, had become the first
Lord Erskine and had put forward a claim to the earldom of Mar
through his mother, great-granddaughter of Gartnait, one of the
ancient family of Mar.[75] On Colquhoun's death, Erskine seized control
of Dumbarton Castle, which he planned to use as a bargaining counter
in promoting his claim to the earldom of Mar and to possession of
Kildrummy Castle, the chief messuage of the earldom. His action
forced the Earl of Douglas, governor of Scotland, and his council to
come to terms with Erskine, and on August 10th, 1440, they agreed
that as soon as he should receive Kildrummy Castle into his possession
he would deliver up Dumbarton Castle and that he would retain
Kildrummy until the king came of age, when all grants made during the
minority would be reviewed.[76] Unfortunately for Erskine, in his
eagerness to acquire Kildrummy he delivered up Dumbarton Castle
first; and two years later he was still complaining about the non-
delivery of Kildrummy Castle. He was at last driven to take forcible
possession, and in retaliation his castle of Alloa was seized.[77]

In 1443, Dumbarton Castle was being held by two keepers, Robert
Sempill of Fulwood in Renfrewshire and Patrick Galbraith, son of
James Galbraith of Culcreuch, one of the oldest Lennox families. Both
had connections with Lord Erskine, who may have appointed them to
succeed him as a temporary arrangement when he surrendered the
castle in 1440. Sempill's lands of Fulwood were adjacent to those of
Erskine on the Clyde, and Galbraith was related to Lord Erskine.[78]
Sempill had the charge of the nether bailey overlooking the river Clyde
and Galbraith had the charge of the over bailey and the main entry at
the north side of the castle rock. As might have been expected, the two
keepers of Dumbarton Castle quarrelled, perhaps over the question of
seniority but more probably over the sharing of the dues payable to the
keeper. On the 15th December, 1443, Sempill managed to expel
Galbraith. According to one chronicle, this was done with subtlety
and, although no details are provided, Galbraith's departure may have
been on the basis of promises made by Sempill. The following day,
however, with only three or four unarmed men, Galbraith returned,
ostensibly to remove some of his gear. With his intimate knowledge of
the castle, he was able to capture the over bailey and eject Sempill from

the nether bailey. One of the chronicles states that Sempill was killed, which would have been the easiest way for Galbraith to effect his purpose, but there is no corroborative evidence of Sempill's death.[79]

During the period of James II's minority, the custody of the young king was a source of rivalry and was part of the struggle for power between Sir William Crichton, who was keeper of Edinburgh Castle, and Sir Alexander Livingston of Callendar, who was keeper of Stirling Castle; and both of these ambitious knights were in turn jealous of the powerful house of Douglas. Galbraith, who had ousted his fellow-keeper from Dumbarton Castle, had been 'very familiar' with the Earl of Douglas, who in 1443 was planning to increase his power by using Sir Alexander Livingston against Sir William Crichton.[80] Douglas and Livingston may not have instigated the quarrel between the two keepers but the outcome suited Livingston, who replaced Galbraith by Robert Callendar, a cadet of the Livingston family. Galbraith seems to have relinquished the keepership voluntarily or as part of a bargain: at any rate, in the following year he received £6. 13s. 4d. in payment of his expenses as keeper of Dumbarton Castle.[81] About the same time, he was also confirmed in a grant of the lands of Garscadden by his uncle, Lord Erskine, the self-styled Earl of Mar, presumably in recognition either of his action in seizing the castle or of relinquishing it in favour of a Livingston nominee. Erskine's chief aim was to establish his claim to the earldom of Mar and his motive in rewarding Galbraith may have been to propitiate the dominant party in Scotland at the time, that of the Livingstons.[82]

Robert Callendar was not the only one to benefit from the upturn in the Livingston fortunes; members of the Livingston family were appointed to some of the great offices of state and held the castles of Stirling, Doune, Methven and Dunoon as well as Dumbarton. But the supremacy of the Livingstons lasted only a few years. Their downfall was cataclysmic. At the time of James II's marriage in July, 1449, James, the eldest son of Sir Alexander Livingston of Callendar, was appointed Great Chamberlain of Scotland; but on September 23 he was arrested by order of the king at the bridge of Inchbellie on the Kelvin near Kirkintilloch along with a number of Livingstons and their adherents, including Robert Callendar, keeper of Dumbarton Castle. All those appointed to offices during the Livingston supremacy were dismissed and either beheaded or imprisoned. Sir Alexander Livingston himself and Robert Callendar were among those imprisoned in Dumbarton Castle. It has been suggested that a Livingston plot was being prepared in the castle of Dumbarton and that it was nipped in the bud by the capture of the leading Livingstons at Inchbellie on their way either to or from Dumbarton. The plot, if there was one, may have been to forestall action by the young king, James II, whose financial difficulties were such that the expulsion of the Livingstons from their many lucrative offices seemed to offer a solution.[83] The new keeper, a royal nominee, was Patrick, the first Lord Graham, who held the lands of Mugdock in the Lennox and who was succeeded after a short time by Sir John Colquhoun of Luss, a grandson of the keeper murdered at Inchmurrin in 1439.

The death of James II in his thirtieth year at the siege of Roxburgh in 1460 meant another period of minority rule as his successor, James III, was only eight years old; and once again the opportunity to enrich themselves was seized by some of the lesser families, notably the Kennedies and the Boyds, one of the latter, Sir Alexander Boyd of Drumcoll, being keeper of Dumbarton Castle for a short period.[84] Sir John Colquhoun of Luss, who was keeper of Dumbarton Castle, sheriff of Dumbarton and custumar of Dumbarton in several years from 1455 onwards, had connections with both the Boyds and the Kennedies and managed to carve out a successful career for himself. He was married to a lady of the family of Boyd and was for a time one of the entourage of Bishop Kennedy, who wielded great power during James III's minority. Colquhoun's prudence enabled him to steer a middle course between the two factions. His financial ability was recognised by his appointment in 1460 as comptroller of the exchequer, an office he held for nine years.[85] He stood in high favour with James III, who appointed him chamberlain of the royal household in 1474 and granted him the custody of Dumbarton Castle for life in 1477, the year before his death at the siege of Dunbar and two years after his son, Robert, was created bishop of Argyll.[86]

The Castle Besieged

James III's personal rule lacked the firmness essential in a medieval king. His reign came to an end in 1488, when he was murdered after the battle of Sauchieburn, a battle in which his fifteen-year-old son, James, fought along with rebel nobles against the king. For a time after his accession, James IV reigned over a divided Scotland. Some nobles, who had supported James III or, at any rate, had not rebelled against him, resented the preferential treatment shown to those who had aligned themselves with the young prince during the latter part of his father's reign. Among the discontented was the Earl of Lennox (formerly Sir John Stewart of Darnley) despite the fact that he and his son had been granted custody of Dumbarton Castle soon after the young king came to the throne. In 1489 they joined in a conspiracy against the king.[87]

One of Lennox's associates was the Great Justiciar of Scotland, Lord Lyle, whose sister had married Matthew, the eldest son of the Earl of Lennox. In addition to the ancestral domains of Duchal in Renfrewshire, the Lyles held lands in the Lennox, Auchentorlie and Dunerbuck in the parish of Kilpatrick and Wester Ardardan (now known as Lyleston) in the parish of Cardross.[88] Lyle took over command of Dumbarton Castle, while Lennox gathered his vassals to him, Andrew MacFarlane of Arrochar, Thomas Galbraith of Culcreuch, Patrick Colquhoun, brother of the Laird of Luss, the Stewarts from the Darnley estates, and their followers. In April, 1489, heralds, pursuivants and macers were sent to demand, with due ceremonial, the surrender of the castles of Dumbarton and Duchal. When the summons to surrender was ignored, couriers were then despatched to the 'west lands, Teviotdale and Galloway', asking the lords of these parts to muster at Dumbarton. Another courier was despatched with similar orders for the bishops of St. Andrews, Brechin and Dunblane and the abbots of Arbroath, Dunfermline, Scone and Lindores. Lennox and Lyle defied the summons to appear before Parliament in July, when they were found guilty of treason and sentenced, along with their abettors, to death and forfeiture of their lands and goods. Couriers were again sent out on the 10th of July to Lothian, Teviotdale and the south to warn the country 'to the siege of Dumbarton', and on the same day preparations were begun for transporting the great bombard called 'Mons' from Edinburgh westward. Lord Lyle's castle of Duchal surrendered before the end of the month, but at Dumbarton Castle, where Lord Lyle was still in command, the Earl of Argyll, in charge of the besieging force, had to content himself with occupying the town. He was driven out of it by a sally of the castle garrison, who then set fire to the houses of the town. Argyll was forced to withdraw to Dunglass, the castle of the Colquhouns, two miles up-river from the Castle Rock.[89]

Before the siege of Dumbarton Castle was resumed, another rising broke out in the north. Lord Forbes, the Earl Marischal and the Master of Huntly, adopting as their banner the 'bludy sark' (bloody shirt) of

the murdered James III, denounced the king and his government at
Aberdeen on September 12th. Lennox, with a body of about 2,000
men, left Dumbarton and marched north to join up with Huntly.[90]
Lennox's advance was halted as the king's force held the bridge at
Stirling and he decided to cross the Forth by a ford nearer the source of
the river. Alexander MacAlpine, who was in Lennox's camp at
Gartloaning near Aberfoyle, was a vassal of Lord Drummond, one of
the king's supporters, and he left the camp secretly to report to him the
location and disposition of the weakly guarded camp. On the night of
October 11-12, Lord Drummond led a surprise attack upon Lennox's
sleeping camp and routed the rebels. Galbraith of Culcreuch was one of
those killed, and the rest of the leaders fled for safety to Dumbarton.[91]
A week later, the king appeared before the castle of Dumbarton but
Lennox and Lyle did not surrender until mid-December. James wisely
did not insist on the dire punishments imposed earlier on Lennox and
his associates. The sentences of death and forfeiture were annulled and
pardons were granted to more than 130 persons who had held the castle
against the king and had burned the town.[92] As keeper of Dumbarton
Castle, James appointed Sir Baldred Blackadder, nephew of the Bishop
of Glasgow, Robert Blackadder, who had been at one time rector of
Cardross on the opposite side of the river Leven from the castle and
who had accompanied the besiegers of the castle at various times.
Lennox's son, Matthew, who succeeded to the earldom in 1495, was
made sheriff of Dumbarton and keeper of the castle in the following
year.[93]

Expeditions to the Isles

James IV, like other Scottish kings before and after him, was faced
with the problem of dealing with the lawlessness, the violence, the
feuding of the clans of the highlands and islands. The Lords of the Isles,
whose independence had at times threatened the security of the Scottish
kingdom, were MacDonalds, to whom allegiance was given not only
by chiefs of the MacDonald clans but also by chiefs of the west and
north-west such as the MacLeods of Lewis and Skye, MacNeill of
Barra, MacLean of Duart in Mull. John, the last Lord of the Isles,
submitted after forfeiture in 1493 but it was not until after many years
of skilful, sometimes devious diplomacy, and several expeditions
against the more defiant or intransigent chiefs that James could claim to

have pacified the west. In his early expeditions of 1493 and 1494, Dunstaffnage Castle near Oban and Tarbert Castle on Loch Fyne were used as bases for the king's expeditions. But later in the reign Dumbarton became the headquarters for his campaigns against the Gaels of the west.[94] The burgh, in the shelter of the king's castle, was conveniently situated for shipbuilding: it lay on the river Leven, a short distance from the river Clyde, and the woods of Lochlomondside provided the necessary timber. It was easily accessible from any part of central Scotland where the king normally resided and far enough from the isles of the west to escape any raids in reprisal.

In the winter of 1494-95 the burgh of Dumbarton was the scene of great activity in preparation for a summer campaign. The king's camp-bed was sent there to be ready for his voyage to the isles, and in the month of May, 1495, with Sir Andrew Wood, the notable sea-captain, in command of the king's ship, the *Flower,* a large force set sail from the Clyde.[95] After establishing an advance headquarters at Mingary, the castle of the MacIains of Ardnamurchan, James forced a number of chiefs to accept charters from him, thus acknowledging his authority.[96]

In 1503 trouble flared up after Donald Dubh, a grandson of the last Lord of the Isles, made his escape from Inchconnel Castle on Loch Awe, where he had been imprisoned since infancy, and was granted protection by Torquil, chief of the MacLeods of Lewis. In 1504 a large-scale expedition was prepared with the main objective that of reducing the MacLeans' castle on one of the Treshnish Isles off the west coast of Mull. James spent some days in Dumbarton in the middle of April 1504, inspecting the vessels which were being repaired and victualled; and, apart from brief visits to Glasgow and Paisley, the king and his court remained at Dumbarton for the first fortnight of June.[97] The expedition to the Treshnish Isles was successful and resulted in the submission of MacLean of Duart and other chiefs. But Donald Dubh continued to hold out, latterly in Stornoway in the Isle of Lewis, until in 1507 he was captured and once again imprisoned, this time in Stirling Castle.

It is usually assumed that James IV resided at Dumbarton Castle when on his visits to the town, and there is little reason to doubt that this was the case. On his frequent travels throughout his kingdom, James sometimes lodged for a night or two in private houses; and on his visits to Dumbarton in 1498 he twice lodged with a 'goodwife', who received 29s. 6d. and 18s. in payment.[98] There is no record however of payment on the king's behalf of a night's lodging on his later visits.

The Treasurer's Accounts provide fascinating glimpses of the King's way of life. He was a generous patron of the church and a benefactor of the poor, his almoner, Sir Andrew MacBreck, being frequently entrusted with sums of money to distribute. On June 8th, 1505, after spending £4. 10s. 'at the cartes', he took to the evensong in the kirk of Dumbarton a purse of 40 French crowns and 4 pounds in silver. On June 10th of the same year the priests of St. Mary's Collegiate Church in Dumbarton received 20 shillings and the priests of the parish kirk the same amount two days later. Entertainment was rewarded with smaller sums than piety — usually 14 shillings, for example on March 19th, 1495, to the man that played the clarsach (harp) and to the piper of Dumbarton; on June 5th, 1505, to the French whistler; and on June 9th, 1507, to 'a woman that sang to the king' (but only two shillings in her case). Presents from loyal subjects were rewarded by gifts to the bearer — on April 24th, 1497, to a child that brought apples to the king from the provost of the Collegiate Church of Dumbarton, 9 shillings; on May 22nd, 1505, to a man that 'brocht in eggs to the king', 9 shillings; on August 22nd, 1505, to a man of the Laird of Buchanan who brought pears to the king, 2 shillings; to a man who brought eels and pikes from the Prior of Inchmahome, 2 shillings; and to a man who brought an ox from the provost of the Collegiate Church, 9 shillings.[99]

Keepers' Fees

The keepers of Dumbarton Castle in the Middle Ages were frequently sheriffs of Dumbarton, whose accounts were normally rendered each year to the king's exchequer. One of the earliest accounts preserved is the account for 1329-1330, according to which Sir Malcolm Fleming, sheriff of Dumbarton, paid £57. 2s. 11d. to Robert Wallace, constable of Dumbarton Castle, presumably for his custodianship of the castle. In 1342, Sir Malcolm, then both sheriff and keeper, was entitled to pay himself 100 marks (£66. 13s. 4d.) for his fee as keeper. The sum of £24 was paid to him out of the revenues of the sheriffdom and the balance out of the fermes of the barony of Cadzow, which had been bestowed by Robert Bruce on the ancestor of the Hamiltons.[100]

The keepers' fees varied from keeper to keeper and from year to year depending on the condition of the royal finances and on the extent to which the keeper enjoyed the favour of the king or the government for the time being. In 1364 Sir John Dennistoun received an annual fee of 200 marks (£133. 6s. 8d.), but when he returned to the post in 1369 after an absence of a few years, he was paid a fee of only £80, a considerable proportion of which, £64, came from the fermes of the barony of Cadzow. Small additional payments were made in some years for watchers or sentinels (*vigiles*). In 1360, 26s. 8d. was paid for the service of one sentinel and in the years following, similar payments for sentinels were made — 40s. in 1361, 33s. 4d. in 1364, £3. 6s. 8d. in 1366. Payments for watchers were made regularly at Stirling Castle in the fifteenth century — £7 for six watchers and one 'garitor' in 1461, £11 for eight watchers, one garitor and two janitors, plus 11 chalders of oatmeal in 1466 and subsequent years. One can only surmise that the watchers or *vigiles* performed sentry-duty at the main entrances. The defence of the castles obviously did not depend on these watchers, apart from raising the alarm, but rather on the garrison made up of retainers of the keepers.[101]

Sir Robert Dennistoun, keeper of Dumbarton Castle from 1376 to 1397, for most of the period of his custodianship received an annual fee of 80 marks (£53. 6s. 8d.), all of which was paid out of the customs of Linlithgow. Sir Walter Buchanan, who succeeded Walter Dennistoun on his appointment as bishop of St. Andrews, was also entitled to a fee of 80 marks but for several years during the regency of the Duke of Albany received only a portion of his fee.[102] In 1415, when he was replaced by the regent's grandson, Sir Walter Stewart, Buchanan received only £4. 2s. 7d, and it was not until 1420 that he finally obtained his arrears of payment. His successor was paid his fee of 80 marks regularly by the custumars of Linlithgow but in 1422, as has been mentioned above, he demanded in addition from the custumars payment in advance for the next year and, on their refusal of his demands, carried them off to Dumbarton Castle, where he kept them imprisoned until the money was paid.[103]

In the fifteenth and sixteenth centuries the keepers' fees were derived from different sources. An act of parliament of 1455 listing the lordships and castles annexed to the crown included 'the castle of Dumbarton with the lands of Cardross, Rosneath, the pension of Cadzow, and the pension of the ferme-meal of Kilpatrick'.[104] The account for 1455-56 of Sir John Colquhoun of Luss, who was both keeper of the castle and sheriff of Dumbarton, gives the keeper's fee as £123. 6s. 8d., made up from the fermes of Rosneath (55 marks), Cardross (40 marks) and Cumbrae (40 marks) and the annual rent from Cadzow (40 marks), and in addition 3 chalders 2 bolls of barley and 10 marts from Cumbrae. The account for 1470-71 shows further changes — the fermes of Rosneath, Cardross and Cumbrae, the annual rent from Cadzow ('now called Hamilton'); 10 marts from Cumbrae; 4 chalders 2 bolls of barley from Cumbrae; the blenchfermes of Kilmaronock, Arthur's Castle, and Baljaffray (nominal payments totalling 10 pence); 4 chalders of oatmeal from the abbot and convent of Paisley.[105] By a charter of 1477, Sir John Colquhoun was given the custodianship of Dumbarton Castle for life, with the revenues of the lands of Cardross and Cumbrae, the annual rent of the lands of Cadzow, and the 'watch-meal' of Paisley Abbey.[106] The 'watch-meal', comprising 5 chalders of oatmeal, came from the lands in the parish of Kilpatrick belonging to the Abbey of Paisley but the 'watch-meal' continued to be paid to the crown long after the dissolution of the abbey.[107] Sir John Colquhoun was also from 1459 to 1469 custumar of Dumbarton, and in 1464 he was responsible for the customs on 1 last of wool (£13. 6s. 8d.), 16 lasts 10 dacres of hides (£46) and 30 dozen pieces of woollen cloth (£1. 10s.). The office of custumar was a lucrative one and after Colquhoun's tenure of office was held generally by a burgess of Dumbarton or the son of a local laird. The expansion of the herring fishery in the late fifteenth century involved an extension of the custumar's duties and he was then generally designated as 'custumar of Dumbarton and the Lowes', i.e. the lochs of western Scotland.[108]

The fees paid to the keepers of Stirling Castle, at one time a fortress comparable to Dumbarton Castle but latterly much more important as a royal residence, also varied from time to time. In 1369, Sir Robert Erskine was appointed keeper of Stirling Castle for life with an annual fee of 200 marks (£133. 6s. 8d.), the same fee as that paid to Sir John Dennistoun for Dumbarton Castle in 1364, but in addition Erskine received 14 chalders of corn and 12 chalders of oatmeal from the lands of Bothkennar. In the period 1465-76, however, Gilbert, Lord Kennedy and Andrew, Lord Avondale, were paid a keeper's fee of only £80 plus £11 for watchers, who also received a chalder of oatmeal each for their victuals.[109]

In the accounts for Stirling and Dumbarton castles there are included the stipends of the chaplains of the castles. Robert Bruce made a grant to the chaplain serving St. Patrick's chapel in Dumbarton Castle but there had been a chaplain attached to the castle at least as far back as 1271. In 1390 Robert III increased the stipend from 8 to 10 marks (£6. 13s. 4d.) to be paid out of the burgh fermes.[110]

Castle Buildings

There are numerous references in the Exchequer Rolls to repairs carried out at the castle buildings on Dumbarton Rock in the Middle Ages, but almost invariably with details only of the expenditure involved. When most of the other castles in Scotland were being dismantled at the end of the reign of Robert Bruce, Dumbarton Castle was repaired and fortified. In 1330, Robert Wallace, constable of the castle, was paid £86. 9s. 11d. for building expenses at the castle and at the king's manorhouse of Cardross; and during the keepership of Sir Malcolm Fleming, a friar, John Carpenter, was granted by David II a liferent of £20 per annum for the work he carried out at Dumbarton Castle and elsewhere. Whether new buildings were erected on the Castle Rock under the supervision of John Carpenter is not clear, and, similarly, nothing is known about the fortifications and repairs carried out by Robert Dunbertane, 'clericus', before 1361, when he was paid £66. 13s. 4d. plus a sum of £40 for necessary materials. At the end of the century, in the 1390's, Sir Robert Dennistoun in four different years received payment for repairs on Dumbarton Castle; the largest sum paid was in 1394 — £88. 3s. 2d., including £12 for materials, 50 deals of timber and 100 stones of iron. In 1451, the vicar of Houston in Renfrewshire, John Fleming, was master of works at Dumbarton Castle, and stone-cutters and carpenters worked for three weeks under his supervision on the repair of a building known as the Red Tower.[111]

The oldest medieval building on the Castle Rock still standing is the portcullis arch, which dominates the narrow passage between the two peaks of the Rock. It is estimated to date from the fourteenth century. According to the account of the seizure of the castle by Patrick Galbraith in 1443, the castle was divided into two parts, presumably by this arch, with the nether bailey on the south side overlooking the Clyde and the over bailey on the north side overlooking the Leven and the town of Dumbarton. An inventory of the gear and goods of the castle in 1510 includes references to the buildings, not all of which are readily identifiable — the Wallace Tower, the Windy Hall, the Hall and St. Patrick's Chapel.[112] The Wallace Tower, which commanded the north entry, as illustrated in Slezer's Theatrum Scotiae, was a four-storey building, regarded as dating from the fifteenth or early sixteenth centuries. If such an estimate of its age is accepted, the Wallace Tower must have been constructed not very long before 1510. The Windy Hall, which contained only a 'waist bed', is probably to be identified as a building in the over bailey at the south end of the space between the two peaks, where in modern times the armoury and master gunner's quarters were situated. The Hall was the main building in the nether bailey in medieval times and contained a 'chalmer of deas'. St. Patrick's Chapel, which also stood in the nether bailey, may have been built in the thirteenth century or even earlier, to judge by two ancient gravestones which were found during excavation of one of the garden terraces behind the modern Governor's House. Not included in the inventory is the Red Tower, repaired in 1451. If it is to be identified with the 'Red Hall' (*Talla Dearg*), mentioned earlier, in the rhyme about the Galbraiths, it stood on the south side of the Rock, that is, in the nether bailey or possibly as part of a curtain wall.

3

The Sixteenth Century

After Flodden

When James IV was killed at the disastrous battle of Flodden on September 9th, 1513, his son and successor, James V, was an infant, only seventeen months old. Scotland faced the prospect of a long minority and the combination of domestic strife and intervention by a powerful neighbour, Henry VIII of England, only too ready to exploit the victory at Flodden. Dumbarton Castle, like other royal fortresses, changed hands time and again; and as the French sought to preserve and strengthen the 'Auld Alliance' against the threat of English domination of Scotland, Dumbarton, which secured one of the main routes to and from France, acquired an importance it was to retain for most of the century.

The choice of a governor or regent of Scotland during the king's minority was obviously of prime importance. The heir-presumptive to the Scottish throne was John Stewart, Duke of Albany, first cousin to the late king, James IV. Born and brought up in France, where he held the office of Lord High Admiral, he was nevertheless regarded as the obvious choice for the governorship, and immediately after Flodden the Lord Lyon King of Arms was dispatched to France to invite him to Scotland.[1] In the period of waiting before Albany's arrival in the spring of 1515, uncertainty prevailed, and in the words of the old chronicle, 'every ane pressed to tak sic possessioun as they mycht obtaine, principallye of that was lyand nearrest unto thame'.[2]

Next in succession to the throne after Albany was his cousin, James Hamilton, Earl of Arran, whose mother, Princess Mary, was a daughter of James II. Arran's sister had been married to Matthew, Earl of Lennox, who was killed at Flodden, and their son, John, the young

Earl of Lennox, was thus Arran's nephew. At the beginning of 1514, Lennox, in order to strengthen his own position and that of his uncle, decided to seize Dumbarton Castle, which was strategically central to his earldom. Robert, Lord Erskine, had in June, 1511, received from James IV a grant of the custody of Dumbarton Castle for nineteen years for himself and his heirs; and, after his death at Flodden, his son John, Lord Erskine, held the castle in the name of Queen Margaret, then acting as governor.[3] On 'ane mirk, wyndy nycht', the 12th of January, 1514, the young Earl of Lennox, along with William Cunningham, son of the Earl of Glencairn, William Stirling of Glorat, and others, undermined 'the nether sole of the yett' of the castle and ejected Lord Erskine and his garrison.[4] Stirling of Glorat, one of the vassals of the Earl of Lennox, was restored to the post which he had held in the reign of James IV and was rewarded by the earl with a grant of the keepership for life and of the lands of Keppoch (near the modern Cardross) in return for 'his labours, travels, costs and expenses in obtaining for us the castle of Dumbarton'.[5]

When the Duke of Albany at last arrived from France with a squadron of eight ships and a large company of French nobles and soldiers, it was at Dumbarton Castle that he landed on the 26th May, 1515, 'to the exceeding joy of all men'; and the next day he left for Edinburgh where he was received with acclaim.[6] The Earl of Arran, Albany's nearest rival for the succession to the Scottish throne, was not at first disposed to accept him as governor, and in the summer of 1516 Arran withdrew to the west country, where his supporters, the Earls of Lennox and Glencairn, fortified their castles and seized the Bishop's Castle in Glasgow. The Countess of Lennox was then pregnant and Lennox brought his wife for safety into Dumbarton Castle, where his son and heir, Matthew, was born on September the 21st, 1516. Shortly afterwards, Albany, who had marched through to the west to crush the incipient rebellion, was able with the help of the Bishop of Glasgow to re-take the Bishop's Castle. Lennox conceded defeat by entering into ward in Edinburgh Castle and only procured his release by surrendering the custody of Dumbarton Castle.[7]

By the time Albany left for France in 1517, there were French garrisons in the fortresses guarding the approaches from France — at Dumbarton in the west and at Dunbar and Inchgarvie (one of the islands on which the Forth Bridge stands) in the east. They were to remain 'stuffed with Frenchmen' during the period of Albany's regency.[8] The custody of Dumbarton Castle was entrusted by Albany not to a Frenchman but to a Scotsman who had served in the Scots Guard of the French king. He was Alan Stewart, son of Alexander Stewart of Galston and a relative of the Earl of Lennox, and was known as the 'Captain of Milan' because of having been in charge of the castle of Milan during the Franco-Italian wars. He did not, however, spend much of his time at Dumbarton, James Nisbet acting as constable under him. Stewart was keeper of the island castle of Inchgarvie on the Forth as well as of Dumbarton, and in addition held the office of provost of Edinburgh in 1523.[9]

After the lapse of four years, Albany returned from France but remained only a year, his ships lying at Dumbarton in the protection of the castle, except when they went cruising in the Clyde. When Albany arrived for the third time from France on September 22nd, 1523, it was for the purpose of leading an invasion into England. He landed at Dumbarton with a large force of Frenchmen and vast supplies of arms and ammunition. Reports of the size of the invasion force varied but it was almost certainly the greatest display of military and naval power ever seen at Dumbarton Castle. According to one eye-witness, the prioress of Eccles, the Duke brought to Scotland 87 ships, 100 barded horses, 500 light horses, 4,000 foot, 500 men of arms, 1,000 arquebusiers, with 16 cannon and nearly 1,000 small guns and gunpowder to the value of 10,000 crowns. According to a French captain, who claimed to have been in charge of 60 ships in Albany's expedition, there were 600 horses, 5,000 foot, 100 men of arms, 8,000 marines.[10] Albany's projected invasion of England was thwarted by the unwillingness of the Scots to cross the border and risk almost certain defeat on behalf of France. Before Albany left Scotland for good in 1524, the Scottish council demanded that all French troops should leave the country and that Albany should deliver up Dumbarton Castle and Dunbar Castle, where he had placed all the artillery of Scotland in the charge of French garrisons. His return to France was delayed for nearly four months by stormy weather, his four ships sheltering at Dumbarton from December, 1523 to May, 1524.[11]

In Scotland, following the departure of Albany, the strife of rival factions, almost inevitable so long as the minority of the king lasted, was renewed. In August 1525, when the Earl of Lennox, who had seized Dumbarton Castle the previous autumn, held the reins of power along with the Earls of Angus and Argyll, a grant of the custody of Dumbarton Castle was given to him, in the name of James V, for the space of five years.[12] The youthful king, who was held in close confinement in Edinburgh Castle by Archibald Douglas, Earl of Angus, entered in June, 1526 into a compact with the Earl of Lennox, whose counsel he promised to accept in all matters.[13] Advancing towards Edinburgh with a large army in an attempt to rescue the king from the Douglases, Lennox met his death at Linlithgow, where he was killed by Sir James Hamilton of Finnart, natural son of the Earl of Arran. When Arran, who was Lennox's uncle, discovered his nephew's body after the battle, he wept and, placing his red cloak over the corpse, said, 'The wisest, the best, the bravest man in Scotland has fallen this day.'[14]

Hamilton of Finnart was nevertheless appointed joint keeper of Dumbarton Castle with his brother-in-law, Lord Avondale, in 1527 but relinquished the post in 1531, after the young Earl of Lennox, then only fifteen years old, had granted pardon to Hamilton for the killing of his father on condition that Hamilton should, clad only in his shirt and kneeling, offer his naked sword to the Earl of Lennox at the market cross of Edinburgh, Stirling or Glasgow as the king might direct, perform the three pilgrimages of Scotland, and should maintain three chaplains in the collegiate church of Hamilton and three in the Blackfriars' church in Glasgow, where the deceased earl was buried, to sing masses continually for the soul of the dead. The young Earl of Lennox was appointed keeper of Dumbarton Castle in place of Hamilton of Finnart, who later became a favourite with James V, and, as master of works, was responsible for the building of Linlithgow Palace and the reconstruction of other royal residences.[15]

Stirlings of Craigbarnet and Glorat

For most of the first half of the sixteenth century the keepers of Dumbarton Castle were the Stirlings of Craigbarnet or Glorat. Craigbarnet and Glorat, small estates nestling at the foot of the Campsie Hills in the eastern portion of the earldom of Lennox, have been for centuries in the possession of the Stirling family, which can claim descent from the ancient earls of Lennox.[16]

The first of the family to hold the post, Sir John Striveling or Stirling, 3rd of Craigbarnet (which is sometimes spelt Craigbernard), was given a grant of the keepership for nineteen years in 1497 by James IV, who on his way to and from Dumbarton sometimes lodged with Sir John at Craigbarnet. On February 9th, 1507, the king received from his treasurer 24 shillings to play at the cards 'that nicht in Craigbernard'.[17]

In 1508, the Earl of Lennox made a grant of the lands of Glorat, about three miles east of Craigbarnet, to Sir John Stirling, and in the same year they passed to Sir John's second son, William, who had been custumar of Dumbarton from 1506. He succeeded his father as keeper of Dumbarton Castle in 1508 but had to resign the post on the appointment of Robert, Lord Erskine, as keeper two years later.[18]

The inventory of goods and gear of the castle in 1510, when William Stirling of Glorat made delivery to his successor, Lord Erskine, has already been mentioned in the description of the castle buildings of the fifteenth century. The furnishings and contents of most of the buildings were scanty. In St. Patrick's chapel, where another member of the family, Mr. John Stirling, officiated, were to be found 'ane auld mess book of parchment', a chalice, a chasuble of 'auld grene saten', an alb, a stole, a maniple, an amice, and a cruet.[19]

William Stirling, 1st of Glorat, returned to Dumbarton Castle as keeper on behalf of the Earl of Lennox after the earl's capture of the castle from Lord Erskine with the assistance of Stirling of Glorat and others in 1514; but after Albany's arrival in Scotland in 1516 he was replaced by Alan Stewart, 'Captain of Milan', mentioned above. When, after Albany's departure from Scotland in 1524, Lennox again captured the castle, Stirling of Glorat returned as keeper, but again his tenure of office was brief as, following the death of the Earl of Lennox in 1526, the custody of the castle was given to the man who had killed him, Sir James Hamilton of Finnart. On September 8th and 9th, 1526, a few days after the earl's death, when Stirling received gifts under the privy seal of the reliefs and non-entries of Portnellan and other lands on Lochlomondside, he was not designated as captain or keeper of Dumbarton Castle, and it may be inferred that these were intended as compensation for the loss of his appointments as keeper of the castle and custumar of Dumbarton. Stirling was later appointed deputy keeper of the castle after paying for the office £300 'usual money of Scotland' to Hamilton of Finnart, his fourth term of office lasting from March, 1527 to April, 1534.[20] In April 1531, Hamilton resigned the keepership to the young Earl of Lennox but Stirling remained in charge and indeed was at the time also curator of the young earl, who was not yet fifteen years of age.[21] Stirling was also restored in 1528 to the lucrative office of custumar of Dumbarton, which was often, but not invariably, associated with that of keeper of the castle. As custumar, he was responsible for the collection of outward customs in the trading area of the burgh of Dumbarton and also in the sea-lochs of the Firth of

Clyde and Argyll, the trade being mainly in hides, fish and woollen cloth. From the customs revenue a payment of £40 per annum was made to Stirling as part of his emoluments as keeper of the castle.[22] In 1533, James V directed the magistrates of Glasgow and Dumbarton to deliver to Stirling of Glorat from the French ships coming within their bounds three or four tuns of the best sort of wine from every ship, Stirling to make payment at the normal price; and in the same year the king gave Stirling and his successors permission to build a mill on the lands of Murroch, one mile up the river Leven from the castle.[23]

On Good Friday, April 3rd, 1534, Stirling of Glorat was on his way from Stirling to Dumbarton when he was ambushed and 'crewellie slayn' by Humphrey Galbraith, uncle and tutor of James Galbraith of Culcreuch. The motive behind the murder seems to have been revenge for Stirling's part in the capture of Dumbarton Castle from Lord Erskine twenty years before. Among the accomplices of Galbraith were two sons of Sir John Colquhoun of Luss and Andrew Cunningham of Drumquhassil, who was married to Lord Erskine's sister. It is difficult to see why Lord Erskine, by this time comfortably installed as keeper of Stirling Castle, should inspire or connive at such a dastardly affair; but it is conceivable that Galbraith, whose family had acquired an unenviable reputation for their unruly and violent conduct, might think he could curry favour with Lord Erskine in this way. Another possible motive for Galbraith and his accomplices could be that of revenge on Stirling as keeper of Dumbarton Castle and custumar of Dumbarton for some official act whereby Galbraith or his friends had suffered loss or injury.[24]

William Stirling, who had been associated with Dumbarton Castle for over a quarter of a century, was succeeded in the office of keeper by his son, George, 2nd of Glorat, who was to retain the post until 1546. By that time, the kings of both England and France had become set on securing control over Dumbarton Castle and, as will be seen, George Stirling's stout defence of the castle against both English and French, as well as against his feudal superior, won him the admiration of his fellow Scots. When it was decided in 1927 to restore the office of keeper of Dumbarton Castle after a lapse of over eighty years, it was fitting that the choice should fall on Sir George Stirling of Glorat, a direct descendant of the sixteenth-century keepers.

'The Key of the North'

The death of James V at Falkland Palace in 1542, only six days after the birth of his daughter, Mary, plunged Scotland once again into the throes of a minority. Three weeks earlier, the Scots had suffered another humiliating defeat at the hands of the English at Solway Moss. Little wonder that when James heard of his daughter's birth he exclaimed, 'It came with a lass and it will pass with a lass' (referring to the Scottish crown, which had come to the Stewart family through Marjorie Bruce), then turned his back to his lords and his face to the wall. It soon became evident that James's uncle, Henry VIII of England, was intent on making himself master of Scotland by means of a marriage between his son, Edward, and the infant queen of Scots. Over a thousand prisoners had been taken at Solway Moss, many of them nobles of standing, who were first hospitably entertained at Hampton Court and then released in return for an undertaking to promote the English marriage and end the traditional link between Scotland and France, the 'Auld Alliance'. Scotland became a hotbed of intrigue as the English and French kings sought to influence Scottish affairs, nobles and men of lower rank accepting English or French bribes and almost all acting as self-interest dictated.

The English king's breach with Rome had already in James V's reign introduced a new factor in Anglo-Scottish relations. In a letter to the English king just before James died, Sir John Dudley had written: 'No perfect reformation (of the church) will ever be had until the King (Henry) has all that part of Scotland on this side the Forth on the East and on this side Dunn Bretayne on the West.' But political domination, not the advancement of reform ideas, was the principal aim of Henry VIII and his council, who considered Dumbarton Castle, guarding the main western gateway to France, as 'a key of the realm', the possession of which by the 'Assured Scots' of the English party would prevent French military aid arriving in Scotland.[25]

In the intrigues of the early years of Queen Mary's minority, Matthew, Earl of Lennox, was to play a prominent role. Lennox was only sixteen years old when he left Scotland in 1532 for France, where he served in the Scots archer guard of the French king; and his return to Scotland in the spring of 1543 was eagerly awaited by the pro-French party, led by the Queen-Mother, Mary of Guise, and Cardinal Beaton, Archbishop of St. Andrews. They hoped that he could be used to undermine the authority of James Hamilton, 2nd Earl of Arran, who as heir-presumptive to the crown had been acknowledged by Parliament as 'second person' in the realm and governor of Scotland but was regarded by the Queen-Mother and Cardinal as unreliable. Lennox, whose father had been killed by a half-brother of the Earl of Arran, stood next in line in the succession to the throne and could challenge Arran's claim to be heir-presumptive as it depended on the questionable validity of a divorce. But Lennox's return from France had wider implications. The decision of Francis I, the French king, to send Lennox to Scotland was also 'a move in the game of international politics', as Henry VIII had just concluded a treaty of alliance with the Emperor Charles V against France and Francis was desirous of securing a hold on the kingdom of Scots.[26]

When Lennox arrived at Dumbarton with only two ships on April 5th, 1543, he was met by the constable or acting keeper of the castle, George Stirling of Glorat. He handed the keys of the castle to Lennox, who was his superior and claimed the keepership by right of an instrument of surrender by its former keeper, Hamilton of Finnart, in 1531.[27] Sir Ralph Sadler, Henry VIII's envoy in Scotland, reporting the arrival of Lennox to his master, feared that the Scottish nobles would turn towards Lennox, as the earl had boasted that 'France would now fill their Scottish purses with gold'.[28] The Earl of Arran, governor of Scotland, considered sending a complaint to the French king about Lennox and dispatched a herald to Dumbarton demanding the delivery of the castle within forty-eight hours 'upon pain of treason'.[29] Lennox replied equivocally that he was willing to do so but that the captain of the castle, Stirling of Glorat, refused to surrender the castle on the ground that he had received an undertaking in James V's reign that he would hold the castle for seven years to come.[30] As the summer went on, Henry VIII bade his envoy, Sadler, advise the Earl of Arran to expel Lennox from Scotland and 'if possible win into his hands the Castle of Dumbarton, the key of the north', which he should then entrust to one or other of the 'Assured Scots', Cassillis or Glencairn.[31]

But the summer passed and on October 6th reinforcements for the French party arrived at Dumbarton from France in a flotilla of eight ships, bearing a papal legate, Marco Grimani, Patriarch of Aquileia, sent by Pope Paul III to collect a subsidy to be spent in the defence of Scotland against the English king and in the protection of the Catholic religion, and two ambassadors from the French king on a special mission to assist the Scots against the English, in support of which they brought a large sum of money and arms and ammunition. The money, amounting to almost 10,000 gold crowns, was to be disbursed as follows — 4,000 crowns to the Queen, 2,000 crowns to Cardinal Beaton, 2,000 crowns to the Earl of Lennox, and the rest to nobles who held lands near the Border (Home, Buccleuch, Cessford and Kerr) and who were known to have been generally hostile to the English.[32]

Lennox had by this time begun to consider the possibility of a marriage with Lady Margaret Douglas, daughter of Margaret Tudor by her marriage with the Earl of Angus and niece of Henry VIII, at whose court she had lived since the age of fifteen. Such a marriage would ensure him the powerful support of the English king and would strengthen his own claim to the Scottish crown. Protesting, however, to the newly arrived French ambassadors that he was 'ready to die in the service of the most Christian King' and that he was associating with nobles of the English faction like Glencairn only in the hope of winning them over to the French side, Lennox received the munitions and money, which for safe keeping he deposited in the castle of Dumbarton.[33] The papal legate, Grimani, who had been impressed by 'the handsome and pleasing aspect' of Lennox, was nevertheless doubtful about the wisdom of entrusting all the money to him; and later the French ambassadors, in Lennox's absence, contrived to remove some of the gold from the castle to the town of Dumbarton, only for Lennox to retrieve it soon afterwards.[34] The French ambassadors were as well aware as Henry VIII of the strategic importance of Dumbarton Castle, the surrender of which to the king of England would involve the grave danger of the realm of Scotland being 'utterly lost', and they proposed to win over Lennox, who held the castle, by arranging a marriage between him and the mother of the infant queen of Scots.[35] Sadler, the English envoy in Scotland, complained in a letter to Henry VIII that 'the world is so full of falsehood, he knew not whom he might trust' but, considering that Lennox could be won over to the English side, informed Henry of Lennox's probable demands — marriage with Lady Margaret Douglas, with a suitable living in England in lieu of what he would lose in France, and assistance in claiming his title as second person in the realm.[36] As for the Queen-Mother and Cardinal Beaton, they wished 'the French gold had all been sunk in the sea than fall into the hands of Lennox'.[37]

By the end of February, 1544, Lennox, in open defiance of the governor, Arran, raised a levy of his vassals and fortified his own castle of Crookston and Glasgow Castle, as well as Dumbarton Castle. But when Arran came through to the west with a superior force,

Lennox betook himself to Dumbarton Castle, leaving the command of his forces to the Earl of Glencairn, who was defeated in battle on Glasgow Muir.[38] Lennox decided to flee to England but his ship was buffeted by contrary winds in the Clyde and he was compelled to return to Dumbarton Castle, where he summoned a conference of his kinsmen and friends. These advised him to send his brother, Robert Stewart, Bishop-elect of Caithness, and the Master of Glencairn to act as commissioners for him in the proposed negotiations for his marriage to Lady Margaret Douglas in England.[39] The earl himself in due course arrived in England and, in fulfilment of an indenture signed by his commissioners at Carlisle, whereby, among other promises, he undertook to serve the English king as his subject and to surrender the Castle of Dumbarton and the Isle of Bute, he became the husband of Lady Margaret Douglas.[40] Their son, Henry, Lord Darnley, was twenty-one years later to marry his cousin, Mary, Queen of Scots.

'A Valiant Gentleman'

Lennox was not able to fulfil his undertaking to surrender Dumbarton Castle to the English. By the contract he made with Henry VIII in June, 1544, the keeper of the castle, George Stirling of Glorat, was to be bribed with the promise of an annual pension of 100 marks (£66. 13s. 4d.) on resigning the keepership, and in July approval was given in London for the grant of an annuity of that amount to Stirling on the recommendation of Lennox 'for advancing the (English) king's affairs in Scotland'.[41] But when Lennox reached Dumbarton in August, 1544, Stirling, 'a valiant gentleman and a true Scotsman' (according to Bishop Lesley) and 'a stout man who bears no affection to England' (according to the English envoy, Sadler), refused to surrender the castle.[42] Lennox landed near the castle with 300 men, mostly English, and proceeded with a small retinue to the castle. He was at first received hospitably but after some discussion, during which Lennox presumably tempted the keeper with the promise of an English annuity, Stirling drove the earl and his companions out of the castle and back to their ships. Stirling of Glorat earned the praise of all 'guid Scottis men' for his refusal to surrender the castle to his feudal superior and for his spurning of English bribes.[43] Lennox, who had overrun the island of Bute and captured Rothesay Castle on his way north to Dumbarton, seized the castle of Dunoon and plundered the lands of Cowal on his return voyage; but these exploits did not compensate for his failure to capture Dumbarton Castle, the principal objective of his expedition.[44] Lennox's campaign in the west, along with the Earl of Hertford's invasion of Scotland by the eastern route, was part of Henry VIII's 'Rough Wooing' of Scotland, which only served to increase the Scots' detestation of the 'Auld Enemy', England.

Glorat, whose defence of the castle was so universally lauded, was probably inspired to some extent by self-interest as well as by patriotism. Surrender of the castle to Lennox would have meant for-feiture, the loss of his lands, and exile in England. His patriotic defence of the castle was rewarded in due course. In January, 1545, he received a grant under the privy seal of the keepership of Dumbarton Castle for nine years. Further, by an agreement in April, 1545, the Privy Council granted him remission for all crimes committed previously against the Queen Dowager and Governor, when Lennox held the castle, and he was provided with guns and munitions, £300 to pay his servants' fees and buy provisions and fuel, and £500 yearly so long as the war with England lasted, in addition to the usual revenues due to the keeper. At the beginning of the following year, he was also in receipt of a pension from the French government.[45]

At the end of May, 1545, an army of 2,000 gunners, 200 archers and 200 barded horses arrived from France at Dumbarton with plenty of provisions for six months and money enough to pay 2,000 Scots for the same space of time.[46] This French expeditionary force crossed over to Edinburgh and, along with a Scottish army, compelled the English to withdraw. A foray into England by a combined Scottish and French force was claimed as a success, but the autumn saw another English attempt to overthrow the pro-French government of Scotland. The south-east suffered grievously from the harrying and burning carried out by the Earl of Hertford but a projected invasion of the west by Lennox with the avowed intention of capturing Dumbarton Castle proved abortive. Lennox, after some delays, had gathered at Dublin a mixed force of Englishmen, Irishmen and Scottish Islesmen (including the claimant to the lordship of the Isles, Donald Dubh) but it did not leave Ireland until mid-November and returned there, having accomplished nothing.[47]

In the first half of 1546, Dumbarton Castle was still held by George Stirling of Glorat. Arran, the Governor, despite the agreement entered into in April, 1545, did not entirely trust Glorat, who was bold enough in August, 1545, to confiscate the horse of the governor's servitor, John

Hamilton of Turnbull, when on a mission to the castle.[48] Arran became alarmed when news was brought at the end of May, 1546, that Robert Stewart, Lennox's brother, who was Bishop-elect of Caithness, had arrived from England at Dumbarton to negotiate terms on behalf of Lennox. Stewart, who was accompanied by nineteen Scotsmen only, may have had reason to expect a friendly reception from Stirling of Glorat, in whose favour he had, as provost of the collegiate church of St. Mary, Dumbarton, made a free gift of the annual duties of the kirklands of Strathblane 'for the good service to us done and to be done'.[49] Immediately before Stewart's arrival at Dumbarton, an event quite unconnected with Stewart or Lennox and of momentous significance had occurred on the other side of Scotland. The Archbishop of St. Andrews, Cardinal Beaton, was murdered in his own castle and his murderers thereafter took forcible possession of the castle. Arran, overwhelmed by the news from St. Andrews and Dumbarton, assumed the worst — that Dumbarton Castle had been surrendered to Stewart and to the English. Later, in September, 1546, in a letter to the Pope recounting the calamities of the spring, he wrote that he had decided 'after deliberation' to concentrate his forces first against Dumbarton Castle, 'the strongest in all Scotland'.[50] On June 29th, a boy was sent out from Paisley 'to espy what they were doing in the town and castle of Dumbarton' and on July 1st another was sent from Dumbarton to Edinburgh with a letter about things necessary for the siege of the castle.[51] While Arran was engaged in the siege of the castle, which lasted fifteen days, part of his force at the Townend of Dumbarton was attacked by over a hundred MacFarlanes, MacGregors and other Highlanders, led by Walter MacFarlane of Ardleish, a younger son of MacFarlane of Arrochar. Ostensibly acting as loyal adherents of the Earl of Lennox, they were primarily imbued with the desire for plunder. Fifty servants of Arran and other lords were killed, 80 horses were stolen and many houses set on fire.[52] The siege was conducted with no great hope of success except by negotiation. By mid-July, Arran and the Privy Council, meeting at Dumbarton, extracted from the lairds of the Lennox a declaration in the presence of the Council that Stirling of Glorat ought to surrender the Castle of Dumbarton, failing which they undertook to assist Arran to recover it. A week later, on July 20th, 1546, the castle was surrendered.[53]

Arran, in his letter to the Pope and Cardinals on September 1st, 1546, claimed to have recovered Dumbarton Castle (the site of which, he wrote, was 'naturally impregnable') by 'a miracle'.[54] But the isolation of Glorat from any help from his Lennox neighbours was combined with the threat of deprivation of his government pensions and fees and forfeiture of all his lands and goods. Stirling had by his admission of Robert Stewart to the castle broken the agreement of April, 1545, in which he had promised not to receive 'an Englishman nor writing out of England nor the Earl of Lennox nor any of his servants nor any favourers of England'; and as one of the conditions imposed upon him had been the delivery of his son and heir and his brother as hostages, the pressure upon him to surrender was overwhelming. According to Lesley, the castle could not be won by force of arms but by the persuasive powers of the Earl of Huntly, who contrived at last to change Stirling's views. The promise of compensation was offered as well as threats, but it fell far short of what he had received in terms of the agreement of April, 1545, and indeed, according to one chronicle, the governor 'never keipit ane word of his promessis'.[55] A year after his surrender, he received in July, 1547, 'for overgiving of the Castle of Dumbarton' 16 bolls of meal, valued at £16. He was also promised the profits from the manor of Cardross valued at £20 per annum, but he was killed at Pinkie on September 10th, 1547, and it was not until 1550 that his widow received payment for the four years since 1546.[56] In addition, as was not unusual in Scotland after periods of civil disorder, he was granted remission for the many acts of plunder committed during his tenure of the keepership of the castle.[57]

Robert Stewart, Lennox's brother, who had been resident in the castle since the end of May, was probably regarded by Arran as the more important person in the negotiations for surrender. Stewart was in 1571 to become Earl of Lennox after the assassination of his brother and, as patron of the historian, Lindsay of Pitscottie, may have given his version of what happened in 1546 to Pitscottie, who wrote of Stewart having been 'betrayed' by Stirling of Glorat.[58] At any rate, Stewart was treated leniently. He appeared before the Privy Council at Dumbarton, charged with having departed into England as hostage for his brother, Lennox, having there engaged in treasonable practices, and on his return having held Dumbarton Castle against the Governor for fifteen days. On Stewart's submission to the Council, the Governor undertook to provide him with as much annual income as he had enjoyed in 1544, but the 'fruits' of the bishopric of Caithness to which he had been nominated in 1541 and never consecrated were granted to Alexander Gordon, who was brother of the Earl of Huntly and who had already been nominated in place of Stewart following the forfeiture of the latter along with his brother in 1544.[59] Thus, by threats and promises, Arran achieved the surrender of the castle in less than three weeks — 'a miracle' as he informed the Pope.

The Hamilton Keepers

The Earl of Arran, after his success at Dumbarton Castle in July, 1546, found himself in a stronger position than he had enjoyed since he became Governor, as although St. Andrews Castle still held out against him, the death of Cardinal Beaton had removed one who had been at best a difficult ally and always a potential rival for supreme power. Not only Arran but his Hamilton kinsmen generally benefited as one lucrative appointment after another came their way as a result of Arran's control of royal patronage. Two of his half-brothers gained preferment to the highest positions in the church in Scotland. John Hamilton, the shrewd Abbot of Paisley and Bishop-elect of Dunkeld, was nominated to the see of St. Andrews, rendered vacant by the assassination of Cardinal Beaton, and when Bishop Gavin Dunbar of Glasgow died in April, 1547, another half-brother, James Hamilton, received the Governor's nomination to the see, although in the end he had to be content with the diocese of Argyll. To Dumbarton Castle Arran assigned as keeper or captain Andrew Hamilton, whose two brothers also received similar appointments to Linlithgow Palace and Dunbar Castle. Arran's patronage also favoured Hamiltons in a more humble station of life. Following the death of the vicar of Kilpatrick near Dumbarton, (Sir) Thomas Hamilton was presented to the vicarage on October 15th, 1547, and within a few months he had also acquired the chaplaincy of the altar of the Blessed Virgin Mary in the parish church of Dumbarton and the chaplaincy of the chapel of St. Patrick in Dumbarton Castle, both of which had been rendered vacant by the death of (Sir) Thomas Jackson.[60] Arran's regard for his family's interests was not something new in Scottish politics, but the lavish generosity with public funds which he evinced exceeded anything of the kind hitherto experienced, and when he surrendered the office of Regent in 1554 he left a deficit of £30,000. In the Treasurer's Accounts are many entries relating to presents for the wives and daughters of Hamiltons, including one to Nanse Crawford, wife of Andrew Hamilton, keeper of Dumbarton Castle, in January, 1547 — 4 ells of French black silk for a gown, 7 ells of lisle worsted and 1½ ells of velvet for a kirtle. The Governor's generosity was not confined to Hamiltons: on a visit to Dumbarton in May, 1547, he gave money to two persons who had suffered loss during the siege of Dumbarton Castle in the previous year — £3. 6s. to a poor woman who had her 'kye slain', 40s. to a poor smith whose house and forge had been burned, as well as 48s. to 'certain minstrels of the town and their Robin Hood', presumably for their performance in the May Day festivities.[61]

Andrew Hamilton, who was keeper of Dumbarton Castle and custumar of Dumbarton from 1546 to 1553, was generally known as Hamilton of Cochno, an estate in the parish of Kilpatrick which his descendants were to occupy down to modern times. For some time after 1525, when John Hamilton, Arran's half-brother, became Abbot of Paisley, Hamiltons without lands in their native Lanarkshire had been infiltrating into Renfrewshire and Dumbartonshire, in which counties Paisley Abbey owned many lands. The new tenure of feuing land benefited abbot and feuar alike, and the process of feuing the abbey lands begun under Abbot John Hamilton was continued and developed by his successor, Arran's son, Claud Hamilton, who was appointed commendator of the abbey in 1553 when he was only ten years of age. Long before the end of the century there were no fewer than seven lairds or feuars called Hamilton occupying abbey lands in the parish of Kilpatrick. Andrew Hamilton, whose connection with Cochno (north of the present Clydebank) began in 1550, was Provost of Glasgow in 1541, 1553 and 1556, and it was during his keepership that the young Mary, Queen of Scots, stayed in Dumbarton Castle prior to her departure for France in 1548.[62]

Hamilton carried out extensive repairs to the fortifications of the castle, the total expenditure from 1546 to 1553, including repairs, furnishings and victualling, amounting to almost £5,000. He also undertook the supply of timber from the forests of the Colquhouns of Luss on Lochlomondside for the Earl of Arran's own houses.[63] Whether in consequence of some action as keeper or custumar or for some other reason, Hamilton was set upon in the High Street of Dumbarton on March 18th, 1564, by a band of Houstons, comprising Patrick Houston of that Ilk, his four brothers, three men from Dumbarton and one from Kilpatrick. He fortunately escaped by finding refuge in a house nearby. The Houstons (with one exception) were found guilty of 'unlawfully convening the lieges' and attempting to slaughter Hamilton.[64] In his latter years, as a loyal supporter of Mary, Queen of Scots, Hamilton suffered hardship and met with disaster. His son was beheaded for his part in seizing the castle of Glasgow in 1571, Hamilton, whose lands had been forfeited and who himself was declared a traitor, dying a month after his son.[65]

Hamilton of Cochno had been succeeded as keeper in 1553 by another of the same name, Andrew Hamilton of Ardoch, who at the time of his promotion was keeper of the castle of Hamilton, the residence of the Duke of Châtelherault as the Earl of Arran had become in February, 1549. Little is known of him, not even which of the many Ardochs in Scotland he possessed. During all the time that Hamiltons were captains or keepers of Dumbarton Castle, the Duke of Châtelherault was nominally the governor of the castle. In April, 1554, he lost the office of Governor or Regent of Scotland, and in 1562, following the discovery of a plot in which his son was involved, the duke had also to surrender control of Dumbarton Castle to the crown.

When the Hamiltons regained royal favour later in the century, the duke's son, Lord John Hamilton (later Marquis of Hamilton), was appointed by James VI in 1585 governor of Dumbarton Castle as part of the reward for his staunch support of the king. During his tenure of the governorship from 1585 to 1597 he appointed deputies as keepers, among them Claud Hamilton of Cochno, second son of the keeper from 1546 to 1553. Claud Hamilton who, like his father and some other keepers, acted as custumar of Dumbarton, was to remain as keeper from 1590 to 1597, when Lord John Hamilton was replaced as governor by the second Duke of Lennox.

Mary, Queen of Scots, at Dumbarton Castle

Arran's first task after the surrender of Dumbarton Castle in 1546 was to lay siege to St. Andrews Castle, but the siege was carried on in half-hearted fashion and was for long ineffective. It was to a French fleet, which sailed up the east coast in July, 1547, that the beleaguered 'Castilians' surrendered, some of them, including John Knox, being sent to France to be galley-slaves. In the autumn of 1547 a well-equipped English army led by Protector Somerset crossed the border and on September 10th ('Black Saturday') inflicted a crushing defeat on a much larger army of Scots at Pinkie Cleugh near Musselburgh. Although Somerset withdrew after his victory, the English fleet which had accompanied the army was used to capture Inchcolm, Inchkeith and Broughty Castle, where English garrisons were installed. In the south-west of Scotland, Dumfries and other places were also garrisoned by English troops. The outlook for the Scots was indeed dark and foreboding. While Somerset was in Scotland, fears for the safety of the young queen were such that she was conveyed from Stirling Castle to the island priory of Inchmahome in Menteith, where she remained for a few weeks until Somerset re-crossed the border.[66]

Scotland, as before on many occasions, looked for assistance to the 'Auld Alliance' with France, where Henry II had just come to the throne. The envoy sent by the Earl of Arran to France was John Hamilton of Millburn. Before he left from Dumbarton early in November, 1547, he was paid £1,238. 17s. 6d., owing to him for his services as master of works for the Queen Dowager; in addition, he was supplied with a fine array of clothes for his mission to the King of France — a riding cloak, a doublet, 9 ells of black velvet to line the neck of the cloak, and $3\frac{3}{4}$ ells of Paris black silk for another cloak, all of which were to be packed in canvas and sent to Dumbarton for him. John Knox recounts with grim relish the tale of his return. After being received favourably by King Henry and the Cardinal of Lorraine, he sailed for Scotland with important letters for the Queen Dowager and the Earl of Arran, but (in Knox's words), 'passing up to the craig of Dumbarton before his letters were delivered, he broke his neck and so God took away a proud, ignorant enemy'.[67]

The unfortunate envoy probably arrived and died on Christmas Day, 1547, when two French ships landed fifty captains at Dumbarton with as much money from the Pope as would pay 10,000 Scottish soldiers for a year, each of the captains to pay the money to his company of Scots. The following day, St. Stephen's Day, three of the chief captains, dressed in white satin, appeared before the Queen-Mother and the Privy Council at Stirling and promised that as soon as 10,000 Scots were mustered, the King of France would send an army of 30,000 to England and that already 6,000 Frenchmen were embarked on ships for Scotland, waiting only for the wind.[68] But the French king was only prepared to provide this assistance on his own terms, which Arran, the Governor, accepted at the end of January, 1548. Arran promised that, in return for a duchy in France, he would arrange for the transport of the young queen to France, for her marriage to the French Dauphin, and for the delivery of the Scottish fortresses to the French.[69]

English garrisons remained in places on the east coast as far north as Broughty Castle through the winter of 1547-48, and a double invasion by the English in February, 1548, threatened both the eastern and western lowlands. In the west, the Earl of Lennox was once again unsuccessful, but in the east the English Commander, Grey of Wilton, seized Haddington, only eighteen miles from Edinburgh, fortified it and held it until 1549.[70] In late February, 1548, Grey wrote to Somerset, the English Protector, that Scotland was 'dismayed at my entry' and that the young queen was taken by her guardians, Lord Erskine and Lord Livingston, from Stirling Castle to Dumbarton Castle for fear of further advance by the English invasion force.[71] The young queen was to remain for over five months at Dumbarton. Soon after her arrival, she fell ill with smallpox (or perhaps measles), and a rumour spread that she had died. Her mother, Mary of Guise, saw to it that her fellow-countrymen were in charge of the castle. A Scotsman was placed as sentry at the gate, but whenever anyone approached from outside the castle, ten or twelve French soldiers of the garrison went to the gate and no one was allowed admission who did not bring a letter from the Queen Dowager. Other fortresses, Dunbar and Blackness, were handed over to French control at this time while the English still occupied most of the south-east of Scotland.[72]

In the month of June, 1548, in response to many petitions from the Queen-Mother, a French fleet arrived at Leith and landed a mixed force of 6,000 soldiers, half of them Germans, under André de Montalembert, Sieur d'Essé, who along with the Scots laid siege to Haddington, still held by Grey of Wilton. It was at the abbey near to the town on July 7th, 1548, that the French plenipotentiaries and the Scottish estates in the presence of the Queen Dowager and the Governor agreed to a treaty whereby Mary, Queen of Scots, was to marry the French Dauphin and in return the French king would maintain the defence of Scotland and guarantee Scottish freedom and laws. Arran, who had nourished hopes of a marriage between the young queen and his own son, in due course received the French duchy which had been promised and henceforth he came to be known as the Duke of Châtelherault.[73] The Treaty of Haddington made Scotland almost a French province. The Queen-Mother herself wrote in a letter that it 'put all things into the hands of the French king', and it is not surprising that when Henry II heard of the signing of the treaty he 'leaped for blitheness and was so blithe that it seemed incredible', exclaiming, 'France and Scotland are now one country.'[74]

Before the Treaty of Haddington was signed, four French galleys under Admiral de Villegagnon set off from Leith Roads as if to make for France but once out of sight of land made their way north by the treacherous Pentland Firth and round to the west of Scotland and Dumbarton. The Queen-Mother arrived from Haddington at Dumbarton in mid-July and began to make preparations for her daughter's departure to France. The young queen, not yet six years of age, went on board the French royal galley, specially commissioned for her, at the end of July.[75] Along with her went her guardians, Lord Erskine and Lord Livingston; her governess, Lady Fleming, an illegitimate daughter of James IV and a half-sister of James V; four young girls all of the same age as the queen, the 'Queen's Maries' — Mary Fleming, daughter of Lady Fleming; Mary Livingston, daughter of Lord Livingston; Mary Beaton, a relative of Cardinal Beaton; and Mary Seton, daughter of Lord Seton; two (possibly three) of the queen's half-brothers, illegitimate sons of James V; and many children, ladies and gentlemen of the noblest families of Scotland.

For a week after embarking, the weather was so stormy that the ships lay at anchor in the Clyde near the castle. During the week of waiting, a west wind driving up the firth made conditions aboard ship so uncomfortable that Lady Fleming demanded to be put on shore 'to repose her' but the ship's captain told her she could go to France and like it, or drown on the way, but she would not be allowed to go back on land. By August 7th, the wind had swung round to the east, the weather had turned fine and the small fleet, under the command of de Brézé, set sail for France. After running through a storm off Cornwall so severe that the rudder was broken on the queen's ship but, according to de Brézé, 'by divine intervention' repaired almost at once, the flotilla reached Roscoff in Brittany on August 13th.[76] Mary's marriage to the Dauphin did not take place until 1558. She was for a brief period queen of France after her husband succeeded his father as Francis II but he died soon afterwards and in August, 1561, Mary returned to her native land.

Queen Mary's Personal Reign

Mary, Queen of Scots, a widow at nineteen years of age, returned to a Scotland very much changed since her departure in 1548. The Treaty of Edinburgh, signed by English and French commissioners on July 6th, 1560 (a few weeks after the death of the Queen-Mother) had transformed relations between England and Scotland. Although Queen

Mary was at first reluctant to ratify the treaty and still retained her contacts with France, French influence steadily declined. The importance of Dumbarton Castle, as guarding the western sea-route to and from France, had already diminished before the Treaty of Edinburgh, and in February, 1560, there was only a skeleton garrison of six soldiers.[77] It was by the east-coast route that Mary travelled from France and it was at Leith that she landed on August 19th, 1561. The support of many of the Scottish people for the new Protestant religion, the question of her marriage, the ambitions of powerful subjects, the determination of Queen Elizabeth of England to intervene in Scottish affairs, made the first few years in Scotland a difficult period for the young queen; but she managed, nevertheless, for a time to establish herself as ruler of her kingdom.

Among those whom she regarded as likely to threaten her security in the early years of her personal reign were the Duke of Châtelherault, next in succession to the throne, and his son, James Hamilton, Earl of Arran. For his son and heir the duke had hoped for a brilliant marriage such as would befit one of royal lineage — at first with the daughter of the Duke of Montpenser in France, then with Queen Elizabeth of England, and, after the death of Francis II of France, with his widow, Mary, Queen of Scots.[78] The Hamiltons were at first optimistic about the prospects of a royal marriage, but even before Mary had rejected Arran's advances the duke became as suspicious of the queen's intentions as she was of his. The duke feared that Dumbarton Castle, of which he had had control since 1546, might be taken from him and that he would thus be left 'without a place of succour' if the queen's enmity to him should increase. He informed the English ambassador, Randolph, in November, 1561 (only four months after Mary's return to Scotland), that he would assure himself by all means available that he would keep Dumbarton Castle, relying on the English queen, 'who hath promised me by her letter never to see me nor my house wrecked'. He claimed that when he captured the castle in 1546 he received a promise by word of mouth from the Queen-Mother that he should possess the castle and its revenues for nineteen years.[79]

In the spring of 1562 the young Earl of Arran, whose aspiration to a marriage with the young Scottish queen had become an obsession, was involved in a plot with James Hepburn, Earl of Bothwell, to abduct the queen by force and transport her to Dumbarton Castle. Arran, who had previously been engaged in bitter rivalry with Bothwell, and had possibly been inveigled into the plot by Bothwell, started to act in a curious fashion, revealing the details of the plot to John Knox and then to the queen herself. Not only his enemies but also his friends and relations began to have doubts about his sanity. According to the English ambassador, to whom Arran sent a letter to be delivered to Queen Mary, men feared that the young earl would 'turn into some dangerous and incurable sickness or play some day some mad part that will bring him into mischief'.[80] His father, the duke, was compelled because of the alleged plot to give up all claims to Dumbarton Castle, which was surrendered to the queen on April 25th, 1562. The Earl of Arran was never to regain his sanity but lingered on until 1609, a close prisoner in one or other of his own castles.

In the following year, Queen Mary visited Dumbarton Castle on a progress through the Lennox and Argyll. On Thursday, July 15th, 1563, she dined at the castle and passed on to Rossdhu, the castle of Sir John Colquhoun of Luss, with whom she stayed until the Saturday, when she returned to Dumbarton Castle. There she remained over the weekend until Monday, July 19th, when she sailed down the Clyde to Carrick Castle, passing from there by Ardkinglas and Dunderave to Inveraray, where she stayed with her half-sister, the Countess of Argyll. The list of eatables for her sojourn at Dumbarton and Rossdhu is interesting for the light it throws on the diet of the period: it included 144 loaves; 5 gallons, 3 quarts of white wine; 2 salt salmon; 2 salt ling; 2 cod; 3 salmon trout; 47 trout; 3 dozen plaice; 150 eggs, and 16 pounds of butter.[81]

The marriage of Mary, Queen of Scots, to her step-cousin, Henry, Lord Darnley, helped to bring about the restoration of his father, the Earl of Lennox, to the lands he had forfeited twenty years before. Even before her marriage to Darnley, Mary was considering handing over the custody of Dumbarton Castle to Lennox but decided instead to place it in the charge of someone less powerful and more likely to be loyal to her — another step-cousin, John, 5th Lord Fleming. Fleming, whose mother, a natural daughter of James IV, had been the young queen's governess and who had himself accompanied the queen to France in 1548, was also appointed Great Chamberlain of Scotland, an office which his father and grandfather had held before him. He was to prove a staunch supporter and loyal servant of the queen.[82]

Mary's troubles multiplied after her marriage to Darnley. The murder of her favourite servant, Riccio, her estrangement from her husband, Lord Darnley, his assassination, and her subsequent marriage to the Earl of Bothwell, strongly suspected of having been

involved in the assassination, led to her imprisonment in Lochleven
Castle and to her deposition in July, 1567, in favour of her infant son,
James. She was however not without support, particularly from those
nobles who still remained faithful to the Catholic Church. When, in
May, 1568, she escaped from Lochleven Castle, she made her way to
the west country, where at Hamilton over 6000 rallied to her cause, an
army vastly superior in numbers to that of her half-brother, the
Regent, the Earl of Moray, who mustered his men at Glasgow on the
north bank of the Clyde. Mary was unwilling to become the puppet of
the Hamiltons, who claimed that the regency rightfully belonged to
their family and who saw in the overthrow of Moray an opportunity to
advance their own interests; and she decided to make for the security of
Dumbarton Castle, held by the trusted Lord Fleming.[83] Safe in the
stronghold of Dumbarton, Mary could hope to find support for her in
the country at large increase. It might have been better for her had she
made for Dumbarton first after escaping from Lochleven or at any rate
avoided conflict with Moray on her way there from the Hamilton
country. But her supporters welcomed the opportunity to inflict a
decisive defeat on Regent Moray. To reach Dumbarton, her army had
to by-pass Glasgow and it was on the south side of the city at Langside
on May 13th, 1568, that the queen and her half-brother engaged in
battle. The queen's army lacked leadership, and before long all was in
confusion. When defeat was inevitable, Mary still hoped to find a place
of refuge in Dumbarton Castle, but her route was cut off by Moray's
troops and, led by Lord Herries, she fled south, first to the Maxwell
castle of Terregles, then to the abbey of Dundrennan, and finally across
the Solway Firth to England.

Mary's arrival in England was the cause of considerable embarrass-
ment to Elizabeth, who was for some time doubtful how to deal with
the exiled queen, at first kept in close confinement in Carlisle. During
the lengthy negotiations between the two queens (Mary wrote more
than twenty letters from Carlisle to Elizabeth), Dumbarton Castle was
more than once a 'troublesome point'. Sir Francis Knollys, a polished
courtier, was despatched by Elizabeth to treat with Mary, who asked
that Elizabeth would either let her go to France 'or else that she will put
me into Dumbarton, unless she will hold me as a prisoner, for I am sure
that she will not of her power put me into my Lord of Murray's hands'
— a statement which Knollys interpreted as a declaration that she
dared not go to Dumbarton by herself if set at liberty. Elizabeth, when
asked in June, 1568, by Mary to permit Lord Fleming to pass to France

to obtain financial assistance for her, expressed herself astonished at the request. 'You surely doubt my wisdom in asking for such a thing as to let the keeper of such a place to go there, being at the moment the only strength where the French can enter — not so much to aid Scotland as to annoy England.'[84] Elizabeth's suspicions about Mary's intentions in regard to Dumbarton Castle and its possible use as a base for French intervention were strengthened by reports from the English envoy in Paris that the Duke of Châtelherault, then in France, had been instructed by Mary to procure arms and money and convey them to Dumbarton Castle and that he had left for Scotland in September, 1568, with 1500 arquebusiers.[85] At any rate, Mary's requests were not granted and she was to remain a prisoner in England for the rest of her life.

A Marian Stronghold

From the time of Mary's flight into England in May, 1568, Dumbarton Castle became a Marian stronghold, a focal point of resistance to Moray's regime. On the 12th of September, 1568, at a conference of Mary's supporters in the castle, they entered into a bond or covenant, the so-called Dumbarton Bond, to defend her cause, forcefully repudiating the charges of complicity in Darnley's murder levelled against Mary and based on what came to be known as the Casket Letters. By this time, according to John Willock, moderator of the general assembly of the Church of Scotland, 'the whole west country is in such a state that no man comes to the parish church without his armour and weapons and every man is ready to avenge his old and new quarrels'.[86]

Lord Fleming, keeper of Dumbarton Castle, having returned from his missions in England on behalf of Queen Mary, proceeded to make ready against the dangers of attack by the forces of Regent Moray. With the help of the Earl of Argyll, he hired about 100 hagbutters, whom he employed to surround the town of Dumbarton with trenches and 'fortify' the parish church of Dumbarton. At the beginning of 1569, his men made attacks on the Colquhouns' castle of Dunglass, situated two miles up the river Clyde from Dumbarton Castle and occupied by the Regent's soldiers, who had been engaged in protecting the people of Dumbarton and district from the 'daily depredations' by men of the castle garrison.[87] It was not until the summer of 1569 that preparations for a close siege were put in hand by the Regent. Queen Elizabeth, whose influence in Scottish affairs had by this time increased enormously since Mary's arrival in England, held the balance between the Marians and Moray's supporters, and she preferred not to let the balance be weighted unduly in Moray's favour. When she heard of Moray's intention of capturing Dumbarton Castle, she wrote to him personally in a letter of August 20th, reminding him of his dependence upon her and forbidding him to engage in such an enterprise: 'Though in words and promises you appear to depend on our favour, in your deeds you seek to fortify your own estate without our advice; wherefore we require you peremptorily to consider our last letter . . . forbearing meantime not only to siege Dumbarton but also to send any force to the west.'[88]

The Regent denied making preparations for a force in the west but he and his council were already from the beginning of August taking measures for the recovery of Dumbarton Castle from Lord Fleming. A tax was levied on landholders in the shires of Dumbarton, Renfrew and the seven parishes of the Lennox in Stirlingshire for the maintenance of a force under the command of Lord Sempill either at Dunglass or in the town of Dumbarton, while the burghs of Glasgow, Renfrew, Dumbarton, Irvine and Ayr were forbidden to pass with their boats to the fishing or otherwise 'doun the watter of Clyde' or come up the same for any reason whatsoever, or resort towards the castle of Dumbarton. In September, 1569, the council ordered the destruction of the castle of Boghall in Lanarkshire, the family residence of John Fleming, a relative of Lord Fleming who played an active part in the defence of the castle.[89] By the end of the year, the Regent still did not consider it feasible to commit himself to an assault on what was regarded as an impregnable fortress and tried other methods to induce Lord Fleming to surrender, sending the Master of Graham, son of the Earl of Montrose, to bargain with Fleming in December. According to Sir William Drury, in charge of the English troops at Berwick, Fleming would have surrendered the castle if Moray had offered a large enough bribe in the form of the revenues of one of the abbeys, now in the gift of the crown; but Drury's opinion was perhaps based only on his knowledge of the many Scottish nobles willing to receive pensions from Queen Elizabeth.[90] At the beginning of January, 1570, the Regent himself went to Dumbarton, but by then Thomas Fleming, brother to John Fleming of Boghall, had arrived at Loch Ryan with 'two greit schippis farth of France, laidin with all manner of furneshing of victualls belanging to the halding of ane castell'; and Lord Fleming, in expectation of their imminent arrival, refused to continue any further discussions about the surrender of the castle.[91]

Regent Moray had another, even more pressing problem which took him back to the east of Scotland: Sir William Kirkcaldy of Grange, keeper of Edinburgh Castle, which contained the regalia, the records of the kingdom and a vast store of ordnance and ammunition, had declared for Queen Mary.[92] Before anything could be done by Moray to deal with the new situation, he was shot dead at Linlithgow on January 23rd, 1570, by Hamilton of Bothwellhaugh, who nursed a personal grievance against the Regent but whose crime was committed with the foreknowledge of other Hamiltons. On hearing the news of the Regent's death, his soldiers in the neighbourhood of Dumbarton made for Stirling, where the infant king, James VI, was living in the care of the Earl of Mar. Fleming, having received the supplies sent from France, was then able to send soldiers from the castle garrison to occupy the town of Dumbarton.[93] It was at this time that Fleming's men destroyed the fortifications at the parish church which had been erected by them a year before but thereafter occupied by the Regent's forces. (Fleming later rebutted allegations that his followers had destroyed the parish churches of Dumbarton and Cardross and also the Collegiate Church of Dumbarton, which last, he maintained, was demolished by the 'congregation' in 1569. He was also accused of taking building material from houses in Dumbarton belonging to John Smollett and others who did not support Queen Mary in order to make new fortifications at the castle, including stables for horses sent from France.)[94]

On March 21st, 1570, there arrived at Dumbarton, Monsieur Vérac, the *valet de chambre* of the French king, Charles IX, with letters to 'every great man' in Scotland, asking them to uphold the authority of Queen Mary and to maintain '*la bonne et ancienne alliance*' with France; and a convention of Marian nobles held in April at Linlithgow was attended by Vérac in order to assess the strength of support for the exiled queen.[95] In a memorandum sent in that month by the leading Marian nobles to Queen Mary's ambassador in France, it was requested that the French king send, together with money to equip 500 to 1000 Scottish light horsemen, one or two hundred German horsemen to 'the landing-place most sure and most convenient', Dumbarton, where the force would immediately obtain security from attack and opportunity to store weapons and ammunition. It was pointed out that although most of the people of the Lennox except the laird of Buchanan

supported the Earl of Lennox, Lord Fleming, provided he was well
supplied and could command 300 foot soldiers and 200 cavalry, would
be able to 'daunt the whole' from Dumbarton Castle. They proposed
also that Fleming be provided with two pinnaces, one to be 'master of
the river' and the other to carry messages to France. It was added that,
in order to minimise the natural antagonism of the Scots to foreigners,
it would be advisable to choose as leader of the French expedition
someone popular among the Scots, the name suggested being
that of Henry of Valois, *le bâtard d'Angoulême*, son of Henry II
of France and Lady Fleming, the governess of Queen Mary, and a
grandson of James IV. Vérac, the French envoy, sailed from
Dumbarton on April 20th, 1570, but the assistance requested was slow
to materialise. On May 28th, the Cardinal of Lorraine wrote to
Kirkcaldy of Grange, who held Edinburgh Castle and also required
French assistance, that ample supplies for the Marian cause were being
entrusted to Thomas Fleming, who had already arrived with two ships
from France earlier in the year. In July Fleming was reported to be in
Brittany with 400 arquebusiers, but his expedition failed to arrive in
Scotland; and he was later blamed for having 'done his duty very
badly'. Vérac himself returned to Scotland on September 7th along with
28 companions and bringing with him oranges, raisins and biscuit
bread.[96]

In the meantime, the Earl of Lennox, who had been resident in
England since 1567, was appointed regent in succession to the
murdered Earl of Moray. The choice of Lennox as regent was given
prior approval by Queen Elizabeth but was opposed by the Marians,
most bitterly of all by the Hamiltons, hereditary rivals of the Lennox
family, and sporadic civil war ensued. Lennox returned to Scotland in
May in the company of the English commander at Berwick, Sir
William Drury, whose troops helped Lennox to devastate the lands of
the Hamiltons, the Flemings, the Livingstons and other Marian nobles,
killing the deer and the white cattle in the forest of Cumbernauld
belonging to Lord Fleming.[97] Drury, the English general, attempted
unsuccessfully to arrange an armistice both at Edinburgh and
Dumbarton. Arriving at Glasgow on May 14th, 1570, he sent a message
to Lord Fleming and Archbishop Hamilton, then in Dumbarton Castle,
proposing a 'parley' with them. They sent a reply to the effect that they
would meet him next day at the village of Kilpatrick, five miles from
Dumbarton, but failed to appear at the appointed time, whereupon
Drury proceeded to Dumbarton Castle. There he was told by a

messenger that the keeper and the archbishop were prepared to discuss the matter with him, but when he was within gunshot of the castle, they sent another refusal. As Drury turned his horse away from the castle walls, several arquebuses and a small cannon were fired at him, an action denounced by the enemies of the Marians as treachery of the most despicable character. A contemporary poem, 'The Tressoune of Dunbartane', published in Edinburgh by Robert Lekprevick in 1570, gave a colourful account of the incident, finding comparisons for the heinous conduct of Fleming's soldiers with that of barbarians such as the Highland chiefs, MacLeod and MacLean, the Turks, and even the 'mekle Deill':

> The General raid with mony Demylance
> Doune to Dunbartane doand na man Ill,
> Quhair furious Fleming schot his Ordinance,
> Willing to wraik him, wantit na gude will.[98]

Lennox, even before his formal appointment as regent on behalf of his grandson, James VI, was particularly keen to gain possession of Dumbarton Castle (in which he had been born) both because it was utilised as a stronghold for the Marians, who could be supplied from France, and also because it lay at the centre of his own earldom. Memories of his own unsuccessful attempts more than twenty years before to capture it from Stirling of Glorat must also have strengthened his resolve to capture the castle. But men, money and munitions were needed, and he found his patron, Queen Elizabeth, refusing to sanction a close siege as she was at the time negotiating with the French king and unwilling to offend him. She still regarded the castle as important to her control of Scotland, and in the negotiations for the liberation of Queen Mary, which still continued, she demanded in August, 1570, that the castles of Edinburgh and Dumbarton, both held by Marians, should be surrendered to her, that four hostages from the Scottish nobility and one hostage from the French royal family be kept in England — demands which the Scottish queen dismissed without hesitation as 'unreasonable', saying she would never bring the realm of Scotland into bondage no matter what the queen of England might do to her.[99] Negotiations about the future of Queen Mary dragged on and fighting between Lennox and the Marians continued, but, at the instigation of Queen Elizabeth, a truce was arranged in September, 1570, between Lennox and the Marians, to last for six months.[100]

Capture of the Castle

By 1571, Lord Fleming had successfully held Dumbarton Castle for six years. He was said to have boasted that he had, as it were, in his hands 'the fetters of Scotland' and that whenever the French king was able to send some small force to Dumbarton he could bring all Scotland under subjection. His confidence in his ability to retain control of the castle had been increased by the defection of Kirkcaldy of Grange, keeper of Edinburgh Castle, to Queen Mary's side and by the knowledge that Lennox was incapable of sustained physical effort. In addition to being troubled with gout, Lennox had suffered injury by a fall from his horse.[101] Fleming's confidence, however, was to be rudely shaken at the beginning of April, 1571, when the six-month truce expired.

In the spring of 1571, Robert Douglas, one of the Lennox family of Douglas of Mains and a kinsman of the Earl of Lennox, was approached by a former soldier of the Dumbarton Castle garrison, a man called Robertson, whose wife had been ignominiously whipped for alleged theft by order of Lord Fleming.[102] Inspired by a desire for revenge, Robertson declared to Douglas that he was prepared to lead a party of soldiers up the rocks of the castle by a route known to him. Robertson was introduced to John Cunningham of Drumquhassil, who offered him a reward if the mission was successful and, lest Robertson was decoying them into a trap, took his daughter and son-in-law into custody as hostages. Captain Thomas Crawfurd of Jordanhill was appointed by Lennox to be in charge of the proposed attempt to capture the castle along with Cunningham of Drumquhassil. Both men held lands in the Lennox and both were soldiers of experience. A son of the laird of Kilbirnie, Crawfurd had been captured at Pinkie in 1547 and had thereafter served in France in the Scots Guard, returning to Scotland in 1561 with Queen Mary. As servant of Darnley during the latter's illness in 1567, he acted as messenger between Darnley and Queen Mary before the fateful journey from Glasgow to Edinburgh. He had, after the murder of Darnley, adhered to Darnley's father, the Earl of Lennox, although his two brothers, Hugh, the eldest, and Patrick, laird of Cartsburn, supported Queen Mary and were denounced as rebels after Langside in 1568.[103] At the hearing of the commission of York in December, 1568, Crawfurd gave evidence relating to the events before Darnley's murder; and in the following year he laid charges against Maitland of Lethington of complicity in Darnley's murder, charges which led to his imprisonment in Edinburgh Castle, although he was later released by Kirkcaldy of Grange. John Cunningham of Drumquhassil was a cadet of the family of the Earl of Glencairn, whose castle in the Lennox, Kilmaronock, was only a few miles away from Drumquhassil. A vassal of the Earl of Lennox, Cunningham was appointed joint-Treasurer of Scotland when Lennox was made Regent in July, 1570, and he obtained another office in December, when he became Collector-General of taxation in Scotland.[104]

Preparations for the capture of the castle went speedily ahead in Glasgow. On the afternoon of April 1st, 1571, Cunningham and Captain David Home left Glasgow with an advance force of horsemen in order to intercept anyone who might be travelling in the direction of Dumbarton, fourteen miles down the river Clyde. They arrived before it was dark at Dumbuck, a hill about a mile from the castle, and were joined before midnight by Captain Crawfurd, Captain Alexander Ramsay and about a hundred men, carrying ropes and ladders as well as weapons. At Dumbuck Crawfurd explained to the soldiers the purpose of the expedition, offering to anyone who wished the opportunity to withdraw, but none of them took advantage of the offer. Ropes and ladders were sorted out and after midnight, when the moon had gone down in a clear, starry sky, the soldiers set off on foot for the Castle Rock. Their route lay across boggy ground with many ditches but Robertson acted as guide, leading the way and the others following in single file, each man coupled with a rope to the man in front. At one stage they became alarmed as a bright light shone and then disappeared — a phenomenon afterwards explained as an *ignis fatuus* or will-o'-the wisp. They again became anxious when they came to a burn, Gruggie's Burn as it is now called, which was bridged only by a tree. As it was fallen down, their suspicions were naturally aroused; but the tree-bridge was put in place and the advance through the darkness continued until the Castle Rock was reached.

The ascent was to be made on the north-east side of the eastern peak, which was called the 'Beak', at a point well away from the main defences, the Wallace Tower on the north side and the lower bailey on the south side.[105] It was a steep, almost precipitous face, broken up by numerous ledges and today would be reckoned, in mountaineering jargon, a 'scramble' or a 'moderate' climb. It was, however, an exceedingly difficult operation in the dark for men unaccustomed to such exertions and called for a high degree of leadership. The ascent was not without incidents. The ladders, when first placed on the ground against the rock, slipped as the soldiers began to climb but fortunately none was seriously hurt and the incident passed unnoticed by the sentinels. Crawfurd and Robertson then climbed up on their own, without ladders, to a ledge on which an ash-tree grew, and from there they let down ropes for the soldiers to climb up, drawing the ladders up to the ledge. From the ledge upwards the ladders were used to good effect. Another untoward incident, which might have ruined the whole enterprise, occurred when one of the men, either overcome with fright or seized by a fit, was unable to move up or down. But someone had the wit to have him tied to the ladder, which was then turned round to allow those below him to proceed.

The rampart at the top of the rock was reached about dawn when a mist which developed gave them an added advantage. The rampart was easily surmounted with the aid of a ladder by Captain Alexander Ramsay and two of the soldiers. They were spied by the sentinels, who raised the alarm and started to throw stones at the intruders. Shouting 'God and the King! A Darnley! A Darnley!', Ramsay leapt from the rampart and was set upon by three of the sentinels but defended himself with vigour and skill until reinforced by the two soldiers, who helped him to dispose of the sentinels. By this time more of the assault party were arriving over the wall, which because of its ruinous condition soon collapsed, making an easy entry for the remainder. When Ramsay and his soldiers had captured some of the castle guns, they turned them on the men of the garrison stationed in the buildings on the Castle Rock — the Wallace Tower, the White Tower, the Windy Hall, and the 'Chamber between the Crags'. But there was no resistance and indeed some of the garrison, helped by the misty conditions, were able to escape over the walls. (According to Buchanan, there were about twenty-five of the garrison 'whoring and drinking' in the town of Dumbarton, an indication of Fleming's lax control based on a mistaken confidence in his security.) Among those captured in the Wallace Tower were John Hamilton, Archbishop of St. Andrews, John Fleming of Boghall, Vérac, the French king's agent, and an Englishman, John Hall. Lord Fleming, roused by the fighting and seeing the castle taken, managed to make his way out at a quiet part of the nether bailey and, the tide being full, escaped by a small boat to Argyll and thence fled to France.

The Regent, Lennox, arrived at the castle before noon. He found the castle well stocked with weapons, munition and victuals: according to a letter sent to John Knox by Captain Crawfurd, there were in the castle

20 tuns of wine, 192 bolls of meal, 10 bolls of wheat, 8 bolls of malt, 11 hogsheads of biscuit bread, 4 puncheons of bacon.[106] Lennox celebrated the daring capture of the Marian stronghold, hitherto considered impregnable, by dining at the castle, and displayed the generosity of the victor by granting to Lady Fleming, the governor's wife, some of her husband's lands to maintain herself and all the silver, domestic utensils and apparel belonging to her. Archbishop Hamilton was not so fortunate. He was taken to Stirling Castle, where he was charged with Darnley's murder, Regent Moray's murder, plotting to kidnap the infant king, and lying in wait for Regent Lennox. He at first denied all four charges but on the scaffold admitted foreknowledge of the regent's murder. He was hanged wearing his episcopal robes, on the common gibbet at Stirling, three days after his capture.[107]

Queen Elizabeth, whose secretary, Lord Burghley, had described Dumbarton Castle as the 'receptaculum to all the Scottish queen's foreign aid', lost no time in sending her congratulations to Lennox, reminding him of the necessity of choosing a keeper who would not be subject to fraud or corruption.[108] Lennox rewarded Cunningham of Drumquhassil for his part in the affair by appointing him captain and keeper of the castle. The earl himself did not live long enough to reap the benefits of the daring capture of Dumbarton Castle, meeting his death in a skirmish at Stirling in September, 1571.

Crawfurd, to whom the major credit was due, received grants of the mill of Partick and lands belonging to the archbishop of Glasgow. He played a prominent part in the capture of the other Marian stronghold of Edinburgh in 1573 and his fame reached the ears of the young king, James VI, who wrote to Crawfurd in 1575, when he was only nine years of age, a letter of congratulation showing a remarkably high standard of calligraphy for one so young:

> Capten Craufurd, I have hard sic report
> of your gud service done to me from ye
> beginning of the weiris agains my onfreinds,
> as I sall sum day remember ye same,
> god willing, to your greit contentment. In ye
> main quhyle, be of gud confort, and reserve
> you to that time wt patience, being assurit
> of my favour. faireweil.
>> Your gud freind,
>> James R.

The king twice ratified this early promise by writing on the letter in

1584 and 1591, presumably at Crawfurd's request, an acknowledgement that he was still of the same mind about his indebtedness to
Crawfurd.[109] In 1576, Crawfurd granted a charter setting up a bursary
at Glasgow University for a student of philosophy, who, on the
recommendation of the principal and the regents of the university,
would receive yearly one chalder or sixteen bolls of good and sufficient
meal, to be uplifted from the mill of Partick and the lands thereof.
Crawfurd, who was provost of Glasgow in 1577, was chiefly
responsible for the building of the bridge of Partick over the river
Kelvin and died in 1603.[110]

Plots and Counter-Plots

James VI was only five years of age when his grandfather, the Earl of
Lennox, was killed, and until he took over personal control of affairs
Scotland was seldom free of plots and rumours of plots. His mother,
Queen Mary, a prisoner in England, was regarded by Scottish
Catholics as legitimate queen of England; and efforts to gain her libera-
tion by English Catholics with the aid of French or Spanish forces
continued to be made. In 1571, the year of the taking of Dumbarton
Castle, the Ridolfi plot, involving the Spanish, came to light in
England. In the spring of 1572, Cunningham of Drumquhassil, keeper
of Dumbarton Castle, was informed by Drury, the English marshal of
Berwick, of a plot to gain control of the castle by bribery; and in the
following year Vérac, the Frenchman who had been captured at
Dumbarton in 1571 and afterwards released, was said to be plotting to
'corrupt' the keeper and garrison of Dumbarton Castle, to seize the
young king at Stirling and bring him to Dumbarton *en route* for
France.[111]

Cunningham, the keeper of Dumbarton Castle, had already
benefited considerably since the capture of the castle in 1571 by grants
of land and revenues — Drumry, which had belonged to the son of the
Archbishop of St. Andrews; Ladyton and other lands of the Collegiate
Church of Dumbarton, which had been feued to him by his son,
Cuthbert Cunningham, appointed provost of the church while still a
youth; a yearly pension for life of 11 chalders 5 bolls 1 firlot of meal
from Shettleston, Dalmarnock and other lands of the Archbishop of
Glasgow. As a further inducement to him to remain loyal to the young
king, Regent Morton suggested to the English envoy, Sir Henry Kille-

grew, that the Countess of Lennox, then resident in England, should be persuaded to make him receiver and administrator of the revenues of the earldom of Lennox.[112] Cunningham, who was custumar of Dumbarton as well as keeper of the castle, had thus little reason for changing his allegiance; and, like most Scotsmen of his time, he placed his own interests first. In a list of persons considered suitable for English pensions in 1574, he was described as 'able to persuade by credit and by counsel, especially about the King and Argyll, and apt to do good by the commodity of his office of Dumbarton (Castle) which he commands', while Sir James Melville, a supporter of Queen Mary, wrote of him as 'ambitious and greedy', using 'the greatest care to advance himself and his friends'.[113]

Cunningham's influence was greatly increased by his appointment as Master of the King's Household in 1577, when the eleven-year-old king had as one of his preceptors George Buchanan, born only a mile or so from Drumquhassil. Cunningham's son, William, was also given a post in the royal household at Stirling as a valet of the king's chamber. But in the following year, 1578, the tide which had flowed so strongly in Cunningham's favour began to ebb. He was charged with failing to render an account of the rents and profits of the earldom of Lennox and was summoned to appear before the Privy Council. When he failed to answer the charges, he was 'put to the horn', but later released from the horning through the mediation of the English ambassador, Bowes.[114] In 1579, Cunningham helped to arrange for the arrival from France of Esmé Stewart, Seigneur d'Aubigny, a cousin of the king's father, Henry, Lord Darnley.[115] Cunningham's motives were presumably connected with D'Aubigny's claim to the earldom of Lennox. Handsome, attractive and with the polished manners of the French court, D'Aubigny won the affection of the youthful king, who had been brought up without any experience of parental care and had always been in the custody of guardians, some of them unsympathetic. Within a year, the king had conferred the earldom of Lennox on his cousin and was depending upon him for counsel and advice. D'Aubigny's arrival in Scotland and his rapid establishment in the royal favour aroused the deepest suspicions in Scotland and England. He was French and a Catholic, and his request for the custody of Dumbarton Castle, which he claimed as belonging by hereditary right to the Lennox family, only served to add to the distrust with which Scottish nobles regarded him. In the night of April 11th, 1580, an alarm was raised at Stirling Castle by the young Earl of

Mar, guardian of the king, and he claimed that there was a plot to kidnap the king and convey him to Dumbarton Castle.

Cunningham, who had been one of those responsible for bringing D'Aubigny from France, at first declined when asked to deliver the custody of Dumbarton Castle to the newly created Earl of Lennox. He informed the English ambassador, Bowes, that he would refuse to surrender the castle 'without the Queen of England's privity and good liking', in return for which promise Bowes recommended that he should be rewarded with a 'good position' from the English queen. By the summer of 1580, some of Cunningham's letters to England had been intercepted and the king, offended by Cunningham's duplicity, appointed Esmé D'Aubigny, Earl of Lennox, captain and keeper of Dumbarton Castle. Cunningham, who had rashly gone to Edinburgh, was taken prisoner by Sir William Stewart of Caberston, brother of Sir John Stewart of Traquair, and was compelled to sign a bond for £40,000 undertaking that he would deliver the castle. He was escorted back to Dumbarton, where the surrender was completed by Cunningham's handing over to Stewart of Caberston an inventory of all the arms, munitions and victuals in the castle.[116] Cunningham's fortunes never recovered. In 1585 he was, along with his son-in-law, Malcolm Douglas of Mains, falsely accused of plotting to abduct the king. The charge was brought by a neighbour of Cunningham and Douglas, Sir James Edmonstone of Duntreath, who professed to be an accomplice and implicated the others in hope of a pardon. The pair were hanged at Edinburgh Cross straight away. Edmonstone, who later admitted that he had made a false confession, lived to be one of the assize at the trial of the Jesuit, John Ogilvie, in Glasgow in 1615.[117]

The transfer of Dumbarton Castle to the Earl of Lennox was most unwelcome to the English government; and the English ambassador in Scotland, Thomas Randolph, made representations to the young king, intimating that Queen Elizabeth was afraid it would 'serve for a gate to receive strange forces', that is, from France or Spain. James replied that, after all, the earl was his cousin and his subject, and that 'Dumbarton Castle has been an ancient and kindly possession of the earls of Lennox, standing in the country where they have their title and where their friends and living lie.'[118] For a year or so, the Earl of Lennox, for whom Stewart of Caberston acted as keeper of Dumbarton Castle, continued to 'guide all as if he were king'. On December 31st, 1580, the Earl of Morton, Regent of Scotland from 1573 to 1577, was charged with complicity in Darnley's murder and imprisoned first in Edinburgh Castle for a few days and thence removed to Dumbarton Castle. There he was kept in close confinement as his nephew, the Earl of Angus, and his friends were known to be considering how to effect his escape. During the time of his imprisonment in Dumbarton Castle, Morton's servants were subjected to torture by the boot (an iron contraption which crushed the leg of the unfortunate victim) and confessed against their master. He was at last brought from Dumbarton to Edinburgh, sentenced to death and beheaded by the 'Maiden', a device similar to the modern guillotine and said to have been invented by Morton himself.[119]

Although Lennox, who was given the title of 'Duke' in 1581, was strongly suspected of pro-French and pro-Catholic leanings, he was mainly intent on advancing his own interests and actually professed the new Protestant religion in order to allay suspicion. But his unpopularity increased as time went on and provoked a coup by a band of Protestant nobles, who in August 1582 kidnapped the young king at Perth and carried him off to Ruthven Castle, the seat of the Earl of Gowrie.[120] James, only sixteen years of age, overwhelmed by the rough treatment and the indignity of his capture, started to weep when he realised his situation, only to be told by one of his captors, 'Better bairns greet than bearded men.' Following this Ruthven Raid (as it was called), the king remained a prisoner for ten months and the effective government was in the hands of the 'Ruthven Raiders', who divested the Duke of Lennox of his office, ordering him to surrender the Castle of Dumbarton and leave the country within fifteen days. Lennox was deserted, except for some Catholics, and was so 'desolate and sorrowful' that, according to John Colville, who had taken part in the Ruthven Raid, 'all good men' (i.e. the Protestants) 'praise God and rejoice greatly thereof'.[121] He betook himself to Dumbarton Castle but delayed so long in preparation for his departure to France that the Protestant nobles and the English ambassador became suspicious of his intentions. Mary, Queen of Scots, angered by the Ruthven Raid and the detention of her son, hoped that soldiers and money would be sent by the king of France to Lennox at Dumbarton. But the duke had lost heart. At Dumbarton Castle, in contrast to the luxurious living he had enjoyed at court, where the kitchen was so sumptuously provided that lumps of butter were cast upon the fire when it grew dull, he had to put up with an even more scanty diet than that of the Earl of Morton when a prisoner, and was 'fain to eat of a meagre goose scoudered (scorched) with barley straw'. In a pathetic letter to the king from Dumbarton Castle on December 16th, 1582, he described himself as 'the most unhappy man in the world on seeing the bad opinion which your majesty has conceived of me'. He made his way finally through England to France, where he died a few months later.[122]

His son, Ludovick (or Louis), who succeeded as Duke of Lennox, was brought over to Scotland at the request of the king in 1583. But, although he won the king's favour, receiving the appointment of Lord High Admiral and governor of Dumbarton Castle, he lacked the ambitiousness of his father and was content to be a courtier, accompanying King James in 1603 to England, where he acquired another title, that of Duke of Richmond. The title of hereditary governor of Dumbarton Castle was to remain in the family for most of the seventeenth century.

James VI and Dumbarton Castle

King James VI paid frequent visits to Dumbarton in the years before his accession to the English throne. As a child, he had generally been kept in close confinement at Stirling Castle under the supervision of the Earls of Mar, hereditary guardians of the princes of Scotland; but, when only seven years of age, James had visited Dumbarton Castle and, curiously enough, was said to have taken ill with smallpox, like his mother Mary, Queen of Scots, before him.[123] In the dozen or so years before 1603, James almost invariably came through to the west in August in order to indulge in his favourite pastime of deer-hunting, and from Dumbarton would pass northwards to Inchmurrin, the island on Loch Lomond where his ancestors, the earls of Lennox, had their castle and where deer were preserved down to modern times. It may be assumed that on his visits to Dumbarton he resided at the royal castle. There is, at any rate, no record, either contemporary or of a later date, of any house in the burgh of Dumbarton which was used as a royal lodging.

In 1592, James arrived at Dumbarton earlier than usual, in the month of February, in pursuit of the Earl of Bothwell. Francis Stewart, the brilliant, dashing, impetuous Earl of Bothwell, was a nephew of Queen Mary's third husband and son of an illegitimate son of James V and therefore a cousin of the king. He had been imprisoned in 1591 for allegedly employing witches to sink the ship carrying his cousin, King James, to Denmark for his marriage. Escaping from prison in Edinburgh Castle, he remained at large for six months and then on December 27th made a raid on Holyroodhouse in order to seize the king. But the alarm was raised, the town bell was rung to summon loyal citizens, and Bothwell was compelled to flee.[124] He made his way westwards to Dumbarton, where he hoped to obtain a passage by boat to the Hebrides or to Spain. Clad in beggar's apparel, he managed to escape, but among those of his followers arrested in Dumbarton was John Smollett, a Dumbarton merchant, who had been involved previously in a plot with Bothwell to assassinate the king. Smollett, under pressure, acknowledged his complicity in Bothwell's most recent escapade and offered, if his life were spared, to provide sufficient evidence at Bothwell's trial to ensure his conviction. King James remained at Dumbarton for four days, pursuing his inquiries. He would have had Smollett hanged, but on Lord Hamilton and the Chancellor interceding for him, his life was spared.[125]

In the last few years of the century, James was faced with the problem of dealing with the rival claims of two of his leading nobles to the custodianship of Dumbarton Castle. It had been held since 1585 by Lord John Hamilton, acting head of the Hamilton family, his elder brother, the Earl of Arran, having been insane since 1562. The Duke of Lennox based his claim to Dumbarton Castle on hereditary right by virtue of the ancient grant to his ancestors, the earls of Lennox. The strategic value of Dumbarton Castle as controlling the gateway to France had diminished as the French connection had long since ceased to be of importance to Scotland. Catholic nobles such as the earls of Huntly and Errol, intent on the restoration of the Roman Catholic church, looked to Spain rather than to France for support. The English, who were at war with Spain, naturally regarded very seriously the possible threat of an invasion of Scotland in support of a Catholic rebellion there. Elizabeth and her advisers therefore strongly favoured a Protestant and pro-English keeper of Dumbarton Castle (such as indeed was Lord Hamilton) in order to prevent a Spanish landing on the Clyde. As for James himself, who maintained rather an ambivalent attitude to the Catholic nobles, he did not in the least desire Spanish intervention in Scotland as it would, he considered, impair his chances of succeeding Queen Elizabeth on the throne of England, and thus Lord Hamilton, Protestant and pro-English, was for James also a suitable keeper of Dumbarton Castle until the Duke of Lennox began to press his claim.

Rumours of Catholic plots, involving a Spanish descent upon the west of Scotland, had existed since the year of the Spanish Armada, 1588. In 1589, letters from Huntly and other Catholic nobles to King Philip of Spain had been intercepted and were found to contain expressions of sympathy for the Armada's failure and promises of support in the event of a Spanish invasion of England. Three years later, blank papers bearing the signatures of Huntly, Errol and other leading Catholics (the 'Spanish Blanks') were seized from a Catholic agent, George Ker, just as he was about to sail from the Clyde to Spain, and under torture he revealed a plot whereby the Catholic nobles were to lend their support to a Spanish invasion of the west of Scotland. Such an attempt would inevitably involve first gaining control of Dumbarton Castle which, according to Lord Burghley, Queen Elizabeth's secretary of state, was 'the only place for descent of Spaniards in the west of Scotland'.[126] Another Catholic agent, Robert Bruce, who had been given 22,000 crowns from the Duke of Parma in Flanders in 1590 for distribution to various persons in Scotland (including the king), was said to have sent information by his servant, Andrew Small, to Lord Hamilton, the governor of Dumbarton Castle, about a plot to subvert the loyalty of the keeper and garrison of the castle, which was to be surrendered to a Spanish force. Lord Hamilton thereupon dismissed the keeper, his natural son, Sir John Hamilton, replacing him by Claud Hamilton of Cochno, son of a former keeper. In a long indictment of Bruce's double-dealing, drawn up by Scottish Catholics in Flanders much later, Dumbarton Castle was described as an impregnable fortress, 'a miracle of nature', with a well which never ran dry and a wine-store, and offering complete security for a Spanish bridgehead in Scotland. In 1594, when there was a Catholic rising under Huntly and Errol, all the fighting took place in the north, and Dumbarton Castle was neither attacked by Spanish forces nor betrayed by its keeper. Even as late as 1601, however, the exiled Earl of Bothwell, by this time a Catholic, was willing to promise Philip III of Spain the surrender of Dumbarton Castle in return for aid to a Scottish Catholic rising.[127]

The possibility of the surrender of the castle to the Spanish was therefore still present throughout the last decade of the century but the danger was exaggerated by Lord Hamilton in his letters to the English ambassador and the English secretary of state, when the prospect arose of his replacement by the Duke of Lennox. Ludovick,

2nd Duke of Lennox, had lived in France until he was nine years of age and was regarded by the English and most Scots as pro-French and pro-Catholic. An English agent described him in 1592, when the duke was fifteen, as 'for his years wise and wary, yea wily' and 'guided by Papists'.[128] In 1593, Lord Hamilton was informed that Lennox and the young Earl of Mar had been attempting to corrupt some of the garrison with a view to effecting the surrender of the castle.[129] But it is doubtful if the Duke of Lennox, despite his Catholic upbringing, seriously considered becoming involved in a Spanish invasion attempt. He was to prove a loyal adherent of his cousin, King James, both before and after 1603, when he accompanied him to England. For both Lennox and Hamilton, the custody of Dumbarton Castle was a matter of prestige and honour. King James tried to effect a peaceful and honourable settlement and finally, in 1598, decided in favour of his cousin, the Duke of Lennox, compensating Hamilton with the revenues of the abbey of Arbroath. The title of governor of Dumbarton Castle remained with the ducal house of Lennox during the seventeenth century, but as the dukes of Lennox invariably resided in England, keepers or captains were appointed by them in charge of the castle.

James VI, like his great-grandfather, James IV, considered Dumbarton the obvious base for expeditions to pacify the warlike clans of the Highlands and Western Isles. Clan feuding was probably at its worst in the last quarter of the sixteenth century as there had been no real attempt for two generations to suppress disorders. The incessant warfare in Ireland, where Angus MacDonald of Dunnivaig, chief of the MacDonalds of Islay and Kintyre, also held lands in Antrim, provided an opportunity for the clansmen to earn a living as galloglasses, professional soldiers. But it was in the rivalry between the MacDonalds of Islay and Kintyre and MacLeans of Mull that the clansmen exhibited the worst features of clan feuding — murder, treachery, pillage. In 1588 Sir Lachlan MacLean of Duart actually hired a hundred Spaniards from the *Florida*, a galleon moored in Tobermory Bay, to fight Angus MacDonald of Dunnivaig, who was said to have hired English soldiers. But the fighting went on for years without foreigners. James and his council tried different methods of dealing with the lawlessness of the clans. One method was to imprison the chief, release him on a promise of good behaviour of himself and his clan, guaranteed by leaving a son as hostage and by some other person of good standing acting as cautioner. Another was to insist on the chief obtaining a title-deed or charter in order to settle the question of lands claimed by a rival clan. Still another was to have the chief's lands forfeited and entrusted to a more powerful and law-abiding neighbour.

None of these expedients proving successful for more than a brief period, James decided on an expedition to Kintyre and Islay in order to deal with the turbulent MacDonalds. But the king had no army, and his summons in 1596 to the men of the western shires to muster at Dumbarton on August 1st met with such a poor response that it was only in November that Sir William Stewart of Houston, who had been appointed the king's lieutenant, arrived with a small force in Kintyre. He was able to procure the submission of Angus MacDonald of Dunnivaig, who was detained in Dumbarton Castle with his wife and family for nearly six months. Angus was not long back in his own country before he was nearly murdered by his son, Sir James MacDonald, who has been described as a 'polished ruffian', having spent years as a hostage in Edinburgh and having been knighted by the king in an effort to secure his loyalty. Another levy of the active men in the western shires was ordered and a rendezvous fixed for August 20th, 1598, at Dumbarton; but again delays occurred and no expedition sailed. In the meantime, Sir Lachlan MacLean of Duart, chief of the MacLeans, was killed when fighting the MacDonalds. A third muster of the western shires was ordered by James on April 2nd, 1600, to meet at Dumbarton and Kintyre in July, but again no expedition materialised.[130] The men of the Lennox, Renfrewshire and Ayrshire had no stomach for such an enterprise and pleaded that the expense involved could not be undertaken by them. James VI was resident in London before the first really successful expedition to the Isles sailed in 1608, to be followed by the imprisonment of a number of chiefs and their agreement to the Statutes of Iona of 1609 regulating their conduct. James returned to Scotland only once after his accession to the English throne. In 1617 he passed through Dumbarton on his way to Inchmurrin, where he was entertained by his cousin, Ludovick, Duke of Lennox, and the town councillors of Dumbarton celebrated the occasion as was their wont in those days by the consumption of 13 quarts of wine and 4lbs. 6oz. of sugar.[131]

Keepers and their Revenues

Throughout most of the sixteenth century the keeper of Dumbarton Castle was generally designated 'captain' or 'captain and keeper' and was appointed by the crown or by a regent acting in the name of the crown. At the end of the century, the Dukes of Lennox and Lord Hamilton, when in charge of the castle, appointed keepers to act for them, much in the same way as the medieval keepers appointed constables as deputies. The old association of sheriff of Dumbarton and keeper of the castle was maintained only in name, the Earls of Lennox considering themselves entitled to claim both offices by virtue of the charter granted by Robert Bruce in 1321.[132] When Matthew, Earl of Lennox, was infeft as heir of his father in the earldom of Lennox in 1532, the infeftment included both the offices of keeper and sheriff. But he was to spend many years in exile in England. During his exile, one of his kinsmen, James Stewart of Cardonald, is on record as sheriff of Dumbarton in 1559 and 1563.[133] He may have been nominated by the exiled Lennox but the keeper in 1559, Andrew Hamilton of Ardoch, was appointed by the regent, the Earl of Arran, and the keeper of 1563, Lord Fleming, by Queen Mary. After Lennox's death and during James VI's minority, James Galbraith of Culcreuch was sheriff of Dumbarton, and his son, Robert Galbraith of Culcreuch, is on record as sheriff depute under the Duke of Lennox as sheriff principal in March, 1597. Later in the same year, William Stirling (probably of the Glorat family) acted in the same capacity, but neither of the Galbraiths nor Stirling was at any time keeper of the castle. In a case of assault on the MacAulays of Ardincaple and their friends in 1590, two of those accused were actually sheriffs depute, Thomas Buchanan in Blairlusk and John Buchanan in Ballagan, both denounced as rebels. In the seventeenth century, the Dukes of Lennox were still entitled hereditary sheriffs, while the acting sheriffs were invariably lairds of the shire, appointed by the Privy Council and holding office for one or two years at a time.[134]

By the beginning of the sixteenth century, the revenues assigned for the keeping of Dumbarton Castle had become more or less fixed — the fermes of the crown lands of Cardross, an annual payment of 40 marks (£26. 13s. 4d.) from the barony of Cadzow (or Hamilton as it came to be called), 10 marts and victual from Meikle Cumbrae, and 5 chalders of oatmeal from the lands in Kilpatrick belonging to Paisley Abbey. The fermes of the crown lands of Rosneath, which had formed part of the revenues in the fifteenth century, ceased to be paid to the keeper of the castle even before 1489, when Colin Campbell, 1st Earl of Argyll, received a crown charter of the lands of Rosneath. The annual payment from the barony of Cadzow also disappeared before the middle of the sixteenth century during the regency of the Earl of Arran, in whose family Cadzow had been for over two centuries.

The revenues were listed in 1565, when Lord Fleming was appointed keeper; in 1571, when Cunningham of Drumquhassil was appointed; in 1580, when Esmé, Earl of Lennox was appointed; in an act of Parliament of 1584, specifying the 'money and victuals' assigned for 'keeping the castles of Edinburgh, Dumbarton, Stirling and Blackness'; and in 1585, in a ratification of the grant of the 'captainry' to Lord Hamilton.[135] In the appointments made in 1571 and 1580, the grant included the customs of Dumbarton and also 20 chalders of meal from the fermes and teinds of the parish of Kilpatrick. The Earl of Lennox in 1580 and Lord Hamilton in 1585 were granted, in addition, 550 marks per annum; both nobles appointed deputies as keepers, who also acted as custumars of Dumbarton. Earlier in the century, during the regency of the Earl of Arran, Andrew Hamilton of Cochno had received as keeper an annual fee of 700 marks (£446. 13s. 4d.) in 1552 and 1553, when the fee of Stirling Castle's keeper was 800 marks (£533. 6s. 8d.); but whether they also received the dues formerly payable to the keepers is not clear.[136] The fermes and feu-duties were presumably paid as of yore, but to the crown or to the regent in the name of the crown and not to the keeper.

The crown lands of Cardross, which had been acquired by Robert Bruce and the revenues of which were assigned to the keepers of Dumbarton Castle, are listed in a grant in feu-ferme in 1567 to the keeper of the castle, Lord Fleming, who was destined not to possess them for long. When Fleming held the castle for Queen Mary, his own lands of Cumbernauld were plundered, and in 1570 John Smollett, burgess of Dumbarton, received a gift from the regent, the Earl of Lennox, of the maills, fermes, profits and duties of the 'castellandis' of Dumbarton in the parish of Cardross and also of the lands in the Isle of Cumbrae which were assigned to the castle. The 'castellandis' in Cardross parish were — Walton, the two Kipperminshochs, Pillanflat, Dalmoak, Succoth, Hawthornhill, Blairshalloch, Hole, Castlehill, Clerkhill, Kirkton, Mains of Cardross, and Cunningpark, extending in annual rent to £45. 6s. 8d. of money and 22 bolls of meal.[137] Feu-charters of these lands granted during the sixteenth century stipulated the payments to be made to the keeper of the castle. In 1542, the master of the royal cellar and vineyard, Archibald Campbell (son of Duncan Campbell of Clachan in Rosneath), in return for his services in Scotland and in France, had been granted in feu-ferme the lands of Walton, Dalmoak, Hawthornhill, Castlehill, the payment of 33 marks (£22) and 22 bolls of meal to be made yearly to the captain of Dumbarton Castle, 'as long as the fermes of the said lands are assigned for the custody of the said castle'. In 1591, the king granted in feu-ferme to Robert Bontine, son and heir of John Bontine in Succoth, the lands of Succoth, Hawthornhill and Blairshalloch in the lordship of Cardross where 'the said Robert, his father and their predecessors were native tenants and rentallers beyond the memory of man', for an annual payment to the king, the captain of the castle of Dumbarton or a royal chamberlain, for Succoth, 4 marks, 6 fowls, with other dues owed to the castle; for Hawthornhill, as for Succoth; and for Blairshalloch, £4, 6 fowls and services due. In the following century, when Quentin Lindsay of Bonhill obtained a grant of the lands of Pillanflat in 1622, the annual payment exacted was £4, 'with the services and multures accustomed to be paid to the castle of Dumbarton'.[138]

In the fifteenth century, the Isle of Meikle Cumbrae provided a greater proportion of the keeper's revenue than the crown lands of Cardross; in 1455-56, when the fermes of Cardross were £26. 13s. 4d., those of Cumbrae were £33. 6s. 8d., with, in addition, 3 chalders 2 bolls of barley and 10 marts. (In the Exchequer Rolls of 1593 and 1594, the keeper's revenues from Cardross and Meikle Cumbrae are given as worth £60.) Of the lands of Cumbrae, only one, South Kames, is specified in the charter granted to Lord Fleming in 1567. It was occupied by John and Johanna Hunter, two men called Robert Hunter, and provided an 'annual rent in all profits' of £4. 2s. money, 7½ bolls of oatmeal, 1 boll of barley, 1½ marts. It was from Cumbrae that hawks were collected for the Scottish kings, even after the union of the crowns. The Cumbraes had belonged to the Stewarts for centuries and in 1606 the fermes of another part of the ancient patrimony of the Stewarts, the Isle of Bute, were assigned to the keeper of Dumbarton Castle. They amounted to £140 'silver maill', 10 chalders of oats, 24 bolls of oatmeal, 15 bolls of barley and 41 'sufficient marts', a considerable addition to the keeper's revenues, which still included the 550 marks granted in 1580 to Esmé, Earl of Lennox, and in 1585 to Lord Hamilton.[139]

The 'watchmeal of Kilpatrick' (5 chalders of oatmeal), which had been paid since the fourteenth century by the tenants of the lands belonging to Paisley Abbey in the parish of Kilpatrick, was increased in 1561 to 20 chalders of oatmeal, to be taken up yearly from 'the readiest of the fruits and teinds of the parish of Kilpatrick' from the third of the income of the Abbey of Paisley, to which the parish church had been appropriated in the thirteenth century. By the end of the century the watch-meal seems to have been payable only by the tenants of the old abbey lands. A grant in feu-ferme to James Edmonstone, younger, of Duntreath in 1590 of the lands of Boquhanran stipulated the payment of the accustomed ferme to the keepers of Dumbarton Castle 'according to the tenor of the old infeftment'. In 1706, an action was raised by the Duke of Montrose (who had purchased the superiority of the lands of the Dukes of Lennox) for payment by 'the heritors, vassals and portioners of the fourteen tounes within the royalty of Kilpatrick' of 5 chalders and a half-boll of oatmeal. The 'towns' listed in the action, which was settled in favour of the Duke, were identical with those listed in the rentals of Paisley Abbey.[140]

In addition to the revenues mentioned above, many of the keepers received grants of escheats and non-entries and, as custumars of Dumbarton, were able to augment their statutory income considerably. Payments for the maintenance of prisoners are sometimes mentioned. They were not always at the same rate but depended on the rank of the prisoners. In 1555, the expenses of warding the chief of the clan MacKay were set at 2s. a day while Quintin Armstrong and Robert Elliott, border reivers, were on a lower rate of 18d. a day. In 1581, the expenses of keeping the Earl of Morton and his servants were fixed at 20 marks (£13. 6s. 8d.) a day, to be recouped from his escheated estates; and in 1597-98 the rate for keeping Angus Mac-Donald of Dunnivaig 'and his family' varied from £5. 14s. a day in the castle to £8. 10s. a day while at an inn in Dumbarton and £9. 5s. while staying in the house of Stewart of Cardonald, the total cost for the period August 25th, 1597, to January 2nd, 1598, amounting to £953. 4s. 2d.[141]

Customs of Dumbarton

Customs duties levied in Dumbarton in the sixteenth century were of two kinds — the great custom, which belonged to the crown and was paid on goods exported from Scotland, and the petty customs, which belonged to the burgh and included a variety of dues paid by merchants and others who came to the burgh markets. The petty customs in the sixteenth century represented a considerable proportion of the burgh's income, while the receipts from the great custom, like other crown revenues, were remitted to the Exchequer by the sheriff.

In the fifteenth century the staple exports had at first been wool, woollen cloth and hides, but before the end of the century the fisheries in the Firth of Clyde and in the sea lochs of Argyll were producing vast quantities of herring, which were consumed locally or were exported. Throughout the sixteenth century, the customs on salt herrings always figured in the Dumbarton custumar's account, often as the largest single item. A typical account of the early part of the century is that of Peter Colquhoun in 1504 — 4 lasts, 11 dacres, 5 hides, £12. 4s; 75 lasts 4½ barrels herrings, £45. 4s. 6d; 92 dozen 4 ells woollen cloth, £62. 0s. 10d. In mid-century Archibald Campbell, custumar of Dumbarton, remitted £97. 10s. 4d. (less his fee of £1. 12s. 6d.) in 1556 for duty on 45 lasts 2 barrels herring, £27. 2s; 14 lasts 11 dacres hides, £38. 17s. 4d; 7 chalders 12 barrels coal, £1. 11s; 12 lasts 6 barrels salmon, £30. At the end of the century, in 1597, Claud Hamilton, who was keeper of the castle and custumar of Dumbarton, presented an account showing a great variety of exports: 4 lasts 4 barrels salmon, £10. 8s; 501 lasts herring, £360. 12s; 140 dozen woollen cloths, £8; 1802 dozen goat fells, £3. 8s; 1200 lamb skins, £2; 2000 rabbit skins, £1; 40 tod skins, 6s. 8d; 20 otter skins, 5s; 20 chalders smithy coal, £4 — a total of £389. 19s. 8d.[142]

Most of the custumars of Dumbarton in the sixteenth century were, like Claud Hamilton, also keepers of the castle. After 1571, when John Cunningham of Drumquhassil received the gift of the 'captainship' of the castle and the customs of the burgh, the customs formed an important part of the keeper's income.[143] The castle, of course, was strategically well situated to enable the keeper with his garrison to observe and control the movement of ships on the Clyde. For very brief periods, the customs of Dumbarton were in the hands of someone other than the keeper. George Stirling of Glorat was acting as custumar for the year before his father, William Stirling, keeper of Dumbarton Castle, was murdered in 1534; but, after his appointment as keeper in succession to his father, he failed to present the customs account for four years, at the end of which period Archibald Campbell, son of Duncan Campbell of Rosneath, was appointed as custumar. He held the office for two years and was succeeded in 1540 by Colin

Porterfield, a burgess of Dumbarton, who was in turn succeeded after a year by his son, Patrick. George Stirling of Glorat was again responsible for collecting the customs in 1542 and again for four years failed to present returns to the Exchequer. There was some excuse for him, however, as the years 1542-1546 were made very difficult for the keeper of Dumbarton Castle by the actions of Matthew, Earl of Lennox. It is not surprising that his successor as keeper of the castle, Andrew Hamilton of Cochno, was given a tack or lease of the customs (for the small sum of £10 a year), and for the next eight years he enjoyed the benefit of the customs revenues of Dumbarton and also of Irvine, for which he paid £20 a year. In 1555, the year after Hamilton's tack expired, the great custom of Dumbarton produced £79. 13s. (for 8 lasts 12½ dacres hides and 94 lasts 5 barrels herring) and the custom of Irvine £25. 19s. (for 166 dozen woollen cloths, 2 lasts 3½ dacres hides, 17 lasts 1 barrel herring, 3 barrels salmon). Hamilton's successor as keeper was his namesake, Andrew Hamilton of Ardoch. For the first three years of his keepership, the customs were again in the hands of Archibald Campbell, but in 1558, Hamilton obtained a tack of the customs for a term of three years. It was fixed at £50 a year by mistake as it was based on the estimated income from the customs of both Dumbarton and Glasgow, and when he was summoned to pay for his tack, he was allowed a remission of £83. 6s. 8d. on the £150 due, the Glasgow custom being valued at that amount.[144]

By the end of the century, the Clyde had become a busy waterway. Some idea of the sea-borne trade may be gathered from the Exchequer Rolls and from a register of ship entries made in Dumbarton in the town clerk's office, where every merchant or master of a ship bringing goods into the Clyde had to declare his cargo and pay his dues to the custumar of the petty customs of Dumbarton. In 1596, four ships brought wine from La Rochelle or Bordeaux, one of them, the *Providence*, a Dumbarton ship owned by John Smollett, and the others from Glasgow, Leith and Pittenweem. In the following year, 1597, there were again four ships carrying wine from France, the Dumbarton ship, *Providence*, and the others from Glasgow, Leith and Crail; nine ships (two French and the others Scottish) carrying salt from Brittany; and one ship from Ayr with a mixed cargo of iron, pitch, tar and cordage. Only two ships brought cargoes of wine in 1598, one of them again the *Providence* of Dumbarton; ten ships (three French and seven Scottish) brought salt from Brittany; and seventeen ships, all from east coast ports in Scotland, carried cargoes of timber. Most of these ships, if not all of them, on their outward voyages from the Clyde, would carry salt herrings, hides, skins, woollen cloth, as listed in the account of the custumar of Dumbarton. The expansion in trade at the end of the century reflected the growing prosperity of the Glasgow merchants, whose enterprising spirit enabled them to thrive despite the obstacle of the shallowness of the Clyde and their lack of a proper harbour.[145]

In addition to the collection of the great custom on exports, the keepers of Dumbarton Castle claimed the right to levy a duty or toll on cattle passing from Argyll to Glasgow. In 1577, in response to a complaint from the Earl of Argyll that drovers from 'Argyll and Tarbertshire' were being forced to deliver 'some of their greatest and fattest kye' to the keeper of the castle at the keeper's price, Regent Morton issued a warrant prohibiting such actions on the part of the castle garrison. The practice does not seem to have ceased, as in 1582 the Earl of Argyll wrote a letter to Esmé, Duke of Lennox, complaining that men of Dumbarton Castle garrison had taken 12 kye from drovers as they passed by and 'menaced them to take more forsooth'. The Duke, nominally governor of the castle, was on the eve of departure from Scotland to France but replied, professing his grief that the soldiers of the garrison should have contravened the agreement made between the Duke and the Earl that the keeper of the castle should have yearly ten of the fattest cattle for two marks a pair more than the price of one. The Duke promised that the soldiers of the castle garrison would be prevented from repeating their 'great boldness'.[146]

The Argyll traders in plaidings or woollen cloth also had their troubles at Dumbarton Castle. In 1592, the Bishop of Argyll and the Isles complained to the Privy Council that Donald MacDonald Roy from Iona and two companions, travelling to Glasgow with plaidings, had been held up on the highway beside Dumbarton Castle by George Smollett, a burgess of Dumbarton, who claimed to be acting by right of a commission from the king and 'violently reft' 85 ells of plaiding, 22 hides and 11 otter skins from the three traders from Argyll. The provost and magistrates of Glasgow and Renfrew lodged a similar complaint in the following year against Smollett, who, it was stated, had gathered a number of 'deboshit men and vagabonds' around him. He was denounced a rebel and his commission, which seems to have been granted by the king but without consent of the Privy Council, was withdrawn.[147]

4

The Seventeenth Century

The Hereditary Governors

For most of the seventeenth century, the Dukes of Lennox were governors of Dumbarton Castle, with power to nominate the captains or keepers, who were latterly called lieutenant-governors. In 1614, William Middlemist, keeper of Dumbarton Castle, was admonished by the Privy Council for 'very disdainfully and proudly' refusing to acknowledge the council's warrant for the transfer of the Earl of Orkney to Edinburgh as it was not made out in the name of the governor, the Duke of Lennox. He was reminded that he had been appointed by the king, although in fact he was the nominee of the Duke of Lennox.[1] Ludovick Stewart, 2nd Duke of Lennox, who had succeeded in regaining custody of the castle for the Lennox family in 1597, accompanied James VI to London in 1603 and thereafter spent most of his time in England. His three nominees had little connection with the Lennox but two of them bore the name of Stewart — Sir William Stewart of Eildon and Sir John Stewart of Methven (the duke's natural son) — and the third, William Middlemist, was a grandson of Francis Stewart of Traquair. Ludovick was made Earl of Richmond, was appointed master of the royal household and first gentleman of the king's chamber, and created knight of the garter. With a mixed French and Scottish background, he became the complete Englishman. His visits to Scotland were few. In 1607 he acted as King James's commissioner to the Scottish parliament, and in 1617, when James paid his one and only visit to Scotland after his accession to the English throne, the duke entertained his royal cousin on the isle of Inchmurrin on Loch Lomond, the ancestral home of the Lennoxes. On July 23rd of that year, the Duke of Lennox wrote to Sir William Livingston of Kilsyth,

Plate 17. Gunners, 19th century

Plate 18.   Soldier, 74th Regiment, *c.* 1800

Plate 19.   Soldier, 93rd Regiment, *c.* 1850

Plate 20. View of Dumbarton Castle and Castle Green, c. 1800

Plate 21. P.S. *Loch Lomond* passing Castle Rock, 1845

Plate 22.　Royal Visit, 1847

Plate 23. Royal Visit, 1937

Plate 24.　Royal Visit, 1953

Plate 25. Royal Visit, 1953

Plate 26.   Opening of Castle Pier, 1874

Plate 27.   Castle Rock from west

Plate 28.   Castle Gate

Plate 29.　Sundial, Governor's House

Plate 30. Western Rampart

Plate 31.   Guard House

Plate 32. Portcullis Arch

Plate 33. French Prison

Plate 34.   Magazine

Plate 35. Sentinel Box

Plate 36.

Aerial view of Castle Rock, showing (*above centre*) the distillery of Hiram Walker & Sons (Scotland) Limited

who was in charge of arrangements, informing him that the king had changed his plan of 'breaking his fast at the castle of Dumbarton, now he had concluded to dine at Inchmurrin, where his dinner shall be sent, and there are tents to be provided for that effect as you told me; and you must expect a good number of sharp stomachs'.[2]

The third duke of Lennox, Esmé, brother of Ludovick, survived his brother by only a few months and was succeeded by his son, James. He was only sixteen years of age when he first visited Dumbarton in May, 1628, accompanied by English servants. They were duly entertained by the magistrates and council, who conferred upon them the honour of burgess of Dumbarton, thereafter celebrating with wine, sugar, sweets, bread and beer in the house of George Buchanan. When he visited Scotland in September, 1637, for his mother's funeral at Paisley, he arrived at Dumbarton with a splendid company, including the Earl of Argyll, the Earl of Traquair and the royal physician, William Harvey, discoverer of the circulation of the blood. The previous year the duke had surrendered to the king 'the whole right of the sheriffship of Dumbarton'.[3] James, 4th Duke of Lennox, who had married a daughter of the Duke of Buckingham, was, like all his family, a staunch royalist. Three of his brothers were killed during the Civil War and he himself is said to have contributed £30,000 to the royal cause. He died at an early age in 1655 and his son, Esmé, 5th Duke, died five years later in Paris, to be succeeded by his cousin Charles, the sixth duke and last of the Stewart Lennoxes. It is doubtful if he ever visited Dumbarton. In August, 1662, the town council of Dumbarton empowered the magistrates to 'do as they think fitting' in view of the expected arrival of the Duke of Lennox 'to see the castle'. In 1670, it was reported to the town council that the duke intended to 'make his abode and residence' at Dumbarton Castle 'ane certain time'. For welcoming and entertaining the duke and his retinue, the town council on August 25th of that year ordered from Glasgow a hogshead of claret, six dozen glasses, and a marvellous assortment of delicacies — raisins, almonds, caraway seed, lemons, oranges, pears etc. But a week later word came that the duke had 'fallen sick by the way' and would not visit Dumbarton that summer. The town council thereupon decided to auction the hogshead of claret at the mercat cross; what was done with the food is not recorded.[4]

Charles, 6th Duke of Lennox, died at sea off Elsinore in Denmark, where he had been sent as English ambassador. He married three times but left no children; and his nearest heir was Charles II himself, who

G

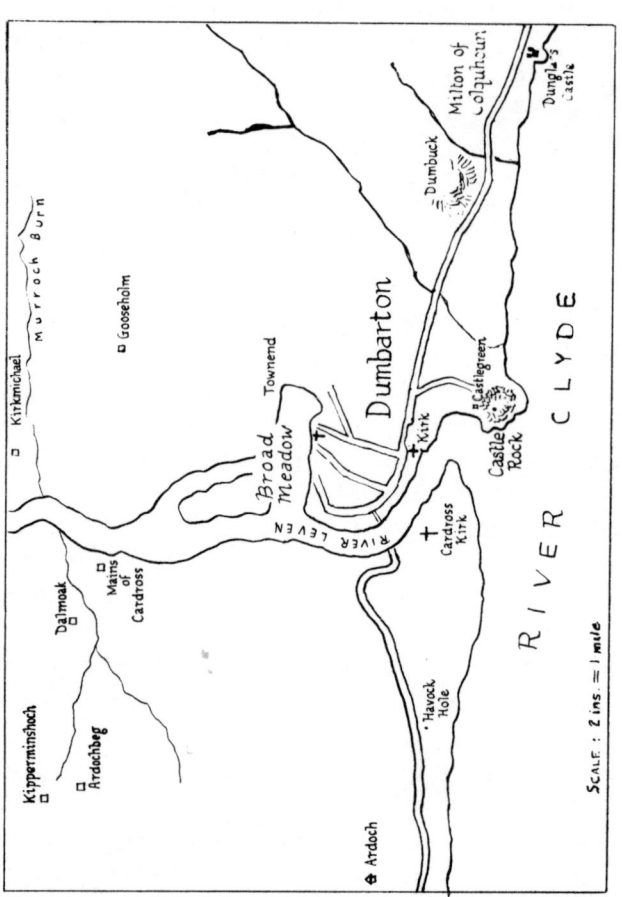

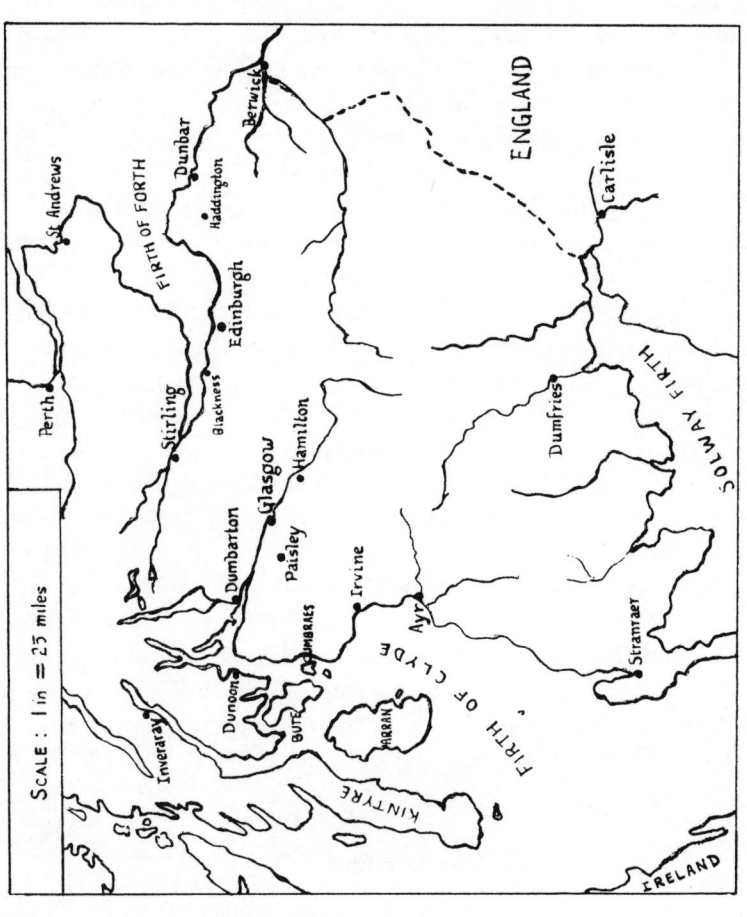

bestowed the titles of Duke of Richmond and Lennox on his illegitimate son by Louise de la Quérouaille, Duchess of Portsmouth. Although the title of hereditary governor of Dumbarton Castle was included in the honours Charles bestowed on his natural son, the appointment of governor and keeper from thenceforward was in the hands of the crown. The widow of the sixth duke was Frances Theresa Stewart, grand-daughter of the first Lord Blantyre. 'La belle Stuart' was regarded as the most beautiful lady of Charles II's court. The king himself was one of her greatest admirers and was said to have considered divorcing his queen, Catherine of Braganza, in order to marry her but was forestalled by the Duke of Lennox. It was at the king's direction that the Britannia engraved on the old copper penny was modelled on her.

The dowager Duchess of Lennox and Richmond had a life-rent of her husband's estates, including the revenues of Dumbarton Castle; but the sheriffship of Dumbarton and the governorship of Dumbarton Castle passed to King Charles, who appointed his natural son, the Duke of Richmond and Lennox, while still a boy, governor of Dumbarton Castle in 1681.[5] When he succeeded in 1702 (on the death of the dowager duchess) to the estates of the duchy of Lennox and Dumbarton Castle revenues, he immediately sold them to Queen Anne's physician, Sir David Hamilton, son of John Hamilton of Dalyell. He held them for only a short time, disposing of them in 1704 to James, 4th Marquis of Montrose (later first duke). By act of parliament in that year, the transfer to the Marquis of Montrose was confirmed of the feu-duties of the lands of Bute and Cumbrae, the ferme and watchmeal of Kilpatrick, the Mains of Cardross, the feu-duties of Cardross, and 'the Castle Green of the Castle of Dumbarton', but with the reservation that 'the rock and the haill fortification' of the castle, with the office of heritable keeper and constable, should be resigned to the crown.[6]

Castle Finance

The revenues of Dumbarton Castle were estimated in 1693 at about £300, payable to the duchy of Lennox (those of the castles of Edinburgh, Stirling and the Bass at £400, £480 and £80 respectively, the last a 'rent of solan geese').[7] The traditional revenues of the keeper of Dumbarton Castle have already been described. They were detailed in the act of parliament of 1704, confirming the transfer of the estates of the duchy of Lennox in 1702 to the Marquis of Montrose mentioned above. These revenues were regarded as part of the private income of the hereditary governors, the dukes of Lennox. As for the actual keepers or lieutenant-governors, in the early part of the century, they had little share of these revenues. When Sir John Maxwell of Pollok was appointed captain of the castle by James, 4th Duke of Lennox, in 1634, the post was described by his uncle, Sir William Hamilton, as 'very uncertain and chargeable', for 'if a man design to have greater preferment, he shall be forced to spend more nor all the benefit he can make by his place, howbeit he was punctually well paid, as we are not'. Shortly afterwards, Maxwell, in a letter to the Treasurer-Depute, the Earl of Traquair, complaining about the state of disrepair of the castle buildings, claimed that the 'outward customs' on the Clyde, paid to the keeper to enable him to provide a salute of guns in honour of noble visitors, had been allowed to lapse through the negligence of a former keeper, Sir John Stewart, and should be restored to the castle.[8] William Middlemist, keeper from 1611 to 1620, petitioned the Treasurer, the Earl of Mar, in 1622 and 1625 for payment of money due to him for the upkeep of prisoners in the castle; and long afterwards, in 1649, his widow presented a supplication to parliament for payment of the 1900 marks still unpaid of the 4500 marks due to her husband for the maintenance of the Earl of Orkney while a prisoner in Dumbarton Castle.[9]

From 1639, when the castle was seized from the duke's keeper by Provost John Sempill, until 1660, when it was restored to the Lennox family, there was no regular source of revenue for the keepers of the castle. Sempill, who held the castle for a few months in 1639 and again from 1644 to 1648, claimed to have spent nearly £14,000 (Scots) as keeper of the castle without being reimbursed.[10] But, after the restoration of Charles II in 1660, when a standing army came into existence and a military establishment was set up, a degree of stabilisation was achieved. Remittances arrived more or less regularly (seldom at intervals greater than three months) from the Treasury for the pay of the garrison. From at least 1667 onwards, the monthly pay for the castle garrison was £621. 12s. (Scots), which by 1682 was converted to £51. 16s. (sterling). In 1690 the pay account of the garrison for a three-month period amounted to £171. 19s. 4d. (with a small deduction for soldiers' pensions). In addition, there was an annual payment of £15 for coal and candle money, bringing the total pay and fuel allowance to approximately £700 for the year, of which £243 went to the lieutenant-governor, Lord Neil Campbell.[11]

Repairs to the castle were generally a matter for separate accounts as in previous centuries and involved considerable sums of money, those of 1617-18 (which included some works at Glasgow in preparation for the king's visit) amounting to £3,802. 9s. 2d. (Scots), those of 1674 and 1676, £2,591. 16s. and £3,316. 7s. 8d. respectively.[12]

The Cattle Impost

The castle garrison's right to levy an impost or custom duty on cattle from Argyll was still a grievance in the seventeenth century. In 1604, the Privy Council forbade the keeper of the castle to take more than ten cattle annually from the drovers of Argyll.[13] From 1600, the burgh of Dumbarton had been empowered, by a grant under the privy seal, to collect a toll of eight pence for 'ilk cow, ox, horse or stot' passing through the town, the grant being one of several given to the burgh in order to provide funds for protecting the town from the frequent inundations caused by the river Leven. The double toll in the burgh and at the castle must have proved a constant source of irritation to the men of Argyll. John Lindsay, who was in charge of the petty customs of Dumbarton in 1628, explained to the town council that the decrease in the revenue from the impost on cattle from Argyll was due to the drovers not using the 'auld accustomed way' but going instead by the castle of Dumbarton. It seemed as if thereafter some arrangement was made by the town council with the keeper of the castle (there are gaps in the burgh records of the period) as in April, 1632, Duncan Mac-Kellar (obviously an Argyllshire man from his name) appeared before the magistrates, charged with taking 'Hieland Kye' past the castle 'without giving the said castle their due', and was admonished after promising 'amendment in time coming'.[14]

The soldiers of the garrison, who had probably little to do apart from collecting the imposts, which would only be at certain seasons of the year, were not averse to using force. In the same year, 1632, John Cochran, servitor to Sir George Elphinston of Blythswood, captain of the castle, was charged with assaulting John Pittullo, a burgess of Dumbarton, and bearing loaded pistols on the streets of the burgh. He defended himself on the second charge by stating that he was out to poind victuals for the castle.[15]

In 1661, a petition on behalf of Charles, 6th Duke of Lennox, hereditary governor of the castle, was presented to the Privy Council, asserting the rights, 'constantly used' by his predecessors as governors of the castle, to receive 4 shillings (Scots) custom duty for 'ilk ox, cow, bull or stot' brought furth of Argyll and passing by Dumbarton Castle, or, alternatively, one cow out of every thirty for the price of £8 Scots for each cow. (The agreement between the Earl of Argyll and Esmé, Duke of Lennox, had been that the garrison should have yearly ten of the fattest cattle for two marks a pair more than the price of one; and it was the burgh of Dumbarton which from 1600 possessed the right to collect a toll of eight pence for 'ilk cow, ox, horse or stot'.) There had, of course, been a long interregnum during the period of the wars of the covenant and the Cromwellian occupation, and the drovers, according to the petition, were 'most wilfully' refusing to pay, taking their cattle by another way instead of past the castle. The Privy Council duly issued an order forbidding the Argyll drovers to pass the castle without paying, under pain of having their cattle seized and themselves arrested until the custom was paid. The duke's agent, John Stewart of Kettleston, who appeared before the council, had maintained that proof of the duke's right in the matter was in the duke's charter-chest, the keys of which were in the duke's possession; but it would appear that over the years the castle keeper and garrison had become more interested in extorting money than in buying cattle.[16]

The Highland drovers continued their attempts to pass by Dumbarton Castle without paying an impost. In 1664, they presented a petition to the Privy Council, protesting that the council's decision in 1661 in favour of the Duke of Lennox had been taken without allowing them the opportunity to make representations. Separate complaints were lodged in 1664 by six drovers, Alexander MacMillan, Hector MacNeill, John MacNeill, Nicol (Neil) MacNeill, Archibald MacNeill and Walter Colquhoun, against Lord Blantyre, tacksman of the custom to the Duke of Lennox, and John Mathie, ferryman at the Boat of Bonhill, claiming that they had been responsible for the unwarrantable 'spulzie' of their cattle. Bonhill, where drovers then and for long afterwards preferred to cross the river Leven, was three miles from Dumbarton but it was a suitable control point for the soldiers from the castle. The litigation dragged on but finally, in 1673 (the year after the death of the sixth duke), by a decreet of the Lords of Council, the drovers were declared free from the obligation to pay to the castle garrison, 'there being another custom due to the town of Dumbarton'. In 1684, however, Major George Arnott, as lieutenant-governor of the castle, made an attempt to obtain the restoration of the impost on

Highland cattle, but once again the drovers were successful in maintaining their freedom.[17]

Sir William Stewart and his Prisoners

Even before James VI became king of England in 1603, Dumbarton Castle had lost much of its strategic value as the gateway to and from France or Spain or as a possible base for invasion forces from these countries. After 1603, its function was to be mainly that of a prison fortress. James, who ruled from London after the union of the crowns, once boasted: 'Here I sit and govern by my pen: I write and it is done, and by a clerk of the council I govern Scotland now — which others could not do by the sword.' James's Privy Council, sitting in Edinburgh, maintained a firm rule over the land although lawlessness and violence still erupted from time to time. The Council took strict measures with the culprits, forcing them to 'enter into ward' in one of the royal fortresses, Edinburgh, Stirling, Dumbarton, Blackness or Doune, and only permitting their release if their good conduct was guaranteed by a person of standing as 'cautioner', under penalty of a severe fine. Dumbarton Castle had housed prisoners many times throughout the Middle Ages, but seldom was it so regularly occupied by notable prisoners as in the early years of the seventeenth century.

Sir William Stewart of Eildon, who was keeper of the castle from 1599 to 1610, had been appointed by Ludovick, 2nd Duke of Lennox. In December, 1602, it was Stewart who, along with a local laird, Sempill of Fulwood, proposed to Colquhoun of Luss that he should arrange for the women of his clan to take to Stirling as many blood-stained shirts as they could procure, after the MacGregor raid on Glen Finlas, in order to gain the sympathy of King James and revenge on the MacGregors.[18] This action did not prevent the massacre of the Colquhouns at Glen Fruin two months later, but the retribution exacted from the MacGregors lasted for a generation. Feuding continued both in the Highlands and Lowlands despite the efforts of the Privy Council. Dumbarton was used as a base for expeditions against the clansmen of the west and Dumbarton Castle as a prison for the clan chiefs, while among Stewart's earliest prisoners was Sir James Johnston of Johnston, whose feuds with the Maxwells and Douglases culminated in his murder by Lord Maxwell in 1608.[19]

In the days before a police force was ever dreamt of, the towns were occasionally the scenes of riots and disturbances which the bailies, responsible for maintaining order, were unable to quell. In September, 1604, five burgesses of Dundee, Robert and Andrew Flesher, Thomas and David Hunter, and Walter Rollock, were warded in Dumbarton Castle by order of the Privy Council for their 'turbulence' during elections in the burgh.[20] In June, 1605, following a 'tumult' in Edinburgh between the supporters of James Wishart and Alexander Lindsay, the latter escaped from custody and, as a result, his father, Sir David Lindsay of Edzell, was warded in Dumbarton Castle.[21] The following month, July 1605, Glasgow was the scene of 'very great trouble and commotion' between the provost, Sir George Elphinstone of Blythswood, and the former provost, Sir Matthew Stewart of Minto. Stewart was warded, along with his son, in Dumbarton Castle (the keeper of which happened to be his cousin) and Elphinstone in Glasgow Castle. The two provosts were banished to Stirling and bound over to keep the peace, Stewart in the sum of £5,000 and Elphinstone in 5000 marks.[22] Prisoners of a different sort arrived later in the year in October — two ministers, Nathan Inglis, minister of Craigie, and James Greig, minister of Loudoun, who were warded for travelling to Aberdeen to attend a prohibited assembly. They were kept in close confinement and were refused visitors for almost two years.[23]

In December, 1606, Sir William Stewart, keeper of the castle, was himself warded in Edinburgh Castle for having allowed the escape of an important Highland prisoner, Archibald Dubh MacDonald of Gigha, natural son of the chief of the MacDonalds of Islay and Kintyre, the redoubtable Angus MacDonald of Dunnivaig, who had bestowed Gigha on his son in 1576. Archibald Dubh (Black Archibald) had entered into ward in September, 1605, as a hostage for his father's good behaviour. Stewart, designated in the records as 'constable' of Dumbarton Castle, appeared before the Privy Council on December 16th, 1606, and admitted his 'oversight and negligence in giving over-meikle trust' to Archibald MacDonald but denied having prior knowledge of MacDonald's attempt to escape. Aulay MacAulay of Ardincaple (near the modern Helensburgh) came under suspicion as MacDonald had been ferried across the Clyde by some of his servants. Another of his servants, Robert Bontine, described as 'a young foolish boy, not capable of any great fraud or malice', admitted that he had been offered the sum of 500 marks by MacDonald to 'help him over the water', but although he had told the ferryman he could transport MacDonald without risk he had declined to accompany him and on his meeting with MacDonald later in the evening had merely exchanged 'good nichts'. Stewart, whose conduct was investigated by a small sub-committee of the Privy Council, was allowed to return after a few months in Edinburgh to his own castle of Dumbarton, in time to pay his respects to the hereditary governor, the Duke of Lennox, on his visit to Scotland as the king's commissioner to the Parliament of 1607. There is a romantic ending to the story of Archibald MacDonald's escape from Dumbarton Castle. His son, 2nd of Gigha, married Elizabeth Stewart, daughter of Sir William Stewart, keeper of Dumbarton Castle.[24]

In October, 1608, six more Highlanders were warded in the castle. They were Hector MacLean of Duart, his brother Lachlan, his cousin Alan and three attendant gillies. They had been captured, along with other leading Highland and Island chiefs, after accepting an invitation from Lord Ochiltree, the king's lieutenant in the west, to dine on board his ship, the *Moon*, at Aros in Mull and to hear a sermon from Andrew Knox, Bishop of the Isles. On February 6th, 1609, Stewart was ordered to produce MacLean of Duart before the Privy Council in Edinburgh by February 20th. Strict precautions were taken to ensure his arrival in the capital. A detachment of the king's guard was sent from Edinburgh to augment the escort from the Dumbarton Castle garrison, and the bailies of the burgh of Dumbarton were instructed to provide a supple-mentary guard as far as Glasgow, the bailies of Glasgow similarly as far as Linlithgow, and the bailies of the latter town to Edinburgh. MacLean duly appeared before the Privy Council and gave promises for the good behaviour of his clan; later, at a meeting in Iona with Bishop Knox, he and other chiefs of the west pledged themselves to obey the king and his council and agreed to the Statutes of Icolmkill (Iona), which proved remarkably effective in bringing peace to the western isles. In the meantime, Stewart himself had received a reprimand from the Privy Council for his 'inexcusable oversight and error' (of which word had reached Edinburgh) in feasting and making merry with his Highland prisoners, conduct which was regarded as particularly reprehensible as he had already been charged with showing undue leniency towards Archibald MacDonald of Gigha. Stewart had been in the habit of taking his prisoners out to dinner with him at an inn in the town of Dumbarton, where presumably the cooking was better than in the castle. He was asked to 'forbear such foolish things' in future, as they might 'imperil his estate and bring further inconvenience'.[25]

Two of the Roman Catholic nobles of the north, who had been engaged in various plots and intrigues, the Earl of Errol and the Marquis of Huntly, were also forced to enter into ward in October, 1608, Errol to Dumbarton Castle and Huntly to Stirling Castle, by the express order of James VI, who, although formerly tolerant towards the Catholics, never forgave them for the Gunpowder Plot of 1605. Errol and the MacLeans were only a week or so in the castle when they were subjected to a most alarming experience. On November 7th, earthquake tremors were felt in various parts of Scotland but nowhere so severely as at Dumbarton, where the people were so afraid that they left their houses and ran to the kirk with the minister to pray to God for fear of imminent destruction.[26]

Before Stewart demitted office at the end of 1610, he had the responsibility of receiving into custody a very different kind of prisoner. Three 'notorious Highland malefactors, Johnne McIlcallum Vc Andro McFarlane' and two others, 'common thieves and murderers', had been apprehended in the Lennox by Alexander Colquhoun of Luss and his friends after they had murdered a John Stewart 'in maist barbarous manner'. They were ordered to be brought to the tolbooth of Edinburgh and were delivered by Sir William Stewart to the bailies of Dumbarton, who conveyed them to Glasgow, where the Glasgow bailies arranged similar guard for them as far as Linlithgow and so on from there to Edinburgh.[27]

The Privy Council, in February, 1609, had decided that MacLean of Duart and his friends were not to be set at liberty until Sir William Stewart was paid for the expense of their upkeep during the time of their warding. But in 1618, after Sir William's death, his son, Walter Stewart, complained to the Privy Council that MacLean, although he had given his bond for the debt of 1000 marks and £100 expenses owed by him to Sir William for his maintenance at Dumbarton Castle, had never carried out his promise. Walter Stewart was, however, unsuccessful in his claim that this money should be paid by Sir Rory MacKenzie of Kintail, who had taken over MacLean's debts in return for acquiring MacLean's lands.[28]

Patrick Stewart, Earl of Orkney

One of the most notable prisoners detained in Dumbarton Castle in the reign of James VI was Patrick Stewart, Earl of Orkney, whose father, Robert, Earl of Orkney, was an illegitimate son of James V by a daughter of Alexander, Lord Elphinstone. Robert Stewart had received a grant of Orkney in 1564 from his half-sister, Mary, Queen of Scots, and had, before he died in 1592, acquired complete power in Orkney and Shetland. His rule of tyranny and oppression was matched, if not surpassed, by that of his son, Patrick, who has been described as 'proud, avaricious, cruel and dissipated'. Fortunately for the northern isles, James Law, a wise and tactful cleric, was appointed Bishop of Orkney in 1606, and in a letter he wrote to James VI in 1608 he narrated the grievances and hardships of the people of Orkney. In less than a month, James instructed the Privy Council to summon the Earl of Orkney before them. He was arrested in July, 1609, and appeared several times before the council in 1610 and 1611. He was allowed a certain degree of freedom in Edinburgh until the summer of 1611, when he foolishly appointed his illegitimate son, Robert, to be sheriff and justiciar in Orkney with powers to collect revenues and retake the castles which the earl had been compelled to surrender. James VI then ordered that the Earl of Orkney be sent to Dumbarton Castle, where he was taken on February 27th, 1612, and where, apart from a period of five months, he was to remain until he was brought back to Edinburgh in October, 1614, to be tried and executed for high treason.[29]

In Dumbarton Castle Earl Patrick spent much of his time scheming and planning how to restore his fortunes.[30] In the summer of 1612 he asked James Lyon (natural son of Sir Thomas Lyon of Auldbar, son of John, 7th Lord Glamis) to come to Dumbarton Castle, where the earl persuaded Lyon to help him 'break ward', i.e. escape from the castle. Michael Mair, the earl's secretary, was instructed to engage the laird of Cluny in the plot, and at a meeting held on the links of Leith, Cluny agreed to assist. Later he withdrew from his undertaking but sent his man, Gardyne, as a substitute. It was decided to use a rope attached to an instrument of iron (probably a grapnel) to allow the earl to make his escape by climbing down the outer face of the rampart. Preparations were made in secret and with thoroughness. A horse was held in readiness for the earl outside the castle and more horses waited at Dumbuck Hill, a mile away, to carry the earl and his rescuers to safety. But when the rope was in position, the earl became 'faint' and unwilling to risk the descent from the castle rampart by such a precarious method. Instead, he suggested bribing the porter at the gate. But when the porter was approached and a bribe offered to him, he at once informed the deputy keeper, John Buchanan of Buchanan, and the earl's escape attempt had to be abandoned.

Soon afterwards his son, Robert, was compelled to surrender the castle of Kirkwall, the capture of which had led to his father's transfer to Dumbarton Castle, and after a short term of imprisonment he was 'relaxed from ward' on a promise of good behaviour. His father was incensed by his son's surrender of Kirkwall Castle and Robert, aware of his father's wrath and, fearing to face him alone, persuaded James Lyon (who had planned his father's escape) to accompany him to Dumbarton to intercede with his father for him. When Robert and Lyon entered the castle, Earl Patrick at first would not even look at his son, calling him 'a feeble, unworthy beast' and cursing him for surrendering Kirkwall Castle. Robert's attempts to mollify his father's rage were met with 'much invective and spiteful speeches'. When Robert said he would do anything his father asked of him, the earl replied that he lacked the spirit and courage to follow any enterprise through to a successful conclusion. In response to Robert's request for some lands in Orkney, the earl said he would give him nothing until he made restitution and played the part of a man by recovering the castle of Kirkwall. At last, goaded by his father's venomous tirade, Robert declared that he would go to Orkney and recover Kirkwall Castle. It was a forlorn hope; and on leaving the castle, Lyon met in the town of Dumbarton a former servant of the earl, James Annand, who said that the earl knew that Robert could not succeed and that he would bring his son to the scaffold and thereby place the responsibility for his death on the king.

By the time that Robert sailed to Orkney to win back Kirkwall Castle, his father was no longer in Dumbarton Castle. In December, 1613, the Privy Council decided to remove him to Edinburgh Castle; but when the guard of the escort arrived at Dumbarton Castle, they found the keeper of the castle unwilling to accept the council's warrant as it did not bear the signature of the Duke of Lennox, the governor of the castle. The keeper, William Middlemist, was later charged with 'very disdainfully and proudly' refusing to accept the warrant and was admonished with a reminder from the council that his appointment as keeper owed its authority to King James, in whose name and on whose instructions the council acted.[31] When news came to Edinburgh that Robert Stewart had captured Birsay Castle in Orkney, it was decided to transfer his father, the Earl of Orkney, back to Dumbarton Castle, where he returned on May 17th, 1614.

On the last day of June, 1614, Duncan Mitchell, the 'post-boy' or messenger for the earl, arrived at Dumbarton Castle with letters from

Robert Stewart about the success of his expedition to Orkney. He found the earl walking in the 'close' of the castle. When the earl learned that his son had captured Birsay Castle, he burst forth — 'The De'il stick him! He might have taken a better house.' With further imprecations, he railed at his son, saying that if he had attacked Kirkwall Castle, the garrison there, composed of former servants of the earl, would have made no resistance. The earl's secretary, James Sharp, wrote two letters to Robert, one from the earl and one from himself; but neither was signed or bore the name of the addressee. Mitchell, the post-boy, was arrested in Edinburgh on his return journey and the earl's letters were discovered. At once, three of the king's guards were sent to Dumbarton to search for letters which might incriminate the earl and also to arrest his secretary. They left Edinburgh on Thursday, July 5th, at ten o'clock at night and, riding hard over the sixty miles to Dumbarton, arrived there on the next day at five o'clock in the afternoon. They demanded immediate entry but were told by some of the garrison from the wall-head that the keeper, Middlemist, was in Edinburgh, that his deputy, Robert Knox, was in the town of Dumbarton and that until his return the gate was not to be opened. Riding into the town, the officers of the guard met Knox, to whom they showed their commission and warrant; but he told them that he would not grant them admission until the next morning at eight o'clock. When they were allowed to enter, they found that Sharp, the earl's secretary, had vanished and that there were only a few papers of little significance belonging to the earl.

There was, however, enough incriminating evidence in possession of the Privy Council to proceed with charges of high treason against both the Earl of Orkney and his 'base son', Robert, who had at last taken Kirkwall Castle but had been defeated by the Earl of Caithness. Most of Earl Patrick's servants were prevailed upon, by one method or another, to give evidence of his having influenced his son in starting a rebellion in Orkney. On August 4th, 1614, Middlemist was instructed to keep the Earl of Orkney close prisoner, removing his servants from him, allowing none but the castle garrison to have access to him, and prohibiting any correspondence to or from him. The earl left Dumbarton Castle for the last time on October 9th, escorted by twelve officers of the king's guard, in charge of the sheriff-depute of Dumbarton, William Sempill of Fulwood, who handed over custody of the prisoner at Linlithgow to the sheriff of Linlithgow, Sir Walter Dundas of Dundas.[32]

The earl's son, Robert Stewart, was hanged, along with five of the ringleaders of the Orkney rebellion, at the mercat cross of Edinburgh on New Year's Day, 1615. Earl Patrick himself, brazenly denying his complicity, was sentenced to death a month later; but a delay of a few days occurred before the sentence was carried out, as it was discovered by the ministers that the earl could hardly say the Lord's prayer. They requested the council to delay his execution until he had some instruction in religion. The request was granted. He received communion on Sunday, February 5th, and was beheaded at the mercat cross of Edinburgh on the following day.[33]

A Keeper Dismissed

William Middlemist, keeper of Dumbarton Castle during the imprisonment of the Earl of Orkney, was succeeded by Sir John Stewart of Methven, who was to be removed from his office for neglect and misconduct. Stewart was a natural son of Ludovick, 2nd Duke of Lennox, the hereditary governor, who seems to have promised the appointment at Dumbarton Castle to him when his predecessor, Middlemist, still held the office. In 1615, Middlemist and Stewart signed a contract (recorded in the Books of Council and Session in 1617) whereby Sir John undertook not to remove Middlemist from the keepership or uplift the dues and casualties payable until he paid Middlemist the sum of 3000 marks. Before the end of 1619, Middlemist must have been persuaded to surrender the castle to Sir John on an assurance that the money was to be paid immediately thereafter. When the money was not forthcoming, Middlemist returned to the castle in February, 1620, during the absence of Stewart in Edinburgh. Accompanied by some former members of the garrison (William Scott, Robert Cairncross, George Buchanan, William Sandilands, Robert Cunningham, Robert Middlemist and Thomas Middlemist), and 'upon auld familiarity and acquaintance', Middlemist ejected Stewart's servants and made himself commander of all the 'ports and yetts', the guns and munitions. When Stewart complained to the Privy Council, Middlemist defended his actions by referring to the contract of 1615, which Stewart had failed to implement. The Privy Council took the view that the contract was not a valid one and should not have been made but ordained that Middlemist should deliver the castle before March 7th, 1620, and that Stewart should find security for the payment of the 3000 marks.[34]

As in the implementation of his contract with Middlemist, Stewart was to prove remiss in the performance of his duties, which to him were of less importance than the revenues attached to the office. But even in the collection of revenues he was careless. One of his successors, Sir John Maxwell of Nether Pollok, complained in 1634 that Stewart had allowed the keeper's right to the outward customs of Dumbarton to lapse.[35] Stewart's income, apart from the castle revenues and an annual pension of 1800 marks from James VI, was derived mainly from the barony of Methven in Perthshire, which he had been granted by his father, and must have been considerable as his wife was granted out of his estates an allowance of 4000 marks a year when he was in prison. His ruthless cutting down of the trees in Methven wood for sale as timber roused the ire of Charles I, who gave peremptory orders that it should cease.[36]

Stewart's duties as keeper included the custody of duplicates of the standard weights and measures of Scotland deposited in the castle at the same time as an identical set was deposited in Edinburgh Castle in accordance with acts of parliament of 1618 and 1621.[37] He did not experience the same difficulty with his prisoners as his predecessors. In his second year as keeper, Stewart received as prisoners two of the Presbyterian ministers still defying the government. Alexander Simson, minister of Mertoun in Berwickshire, preached a sermon in Greyfriars Kirk in Edinburgh on the 22nd July, 1621, violently attacking King James for his personal vices of blasphemy and swearing and the bishops for their failure to supervise the upbringing of the king's sons. He was apprehended the next day by four of the guard, who conveyed him to Dumbarton Castle, there to await trial. On the same day, the Privy Council ordered the imprisonment in Dumbarton Castle of another minister, Andrew Duncan, who had been professor of theology in the Huguenot college of La Rochelle for six years and had been suspended from his ministry of Crail. The ministers spent little more than two months in Dumbarton Castle and seem to have been treated courteously by Sir John Stewart, who provided them with free board.[38]

The only other prisoner recorded in the period of Stewart's tenure of office was a laird of the Lennox, Alexander Douglas of Mains, sheriff of Dumbarton, who had been put to the horn in January, 1625, and warded in the castle at the end of March for an unpaid debt of £359. 11s. and £40 of expenses, due to James Rae, a merchant of Edinburgh.

He was not long in the castle before he made complaint to the Privy Council about the accommodation for prisoners and at the same time informed the council about Stewart's conduct towards his wife.[39] Lady Stewart, who was a daughter of Sir Claud Hamilton of Shawfield (nephew of Lord John Hamilton), had apparently been subjected to cruel and inhuman treatment by her husband. The Privy Council decided to investigate the complaint and ordered Stewart to appear before them to be confronted by his wife. It was then revealed that she had been kept in chains and forced to sleep upon the bare floor of a room without any heating for thirteen days and nights. Stewart had compelled her to sign documents, including one denying that he had committed adultery with two women servants in the castle, Isobel Beaton and Margaret Kilmaurs, and another to the effect that he had always treated her in a loving and kindly manner. He had, however, often threatened to do away with her, vowing that neither God nor the Devil, the King nor the Council, nor all her kin, would save her life. He frequently 'struck and dang' her, threatening to appoint his two mistresses, with their illegitimate children, to be her keepers.[40]

It is not surprising that Stewart was himself warded in Blackness Castle but, as his wife was raising an action of divorce against him, he was released and allowed to return to Dumbarton Castle on his undertaking to compose his differences with his wife, to pay her an allowance of 4000 marks a year, and to maintain a garrison of sixteen soldiers in the castle.[41] Despite this undertaking, the garrison by the end of 1627 consisted of only six men instead of sixteen, without any victuals for their subsistence, as was revealed to the Privy Council in a report by Sir Walter Stewart of Minto and Walter MacAulay of Ardincaple. The council thereupon dismissed Stewart from his office of keeper, replacing him by one of the curators of the young Duke of Lennox, Sir John Stewart of Traquair, who was also a privy councillor. A small sub-committee of the Privy Council which inspected the castle reported on the weakness of its fortifications, which 'lay open to all dangers both of surprise and invasion'; and extensive repairs were set in hand.[42]

Stewart of Traquair delivered custody of the castle after two months to a Mr. Holmes, an English servitor of the Duke of Lennox, and William Young, who had been in charge of the small garrison after Stewart of Methven left.[43] Stewart, in addition to the disgrace of dismissal from his post, had to suffer the humiliation of imprisonment in the tolbooth of Edinburgh while awaiting trial on a charge of adultery.

H

He died not long afterwards, his widow marrying Sir John Seton of Gargunnock in 1629.[44]

Castle Repairs

When Sir John Stewart of Methven was forced to resign the keeper-ship of Dumbarton Castle in 1627, the fortifications were described as much neglected. Yet not long before, during the keepership of his pre-decessor, William Middlemist, extensive repairs had been carried out on the castle buildings. These repairs, so far as is known, were the first since the major reconstruction of 1546-50 when Andrew Hamilton of Cochno was keeper. The repair work during Middlemist's keepership was performed in the summer and autumn months, from April 1st to September 1st, 1617, and from May 18th to November 2nd, 1618.[45] During both years, the supervision of the work was entrusted to Thomas Fallisdaill, the provost of Dumbarton. Fallisdaill, who had been appointed Dumbarton's first provost in 1612, was engaged in similar duties from 1608 to 1615 as one of the overseers of the works to protect the town of Dumbarton from inundation by the river Leven. Fallisdaill, like some other burgesses of Dumbarton, owned land outside the burgh, the small estate of Ardochbeg in the parish of Cardross, not far from Mains of Cardross where Robert Bruce lived and died.[46] For his duties as overseer, Fallisdaill was paid £5 per week but could claim additional expenses, e.g. £3 for two days spent in riding to Edinburgh in search of masons, his expenses including his charges for his boy and his horse; 24s. for the hire of a horse to visit the slate quarries at Camstraddan on Lochlomondside and for arles to the slaters; £22. 6s. 8d. for the hire of a horse (£4), ten days' stay in Edinburgh (£5) and extra charges, including his boy (£13. 6s. 8d.).[47]

During 1617 and 1618, the Wallace Tower, the most important building in those days as it commanded the main north entrance, was the scene of continual activity. The tower was built on the rock itself and one of the first tasks was to level off and smooth the ground floor, which was effected by first lighting a fire on the rock in order to split it. This was done with coal fires which had been kindled by peat fires. Four new iron windows were inserted and an iron stanchion fixed in the 'little window in the cabinet' of the tower. A major operation was the taking down 'to the spout stanes' of the south gable (which was farthest away from the main entrance) in order to give added length to the tower house. Lofts and couples in the roof of the tower were renovated, the roof was slated, and the outer walls 'overcast' with lime, the workers engaged in the last work being suspended in a cradle. The other main building of the castle, the hall in the nether bailey, had its roof stripped and re-slated, the stonework pointed and fifteen windows glazed. Above the constable's chamber at the gate were two chimneys which smoked badly, and 'tirlies' (revolving cans) were fixed in order 'to cause the reek vent'. In addition to the reconstruction work on the buildings, the ramparts were repaired and strengthened.[48]

In November, 1627, following the dismissal of Sir John Stewart of Methven, the Privy Council ordered William Wallace, the king's master mason, to inspect the castle of Dumbarton and prepare a report on the defects in the walls and the bridge and the passage 'between the craigs'. Sempill of Fulwood, a local laird who was sheriff of Dumbarton, Thomas Fallisdaill, and John Sempill, the provost of Dumbarton, were to accompany Wallace on his tour of inspection.[49] In July, 1628, the Earl of Mar, in a letter to James, Duke of Lennox, assured him that the delay in repairs to Dumbarton Castle and other royal castles was due to lack of money but that 'Dumbarton shall not be forgotten but shall be with the first'.[50]

In January, 1629, Charles I wrote to the Treasurer of Scotland about the royal castles. Holyroodhouse, Stirling, Falkland, Linlithgow and Dunfermline had already been attended to, and Charles ordered the Treasurer to proceed with the work on Dumbarton Castle, which was, according to the Privy Council's report, 'altogether out of reparation'. The Master of Works was to be instructed to proceed with the necessary repairs, as Charles intended to visit the castle in the near future, accompanied by some of the principal men of the land.[51] Although Charles did not visit Scotland until 1633, the repairs were undertaken, as instructed, in 1629, when the overseers were Daniel Clerk of Dumbarton and Mr. David Elphinstone, who was appointed minister of Dumbarton in 1632. The south wall at the nether bailey had been allowed to fall into disrepair and Clerk and Elphinstone had it strengthened. Much of the work in 1629 involved the replacement of woodwork — a new door for the Wallace Tower and the roofs of the upper rooms of the hall. Four 'watchmen's lodges' and the brewhouse were repaired and a new iron gate provided for the Windy Hall between the two peaks.[52]

In 1633, when Fallisdaill was again overseer, materials were brought from John Buchanan's 'auld house' in Dumbarton for repairs to the hall

— two hewn doors, two hewn windows, three dozen oak cabers (rafters), and an oak beam for a lintel to the hall chimney. Fallisdaill, as overseer, had to make many journeys in order to engage skilled trades-men and arrange for the transport of materials. In April, 1617, he rode to Stirling and Paisley seeking masons and finally fixed up Robert Welsh and three other masons from Paisley, who were brought along with their tools and bedding by boat to Dumbarton. In 1628, when Fallisdaill was overseer of the water-work at the river Leven and all able-bodied persons in the town were ordered to turn out with spades and shovels, wages were paid at the rate of 5s. a day for men and 4s. for women. The lowest-paid workers at the castle were the women poke-bearers, who earned 30s. a week with an additional 1s. 6d. for drink. In 1617 the poke-bearers received an incentive bonus of 6s. 'to work fast'; and one of them, Christina Buchanan, was given 12s. for getting 'the rest to agree'. With the other workers, wages varied little over the period 1617-33 and the Dumbarton wages were similar to those paid on similar works at Stirling and Edinburgh Castles. The barrowmen who, like the poke-bearers, were recruited locally, were paid 40s. a week. Wrights and slaters received generally £3. 13s. 4d. a week, the same wage as some of the masons, but the leading mason was paid £5 a week. The numbers employed varied from time to time. On an average week in June, 1629, there were 9 masons, 4 wrights, 3 quarriers, 12 barrowmen and 16 poke-bearers. When a large cannon had to be hauled up into the castle, a number of men were hired from the town for three days and the town's drummer and piper were each paid 12s. 'to bring the town's folk out'.[53]

Transport of materials was facilitated by the situation of the castle at the junction of the rivers Clyde and Leven. Stone and lime were brought from Inchinnan, eight miles up the river Clyde; coals from the coal-heughs near Duntocher were taken from 'the burn-mouth of Dalmuir', six miles away; slates were carried by gabbarts from Cam-straddan on Loch Lomond down the river Leven. Timber was bought from merchants in Glasgow and Dumbarton. On June 2nd, 1617, Patrick Bell, a Glasgow merchant, was paid £71. 12s. for 25 deals, 17 double spars and 36 single spars; and on July 14th, 1617, John Sempill, provost of Dumbarton, was paid £53. 6s. 8d. for 80 Scots deals. A supply of timber (22 cartloads) from Glasgow in August, 1617, involved the payment of carters for transport down to the Broomielaw at 2s. 8d. a cartful. In June, 1618, William Wemyss, a Glasgow bailie, delivered a consignment of 500 Scots long deals and 30 spars at the nether bailey of the castle, and his 'mariners' and the castle workers were supplied with drink to the value of 25s. In March, 1629, 100 deals were bought from a Dutch ship in the Clyde and 60 deals similarly from another Dutch ship in 1633.[54]

It might be thought that as a result of the work carried out in 1617-18, 1629 and 1633, the castle had been brought into a state of good repair. But in April, 1634, Sir John Maxwell of Pollok, newly appointed keeper, complained that it was in such a state that 'no honest man could dwell therein'. Maxwell had been appointed keeper by James, 4th Duke of Lennox, when the latter came of age; but when, on October 15th, 1633, he presented his commission to Sir George Elphinstone of Blythswood, in charge of the castle, and Sir Archibald Douglas of Mains, his son-in-law and depute, they refused to deliver custody of the castle. Maxwell complained to the Privy Council, which ordered Elphinstone and Douglas to remove themselves, with their wives, children and servants from the castle within twenty-four hours under pain of rebellion. In his complaint of April, 1634, to the Earl of Traquair, the Treasurer-Depute (who had himself acted as keeper of the castle for a few months after the dismissal of Sir John Stewart of Methven), Maxwell declared that the hall was not 'water-fast' and its north-east corner, which had been taken down as unsafe in 1633, had not been rebuilt; the brewhouse and the bakehouse, the barns and stables 'were down and altogether ruinous'; the walls of the nether bailey were so 'decayed and fallen down' that they could not 'hold out beasts, let be men'. None of the hagbuts or muskets could be used and the only powder in the castle was what Maxwell himself had bought for the purpose of firing appropriate salutes for visitors of importance.[55] Although there is no record of expenditure on castle repairs in the next three years, it is probable that something was done towards the re-habilitation of some of the buildings, as William Stewart, who succeeded Maxwell as keeper in 1636, seems to have resided in the castle with his family.

Wars of the Covenant

Three years before Charles I's arbitrary rule provoked civil war in England, he was faced with a rebellion in Scotland. The publication by royal authority of a new prayer book ('Laud's Liturgy') led to a riot in St. Giles' Cathedral in Edinburgh in July, 1637, and the signing of the

National Covenant in February, 1638. At the end of 1638, the king's authority was openly defied by a General Assembly of the Scottish Kirk in Glasgow, which deposed the bishops and annulled the new liturgy and all the church statutes passed since 1606. Both the Scots and the king realised that war was inevitable and began to make preparations accordingly. Charles intended to advance northwards to Scotland with an army of 20,000 Englishmen, while invasion forces were to be landed at Aberdeen under the Marquis of Hamilton, in Kintyre under the Earl of Antrim (a relative of the MacDonalds of Islay), and at Dumbarton, the landing-place for the army to be sent by the Lord Deputy of Ireland, Thomas Wentworth. As far back as June, 1638, the Marquis of Hamilton, who was acting as the king's lieutenant in Scotland, wrote to his royal master that Dumbarton Castle was in safe custody and was 'the only fit place for the forces that shall come from Ireland to land at', adding that 'it is necessary that the Deputy (Wentworth) should be advised thereof and that he have order to land his men there with as much victuals and ammunition as he can send'.[56]

The planned invasion at four points of entry failed for a variety of reasons, but mainly because the Scots took measures to forestall the projected landings. In one week, Edinburgh Castle, Dalkeith House and Dumbarton Castle were taken, and the Isle of Arran (which belonged to the Hamiltons) was garrisoned by the Earl of Argyll.[57] Charles's advance towards Scotland was half-hearted and stopped short of the border where, faced with a much stronger and better-trained Scots army, he submitted by signing the Pacification of Berwick.

The capture of Dumbarton Castle was undertaken not by a soldier but by the provost of Dumbarton, John Sempill of Aikenbar and Stoneyflat. Sempill, who had been provost several times in the previous twenty-five years, was a member of the body known as 'The Tables' which, in December, 1637, set itself up as a rival to the king's council, and he attended for almost four weeks the General Assembly at Glasgow, which carried through sweeping changes in religion and made war with the king inevitable. As early as September, 1638, the town council of Dumbarton had decided to purchase 30 good muskets with rests and bandoliers, a hundredweight of powder, a hundredweight of good match, and 40 ash pikes. The citizens did not display as much zeal for the forthcoming struggle against the king as did the councillors. On February 4th, 1639, as few or none had bought powder, the council ordained that each person should buy at least two pounds at 18 pence a pound, and on March 20th, as the citizens were not attending the drills, they were ordered to turn out on pain of a fine of 6 shillings, *toties quoties*, and, if need be, have their goods poinded. On March 22nd, a council of war for Dumbarton was set up, comprising the provost and eleven councillors, with powers to raise taxation for defence of the kingdom from foreign invasion and defence of the true religion professed within the kingdom.[58]

On Sunday, March 24th, 1639, Sir William Stewart, keeper of Dumbarton Castle, attended the parish kirk in Dumbarton as he was wont to do. After the service, Provost Sempill invited the keeper to dine at his house and when Stewart declined the invitation, Sempill, who was accompanied by Walter MacAulay of Ardincaple, brusquely informed Stewart that he would remain in his company. Forty armed men (including, presumably, some of the reluctant recruits from the town) surrounded Stewart, who was accompanied by his wife, his son and sixteen soldiers, and escorted him to Sempill's house, where the provost demanded that Stewart should hand over the keys of the castle. 'That I will never do,' replied Stewart, 'as long as I have life.' 'Come,' said the provost, 'be not foolish and obstinate, for if you fail to send for and give us the keys instantly, I vow to God to send the heads of those that are here as a token to deliver them to us for the country's safety'. Whereupon Stewart sent for the keys and delivered them to Sempill. Stewart was next ordered to remove his clothes, which were then donned by one of Sempill's men of about the same height and figure as Stewart. The keeper was also compelled to reveal the password, and when darkness fell it was an easy matter for Sempill's force to approach the castle, give the password and enter the castle.[59]

Stewart, the evicted keeper, writing soon afterwards from Edinburgh to the Marquis of Hamilton, excused his surrender by the lack of 'trusty men and numbers', besides the weakness of the place, about which he had previously warned Hamilton. His garrison, he wrote, were unreliable, almost all of them Covenanters, most of whom were taken on by Sempill for his garrison as 'a reward for their treachery'.[60]

Immediately after the capture of the castle, a letter was sent to the Earl of Argyll informing him of the state of affairs. The Earl of Argyll, who was to play a leading rôle in the wars of the Covenant, held lands in Dumbartonshire and had an obvious interest in the castle of Dumbarton, of which he became governor in 1640. Sempill did not retain the castle in his possession. MacAulay of Ardincaple, his associate in the capture of Sir William Stewart, acted for a short time as keeper and was succeeded by William Crawfurd of Kilbirnie, who had been in charge of the muster of soldiers raised in Dumbartonshire on May 8th, 1639, for service against the king's English army.[61]

As part of the agreement at Berwick between Charles and the Scots, Dumbarton Castle was restored to the king, and Charles appointed as keeper Sir John Henderson of Fordell, whose brother-in-law, Sir Patrick Ruthven, was appointed governor of Edinburgh Castle. According to a memorandum in the state papers of Charles I, written probably in February, 1640, the possibility of the castle being recaptured was considered likely unless the garrison, which stood at between 55 and 60 soldiers, mostly English, was increased to about 200. But even for the small garrison under Henderson, more victuals, clothes and arms were necessary, 'the place being extremely cold'; and, as sentinels during the long winter nights tended to use the matches of their matchlock muskets for lights, it was desirable to have a supply of 40-50 muskets with firelocks. The winter of 1639-40 and the hardships of life in the castle without proper food undermined the health of the garrison soldiers. One of the English ships carrying provisions to the castle 'perished by the way', and the Covenanters sank two small ships (one of them the *Merrie Katherine* of Glasgow) in the mouth of the castle harbour to stop any future supplies coming by sea.[62] At the end of June, 1640, six or seven score of dependants of the Marquis of Huntly arrived to assist the English, by then debilitated and demoralised by scurvy. In a broadsheet, preserved in the British Museum Library, is a poem composed by one of the English garrison of the time, lamenting bitterly their woeful plight. It is entitled 'Dumbriton's Castle Dolefull Commendations to all the Rascall Rogues within this Nation' and was written shortly before the surrender of the castle in September, 1640:

> Most dismall was that day, accurs'd that hour,
> When first we saw Dumbriton's dolefull Toure.

The soldiers were ashamed of their appearance:

> Our carcases most ugly to behold,
> Our sores and sorrows moe nor can bee told;
> Our coal-black faces to the world portend
> Our loathsome lives and most unhappie end.[63]

When Sir John Henderson, the keeper of the castle, arrived at York at the end of September, 1640, he was 'full of the scurvy'. Henderson surrendered the castle to the Earl of Argyll, who from the beginning of August had a force of 200 men in the vicinity of Dumbarton under the command of Major John Maxwell.[64]

In November of the following year, 1641, at the end of Charles's visit to Scotland, Argyll (by this time a marquis) was ordered by an act of the Scottish Estates to surrender Dumbarton Castle to the Duke of Lennox, who was present at the meeting of the Estates, as was also Argyll. The act continued — 'And further for removing of all jealousy and fear that may be conceived by keeping any garrison or ammunition in the said castle . . . the whole soldiers, ammunition and cannon should be transported furth thereof, that no keeper should be appointed in future' and that 'the walls of the castle be never repaired in all time coming'. The reason for this remarkable change of policy as regards Dumbarton Castle is to be found in the jealousy displayed by his fellow-nobles of Argyll's increasing power in Scotland. Dumbarton Castle might be useful to a foreign invader as a base but it was also dangerous in the possession of an over-powerful subject. Dismantled, it could serve neither invader nor rebellious subject. In another act of the Estates in April, 1644, the castle was described as more hurtful than useful to the country in time of trouble and, as nothing seemed to have been done by Argyll as regards demolition of the castle, the houses and walls were to be razed to the ground, John Sempill, provost of Dumbarton, being recommended to see that this was done, and authority being given to him to hire or impress quarriers and other necessary workmen for the work of demolition. A small committee was appointed to dispose of the cannons, carriages and ammunition.[65]

By the spring of 1644, the Scots were already preparing for intervention on the side of the English parliament in the civil war in England in fulfilment of the Solemn League and Covenant. Sempill does not seem to have proceeded with the task assigned to him of supervising the demolition of the castle. At the end of May, 1644, he did however assume responsibility for the castle, which he found ill-furnished and derelict, as his inventory shows.[66] For nearly three months in the summer of 1644, Sempill was in Edinburgh in attendance at Parliament or at Kirkcaldy attending the Convention of Royal Burghs. During the summer, however, over 1600 Irishmen, under the command of the half-Irish, half-Scottish Alasdair MacDonald, landed in Argyll and, joining with the Marquis of Montrose, who raised 800 Atholl men for King Charles, won a resounding victory at Tibbermore (Tippermuir) near Perth on September 1st over a Covenanting army. Montrose and MacDonald proceeded thereafter to win one victory after another. During the winter of 1644-45 when Montrose's forces were in Argyll, the threat of a raid on the Lennox induced the town council of Dumbarton to have a trench dug round the town in December, but later, probably realising their inability to resist the Highlanders and Irishmen, the council decided to have the pikes, muskets and ammunition belonging to the burgh removed to the castle for safe-keeping under John Sempill. The father of Alasdair MacDonald, the famous Colkitto, and two of his sons, captured in the summer in Argyll, were removed from Dunstaffnage Castle to Dumbarton Castle in December, when their fellow-clansmen were devastating the Campbell lands. Sempill complained to the Estates that he had 'neither room nor irons nor other instruments nor men' to keep ward over them, and on February 13th orders were sent to have them transferred to Edinburgh.[67]

After Montrose's victory at Kilsyth on August 14th, 1645, Alasdair MacDonald (by this time knighted by Montrose for his gallantry) set off with his Highlanders and some of the Irishmen for Kintyre to pay off old scores against the Campbells. MacDonald and his men encamped for five days at the beginning of September at Cloberhill, about ten miles east of Dumbarton. The minister of Kilpatrick, the Rev. James Wood, a devoted royalist, who had read Montrose's proclamations from his pulpit and in the burgh of Dumbarton, proceeded to the castle with MacDonald, who demanded of Sempill the surrender of the castle. Wood was later charged at a meeting of Dumbarton Presbytery with making 'opprobrious speeches' against Sempill, who told him, 'There is no loon like a loon minister, as Mr. Rollock said of auld.' Wood's answer, 'There is no loon like a loon provost who keeps the king's castle against those who were sent by the king to receive it', did not help his case at the meeting of the presbytery when he was deposed from his ministerial charge.[68] Sempill was later to complain to Parliament about the ravaging of his crops by the soldiers of Alasdair MacDonald, whose brothers had been Sempill's prisoners earlier in the year, and about the upkeep of Irish prisoners sent to Dumbarton Castle after Montrose's defeat at Philiphaugh on September 13th, 1644. Whether because he wanted payment for his expenses before handing over custody of the castle or not, Sempill refused to deliver the castle to the new keeper appointed by the Duke of Lennox in December, 1646, Sir Charles Erskine of Alva, until the Committee of Estates ordered him in June, 1648, to do so within twenty-four hours.[69] He presented a supplication to Parliament in 1649 for payment of £13,986. 9s. for his expenses in provisioning and repairing the castle and received £4,800 in part-payment. At his death in 1653, he was still being owed a substantial sum, but in this respect he fared no worse than many other devoted Covenanters.[70]

English Occupation

Sir Charles Erskine, to whom John Sempill surrendered the castle of Dumbarton in June, 1648, was still keeper when Scotland fell under the control of Cromwell's army. The subjugation of Scotland, begun after Cromwell's victory at Dunbar on September 3rd, 1650, was completed after his 'crowning mercy', the defeat of the Scots at Worcester a year later. When the 'sad news' of the defeat at Worcester reached Scotland, the Committee of Estates, which had fixed their meeting-place at Dumbarton — considered far enough away from English occupying forces — changed the venue first to Rosneath on the Gareloch and then to Rothesay in the Isle of Bute.[71] Edinburgh Castle was surrendered on December 24th, 1650, after a three-month siege, and Stirling Castle on August 14th, 1651, following a mutiny in the garrison. Cromwell slowly but surely strengthened his hold over Scotland: large forts were built at Leith, Perth, Ayr, Inverness, Inverlochy and even at distant Stornoway in the Isle of Lewis, and the whole of Scotland was brought under military control.

Dumbarton Castle was the last major fortress to be surrendered. Sir Charles Erskine of Alva, the keeper, was the son of John, 7th Earl of Mar and Lady Marie Stewart, daughter of Esmé, Duke of Lennox, and was thus the cousin once removed of James, Duke of Lennox, who as hereditary proprietor and governor had appointed him as captain and keeper of the castle. In 1650, Erskine commanded a much larger garrison than had existed in peacetime — 54 privates at 5s. a day, a lieutenant at £40 a month, a sergeant at £18 a month, a gunner at £30 a month, and a corporal and a drummer at £12 a month. He had also under his command a small garrison two miles up the river Clyde at Dunglass (the old castle of the Colquhouns), where an ensign and a corporal were in charge of 30 privates.[72]

The Scottish defeat at Worcester on September 3rd, 1651 made the surrender of Dumbarton Castle only a question of time. On September 25th, the Dumbarton magistrates hurriedly arranged with the Marquis of Argyll for the town's charter-chest, which had been removed to the castle for safety in November, 1650, to be transported to Carrick Castle on Loch Goil, a Campbell stronghold, where it remained for over a year.[73] The Duke of Lennox, who was known in England by the

title of Duke of Richmond, which he had gained in 1641, was under
strong pressure from the English Council of State to cause Erskine to
surrender the castle, and this the duke agreed to do at the end of
December, 1651. Major-General Lambert, in charge of the English
troops in Scotland, finding Erskine 'dilatory' about obeying the duke's
instructions, decided to 'reduce him by extremities'. Erskine's house of
Alva was occupied and his goods seized, including plate valued at £400
which was found in his other house of Cambuskenneth. Articles of surrender were drawn up to permit Erskine to leave the castle on honourable terms, with his men bearing arms, flying colours and beating
drums.[74] The cannon in the castle were to be at the disposal of the Duke
of Lennox and Richmond, the hereditary proprietor of the castle. The
actual surrender was made on Hansel Monday, January 5th, 1652. By
the end of March, the English Council of State had decided, because of
the lack of ordnance, to have the brass guns removed from Dumbarton
and Stirling Castles and put on board English men-o'-war on the
Scottish coasts, an indication that in Cromwell's view the two fortresses had little military importance.[75]

One of the first tasks of Captain Thompson, in charge of the English
garrison, was to secure the obedience of the civilian population in his
area to the authority of the English government and, in particular, to
the new constitution, which was proclaimed in October, 1651 and
created a united commonwealth of England and Scotland. On February
28th, 1652, Bailie John Smollett, as commissioner for the burgh of
Dumbarton, gave assent in Edinburgh to the union but on April 3rd,
Captain Thompson, whose duty it was to administer to the Dumbarton
magistrates the oaths of allegiance, found them reluctant to take the
oath. In a letter to the English governor of the castle, whom they had entertained four days before at a dinner which cost £38, Provost James
Campbell and the two bailies, John Cunningham and Donald Mac-
Alpine, explained how they had been 'earnest with God' in trying to
reach a decision about the oath. They were prepared to give obedience
to the parliament of England and their authority exercised in Scotland
'in so far as God's word is the rule to lead us therein', but asked for a
postponement of the oath-taking until they would have greater
freedom and light to do so.[76] The magistrates and the people of
Dumbarton (and, for that matter, most of Scotland) before long came
to accept the military government imposed upon them. So far as
religion was concerned, the English army of occupation did not inter-
fere with the practice of the Presbyterian church while it maintained

law and order and allowed trade in the burghs to thrive.

The Scottish royalists, however, were not prepared to accept the rule of Cromwell and his colleagues, whom they denounced as regicides after the execution of Charles I. The Earl of Glencairn, whose castles of Finlaystone and Kilmaronock were only a short distance from Dumbarton, received a commission from Charles II in the summer of 1653 and raised an army, consisting mainly of Highlanders and numbering at one time as many as 5,000 men. In the autumn, Viscount Kenmure, with a force of several hundred Highlanders, advanced southwards by Loch Lomond. Kenmure, nephew of Sir John Gordon of Lochinvar, was said to march with a small cask of whisky in front of him, which his troops called 'Kenmure's Drum'. Colonel Lilburne, writing to Cromwell on October 6th, 1653, expressed the fear that Kenmure would overpower the small garrisons at Buchanan (near the modern village of Drymen) and Cardross (in Menteith) and threaten the towns of Stirling or Glasgow. Lilburne immediately sent seven companies of horse and foot to reinforce the troops on Clydeside, and Kenmure, who had by this time reached Dumbarton, was compelled to retreat. Soon afterwards, Colonel Cobbett, who was in charge of the English garrison at Stornoway, arrived at Dumbarton Castle, having marched through the Highlands with a detachment and successfully repelled attacks from Kenmure's force. Colonel Lilburne, having come through from Dalkeith to Dumbarton, travelled as far north as Loch Fyne in order to intercept Kenmure but found the way 'so impassable for us' that he decided to return to Dumbarton.[77]

The rising started by Glencairn was, despite some minor successes, doomed to failure because of quarrels over the leadership. Glencairn, who was superseded in the command, withdrew from the rebel army and made his way south to Lochlomondside, where he received shelter at Rossdhu, the residence of the Colquhouns of Luss. Glencairn lay at Rossdhu for some weeks suffering from dysentery, from which he was not expected to recover, and decided in April, 1654 to come to terms with General Monk, who was in charge of the English forces in Scotland. Negotiations were broken off by Monk for a time, during which Glencairn, now recovered, led his force in a surprise attack on English dragoons stationed in the town of Dumbarton. The attack was timed for one o'clock in the afternoon when the English soldiers were expected to be at dinner and was completely successful. Over 30 were killed and 20 made prisoners, while the rest escaped by fleeing to the castle.

Immediately on hearing of this success of Glencairn, General Monk re-opened negotiations, and Glencairn was able to obtain more favourable terms. The transactions were concluded on September 4th, 1654, on the castle green below Dumbarton Rock. All Glencairn's officers received an indemnity and were allowed to retain their horses and arms and the liberty of wearing their swords, while the common soldiers were allowed to sell their horses but were obliged to surrender their arms, for which they received full value. Two tables were placed on the castle green, at which officers and men received passes allowing them to travel safely and the men received the money for their arms. On the same day, according to a contemporary account, Glencairn crossed over the Clyde and came to his own house of Finlaystone. Less than a year later, an agreement was reached between General Monk and the Marquis of Lorne, who had taken part in Glencairn's rising, the marquis being compelled to appear at the old parish kirk of Cardross on the opposite side of the river Leven from Dumbarton Castle in order to carry through the surrender of his arms.[78]

During most of the period of English occupation, relations between the garrison of Dumbarton Castle and the townspeople of Dumbarton were on a relatively friendly footing. By 1657 most of Scotland was quiet under English military rule. In that year General Monk, reporting to Cromwell, gave details of the English forces in Scotland. Dumbarton Castle had a garrison of one company of foot (approximately 70 men) and 20 horse, Edinburgh Castle had two companies, while Ayr and Leith each had seven companies of foot and 100 horse.[79] On at least two occasions the town's ladder was borrowed for use in the castle: in May, 1653 John Bontine was paid 4s. for carrying it back along with a water firlot, and in May, 1655 he, along with Robert Leitch and some 'sojours', received 12s. for the same task. Captain William Davies, who succeeded Captain Thompson as governor of the castle, was made an honorary burgess of Dumbarton, along with other English officers, on March 27th, 1656, the sum of £26 being spent by the town council on 'confectiones, wyne and uther necessers' on that day. When Cromwell was proclaimed Lord Protector on July 29th, 1657 in Dumbarton, Captain Davies joined with the magistrates in drinking to the occasion. The goodwill between town and castle was somewhat lessened when the Glasgow magistrates, whose influence with the English was greater than that of the Dumbarton magistrates, decided to challenge Dumbarton's right to levy customs on inward cargoes. Captain Davies, in charge of the castle garrison, was made responsible by the Council of

State for the collection of the dues formerly levied by the burgh of Dumbarton. (The English had already by 1656 appointed a tide waiter at Newark three miles from Dumbarton down the Clyde, where all incoming vessels discharged their cargoes.) In 1660, soon after the restoration of Charles II, the provost of Dumbarton, Walter Watson, and Bailie John Cunningham travelled to Edinburgh to press the burgh's claim to the dues collected by Captain Davies and his subordinate, Lieutenant Richardson. They returned home without a 'satisfactory answer', that is, with no money, but with one of the burgh's charters and the cocket book, which are still preserved in the town's public library.[80]

A Restoration Keeper

The restoration of Charles II in 1660 was greeted with enthusiasm in Dumbarton as in other Scottish burghs. On the day of his coronation in London in April, 1661, the Dumbarton magistrates ordered all the inhabitants of the burgh to 'put on bonfires', and according to the town council minutes 'thair was drums beating and cannons thundering from the castle'. Already in February, 1661, command of the castle garrison had been taken over by Major George Grant, in charge of 'a hundred gallant infantry, all of them approven blades in the royal interest'.[81] Grant was generally designated lieutenant-governor of the castle, the Duke of Lennox being hereditary governor until his death in 1672, after which Charles II appointed William, 5th Earl of Wigton, as governor of the castle and sheriff of Dumbarton.

Grant's brother, James, laird of Freuchie, was to have been created Earl of Strathspey in 1663 but died before the warrant was signed. It was to James Grant of Freuchie that a kinsman once wrote: 'I wiss your mother had borne a grey stone quhen scho did bring forth George.'[82] Major Grant seems to have been possessed of a ruthlessness remarkable even for the times. A chance remark by Lauder of Fountainhall on the occasion of a visit to Dumbarton Castle in 1668 that he was 'so fortunate that Major George Grant was not there' hints at an ungovernable temper.[83] Grant was once so enraged at the claim made by a Dumbarton girl, Margaret MacArthur, against his friend, Mungo Grant, as father of her child that she fled to Ireland to escape his wrath. The kirk session of Dumbarton parish church in 1667 and 1668 tried several times to compel Grant himself to make repentance for his fornication with Jean Clark, mother of two of his children, finally allowing him to do so before the session only instead of publicly before the congregation. In return for the session's leniency, Grant offered to donate 200 fir deals for the roof of the church and promised not to be guilty of such scandalous conduct again.[84]

During Charles II's reign, the Scottish army was placed on a regular footing and gradually an establishment was evolved. Laws and articles of war 'for the government of H.M. forces within the kingdom of Scotland' (the equivalent of the modern Queen's Regulations) were drawn up by General Thomas Dalyell in the autumn of 1666 and ratified by Charles II in January, 1667. The articles concerning Christian and moral duties stipulated the death penalty 'without mercy' for anyone 'so desperately mad as to blaspheme or speak against the Holy, Blessed and Glorious Trinity'. No common or notorious whore was to be tolerated in camp or garrison, and whosoever kept an unmarried woman should be constrained to marry her or put her away. (A long gap in Dumbarton kirk session records from 1668 to 1681 makes it impossible to check on Major Grant's conduct in respect of this article.) Death was also the penalty for any governor who surrendered his castle, fort or garrison; but if forced to surrender by his officers or soldiers, the officers should 'surely die, and the soldiers be decimated for hanging'. The articles concerning camps and garrisons were especially severe, death being the penalty for any sentinel found sleeping on duty, leaving his post before being relieved or going in or out of the camp or garrison by any other ways than were appointed. There is no evidence to show whether these articles were strictly observed in peacetime, and Major Grant, for all his overbearing temper, may not have enforced such a severe discipline as General Thomas Dalyell desired.[85]

Grant's treatment of the soldiers in the garrison of Dumbarton Castle was such, however, that in 1669 a petition was presented to the Privy Council by eighteen n.c.o.'s and soldiers, complaining that Grant had withheld their pay from time to time. The petition claimed that theirs was 'a most miserable and sad condition', 'palpably known to the whole country', and that delaying and detaining pay not only impoverished and ruined them but also the people of Dumbarton and the adjacent countryside to whom they had been in debt. Major Grant, appearing before the council, stated in his defence that of the five months complained of, three months' pay had now been disbursed, another month's pay was in the clerk's hands, and the precept for the fifth was still to be received. Sergeant James Scrymgeour, who appeared in defence of Grant, blamed a corporal, James Strachan, for having got up the petition but added that he had now deserted. Corporal Strachan may have been an early example of the barrack-room lawyer but must have had considerable courage to challenge the conduct of his tyrannical commanding officer. The Privy Council at any rate dismissed the complaint.[86] That Grant's discipline was strict may well be believed. An act of Parliament had been passed prohibiting the import of goods and victuals from Ireland in order to encourage Scottish industry and agriculture; and parties of soldiers were sent out from Dumbarton Castle to intercept any Irish vessels attempting to land such goods. In 1677, four soldiers of the castle garrison were cashiered for accepting bribes from people whose goods had been seized and then released. Their last month's pay was to be forfeited and delivered to the kirk session of Dumbarton parish church for the relief of the poor in the burgh. About the same time, Robert Fleming, clerk to the garrison, who had seized two small Irish boats, one with a cargo of barley and the other with oatmeal, was as a reward given both boats and one third of the barley, while the oatmeal was stored in the girnel of the castle and the rest of the barley given to the poor of Dumbarton.[87] The interest displayed in the condition of Dumbarton's poor may not have proceeded from humanitarian motives so much as from Major Grant's desire to placate Dumbarton kirk session, one of whose responsibilities was poor relief.

Apart from enforcing the embargo on Irish imports, the garrison of the castle was employed in rounding up 'broken and lawless men' in the Highland shires. In February, 1674, the Privy Council granted a commission to Major Grant to apprehend lawbreakers in the Highlands and he was paid £300 sterling per year and £20 for 'ilk notorious thief or murderer he should bring in'. With a small detachment from the castle garrison, he traversed the glens and arrested Highland malefactors with such success that his commission was renewed in 1675 and 1676.[88] Dumbarton Castle during Grant's term of office had little military significance other than as a base for such patrolling activities. It was, however, also used as a secure place where victuals, arms and munitions could be stored for a contingency such as foreign invasion or civil disturbance. After the Pentland Rising of 1666, a proclamation was issued for the disarming of people in the disaffected areas and the storing of arms and powder in the castles of Edinburgh, Stirling and Dumbarton. Again, in February, 1678, arms were collected in

J

Renfrewshire, Lanarkshire and Ayrshire by order of the Committee of the West and sent first to the parish kirks and then to Dumbarton Castle.[89] In 1675, George Maxwell, sergeant in the castle, was ordered to lay up in store 50 bolls of meal and 25 bolls of malt in a new girnel, to be kept there and not used unless by order of the Lords of the Treasury, and also to replenish the store annually with the same amounts.[90] As for the cannon in the castle, they seem only to have been fired in salutes to distinguished visitors or to mark some auspicious occasion. In 1671, Charles II actually granted permission to the Duke of Lennox to transport to England 'his six brass guns at Dumbarton Castle'.[91]

Dumbarton Castle continued to be used as a prison for state prisoners. In the sixteenth and early seventeenth centuries, these were more often than not unruly nobles or lairds, but in the second half of the seventeenth century the main challenge to the government's authority came from the strict presbyterians or covenanters, who opposed the state control of the church. In 1665, two of the Lowland incomers to Kintyre, William Ralston of that ilk and Robert Halkett, were imprisoned in Dumbarton Castle without trial, but after two years, during which they had behaved 'with all silence and submission', they were released. After the Pentland Rising of 1666 Argyll, who was 'cleansing up Kintyre', ordered the arrest of two men who had been sureties for William Wallace, son of Colonel Wallace, leader of the rising. They were James Brown and John Cunningham, both of whom had been elders in Campbeltown (or Lochhead as it was then called), and as young Wallace had escaped to Ireland they were sent, along with a David Muir, to Dumbarton Castle, where they remained for most of the year until released after signing bonds to keep the peace. Robert Ker of Kersland, who had resided in Holland for three years after the Pentland Rising, was captured in Edinburgh when visiting his sick wife and removed to Dumbarton Castle in February, 1670. In September of that year, in a supplication to the Privy Council, he requested a removal to a place 'where his children might have the benefit of schools and colleges', and as a result was transferred to the tolbooth of the new town of Aberdeen, where unfortunately he spent the winter months in a room without any fire. He was then brought south to Stirling, where he lay for seven years, after which he was imprisoned in Dumbarton Castle for a second time. Other covenanters imprisoned in the castle during this period were Robert Bailie of Jerviswood, John Cunningham of Bedlaw, and Hugh Archibald, formerly minister of Symington.[92]

Major Grant's most notable prisoner was William Drummond of Cromlix, major-general of the army in Scotland. Drummond had been a loyal supporter of Charles I and Charles II but, having quarrelled with the all-powerful Duke of Lauderdale, he was imprisoned in Dumbarton Castle in September, 1674 on suspicion of corresponding with Scots exiles in Holland, and there he remained until February, 1676. During this time he was allowed to take exercise because of the effect of close confinement on his 'very sore gravel' and allowed to 'go abroad to the fields in daytime under guard'. On his release, Drummond was restored to his command and was later created Viscount Strathallan by James VII. Another important prisoner, Sir Patrick Hume of Polwarth, who had also incurred Lauderdale's displeasure by opposing the policy of quartering troops in the houses of covenanters, was in September, 1678 removed at his request from Edinburgh tolbooth to Dumbarton Castle as 'a more healthful prison' as he had been indisposed, and a few months later he was transferred to Stirling Castle, where his wife was allowed to be with him.[93]

Major Grant found time, in addition to his military duties, to become involved in a scheme to acquire for himself landed property in the Lennox. According to Buchanan of Auchmar, the historian of the Buchanan family, Grant was an old comrade of John Buchanan of Buchanan, who had inherited the family estates much burdened with debt, and as he had no male issue disponed his estate to Major Grant with various provisions, one of which was that Grant should marry Buchanan's daughter and adopt the name of Buchanan. Grant's suit was spurned by the young lady but he seems to have changed his name to Buchanan shortly before his death. Grant had schemed with Buchanan of Arnprior to sell off much of the Highland portion of the Buchanan estate to the Marquis of Montrose, who in time became possessed of all the patrimony of the Buchanans.[94] Grant, who died in office in 1681, was one of the most active and energetic keepers of Dumbarton Castle known to us. During his time, major repairs were carried out in the castle, much of it on his own initiative.

Rebellions and Revolution

Towards the end of Charles II's reign and during the brief reign of his brother, James VII, Scotland was disturbed by rebellions, culminating in the deposition of James after his flight from London in 1688. The Lennox saw little of the fighting and the garrison of the castle was only slightly involved. At the time of the covenanters' rising in 1679, Major Grant, lieutenant-governor of the castle, considering the defences at the nether bailey ruinous and 'fearing that there might be some attempt made thereupon by the rebels in the west', had a great fort and rampart built at the entry to the nether bailey. He also prepared to withstand a siege by laying in a store of provisions obtained from merchants in Dumbarton; but the rebellion lasted only a few weeks and collapsed after the defeat of the covenanting army at Bothwell Brig on June 22nd, 1679.[95]

James VII, while still Duke of York, acted for his brother Charles in Scotland from 1681 to 1685. When he visited Dumbarton Castle soon after his arrival in 1681, he was welcomed by the new lieutenant-governor, Major George Arnott, who presented the duke with a book in which was detailed the genealogy of the royal Stewarts.[96] At that time the garrison of Dumbarton Castle stood at 35, comprising a captain (the Duke of Lennox), a lieutenant, an ensign, two sergeants, a scrivener or clerk, three corporals, two drummers and 24 private soldiers. In 1683, General Dalyell, lieutenant-general of the forces in Scotland, was ordered by the king to strengthen the garrisons of all the Scottish fortresses: a detachment of ten men out of each foot regiment was to be added to the ordinary garrison in Dumbarton Castle. In 1685, Dumbarton Castle had 44 soldiers, Stirling Castle and Edinburgh Castle 80 each, Blackness Castle 40, and the Bass 24.[97]

The prisoners confined in the castle at this time included William Carstares, who had been arrested in connection with the Rye House plot on his way to Holland and had been subjected to torture by the thumbscrew in Edinburgh before being brought to Dumbarton. Another prisoner was a local laird, John Yuille of Darleith, formerly provost of Inveraray. In 1685 he admitted to having absented himself from divine service and, declining to accept the oath of supremacy, was fined £1000 sterling, which he refused to pay, and was thereupon confined in Dumbarton Castle. His request to visit his ailing wife was refused and it was not until his son and son-in-law stood surety for him that he was allowed to attend his wife's funeral, only to return to the castle immediately afterwards.[98]

On the accession of James VII in 1685, the Earl of Argyll returned from his exile in Holland and tried to rally his clansmen to the opponents of the régime in support of the Duke of Monmouth's claim to the throne. Landing in his own county of Argyll, he set out, after some delays, to reach Glasgow, which was understood to be defended only by a force of the local militia. The direct route by Dumbarton was guarded not only by Dumbarton Castle with its cannons but also by the Duke of Gordon with a force of regular soldiers encamped at the Gooseholm, one mile north of the town, while the shire militia patrolled the approaches to the town. Argyll crossed the river Leven three miles above Dumbarton, and the following day, after marching by Kilmaronock and Finnich to the Blane valley, camped not far from Duntreath Castle, the home of the Edmonstones; and then his small force of less than a thousand, setting off at nightfall with guides for Glasgow, found itself, either by treachery or error on the part of the guides, wandering on the Kilpatrick Hills. Panic and confusion developed and most of the rebels, as daylight broke, sought safety in flight. Argyll himself was captured at Inchinnan and taken to Edinburgh, where he suffered death by the 'maiden', the Scottish guillotine.[99] During the brief rebellion the sheriff of Dumbarton, William Hamilton of Orbiston, who was in charge of the shire militia, requisitioned from the meal girnel of Edmonstone of Duntreath at Boquhanran 83 bolls of meal, which were carried to Dumbarton Castle and stored there as provisions for the militia. The rebellion subsided so quickly that the meal was not required, but it was almost a year later before the Privy Council granted Edmonstone's petition to have the meal restored.[100]

The reign of James VII was ended in Scotland in April, 1689, five months after he had fled to France, by the Convention of Estates in Edinburgh declaring that he had forfeited the crown. James's Privy Council had long since ceased to function and it was the Convention of Estates which ordered Major Arnott, lieutenant-governor of Dumbarton Castle, to supply cannon balls and 400 firelocks to the two frigates which were being fitted out on the west coast for the Scottish navy. Arnott was instructed to replace the firelocks with matchlocks drawn from the Keeper of Public Arms in Glasgow.[101] In April the Dumbarton magistrates were instructed by the Convention of Estates to receive from the store of public arms in Glasgow 300 muskets, 6 barrels of powder and 6 chests of ball to be kept in the tolbooth for distribution to the shire fencibles.[102] Soon afterwards, in May, 1689, Arnott was ordered by the Estates to issue 30 pounds of gunpowder and a suitable proportion of ball to John MacFarlane, younger, of Arrochar, who had offered to raise six companies for the defence of the passes in northern Dumbartonshire, as by this time Viscount Dundee was raising the Highland clans in support of James. The stores of Dumbarton Castle continued to be drawn upon. In June, Arnott was ordered to issue 150 swords from the armoury in the castle to Lord Blantyre, who had promised to raise a regiment of 600 men; and in July, Arnott was authorised to issue 75 bolls of meal to the commissary-general for the army being recruited for defence of the new government against the threatened advance of Dundee and his Highland troops.[103]

Major Arnott, who had loyally carried out the instructions of the new government, was superseded in December, 1689 by Lord Neil Campbell, brother of the Earl of Argyll, executed in 1685. As early as March of that year William of Orange had written to the Earl of Melville of the importance of entrusting the custody of Edinburgh and Dumbarton Castles to reliable persons. Lord Campbell saw in his new appointment to Dumbarton Castle an opportunity of taking measures against the Highlanders still roving and plundering despite the death of their leader, Viscount Dundee, at Killiecrankie. As among these were the Campbells' hereditary enemies, the MacLeans, reported to have gathered 80 boats for a raid into Argyll territory, Lord Neil proposed to use Dumbarton Castle as a base from which two frigates, with about 16 guns each, could operate.[104] The incursions of other Highland raiders, more interested in acquiring booty than in restoring the exiled King James, threatened to be more than what the local fencible companies under the command of the shire lairds could cope with; it was reported in Edinburgh that 500 Highlanders had driven away as many head of cattle within three miles of Dumbarton Castle. Hamilton of Barns, on behalf of the lairds of the shire, made representations to the Privy Council that the garrisons at Drumakill (near the modern village of Drymen) and at Cardross (in Menteith) should be considerably strengthened and that companies of about 50 to 60 men should be formed in each parish ready to march at 12 hours' warning. The town council of Dumbarton, which had distributed to the shire lairds the arms received from Glasgow, found that it had left itself defenceless and, alarmed at the proximity of the Highlanders, requested that the commanding officer of Dumbarton Castle supply 40-50 muskets to be used against the Highland rebels. Twenty-four muskets were actually delivered from the castle armoury; they were not required, as things turned out, but were not returned until 1696.[105]

The Highlands remained unsettled for a long time after the chiefs took the oath of allegiance to the new sovereigns, William and Mary.

In 1696, a merchant from Greenock, John MacFarlane, was imprisoned in Dumbarton Castle as a person with information about a rendezvous of Jacobites on Lochlomondside. At the castle, before the lieutenant-governor, William Ferguson, and Ensign Robert Cathcart, he made a statement that 'being about his merchandising' on the 12th and 13th of March, 1696, at Inversnaid on the east side of Loch Lomond, he had observed several hundred men assembled there, some in Highland dress and some in Lowland clothes. It was a time when the government feared an invasion attempt by the French and on March 7th, the Privy Council, having received a report about the dilapidated condition of Dumbarton Castle, had decided to take the necessary steps to strengthen the castle 'against any invasion presently threatened from France'. MacFarlane, whose misfortune it was to have been a witness, not a participant, was first imprisoned in Dumbarton Castle for eight days, then taken to the tolbooth in Edinburgh. The Privy Council, after an inquiry, accepted his claim to be free of any suspicion of association with the Highland rebels and ordered his liberation. Nothing came of the projected French invasion or Highland insurrection in 1696.[106]

Although threats of trouble from the Highlands continued for some time, the forces of King William were generally successful. The victory over King James at Boyne Water in Ireland on 1st July, 1690 was celebrated by a salute of guns from the castles of Edinburgh, Stirling and Dumbarton by order of the Privy Council; and a year later, when Lord Campbell received word of the Protestant victory at Aughrim, he at once informed the Dumbarton magistrates, who thereupon gave orders for a great bonfire at the cross and for the bells to be rung. In 1692, the English victory over the French fleet at La Hogue moved the Privy Council to instruct the governors of the royal fortresses to fire a salute of all their guns, the Dumbarton magistrates again ordering a bonfire to be 'put on at the cross', and twelve men with firelocks to wait on the magistrates for firing when required, 'as is usual on such occasions'. The revolution had succeeded without much bloodshed, and the despotism of James VII had been replaced by the constitutional monarchy of William and Mary.[107]

It might be taken as a sign of more peaceful times that the minutes of the kirk session of Dumbarton parish church record more frequently than before the dealings of the kirk session with offenders from the castle garrison. In April, 1694, Alexander Campbell, a soldier from the castle, appeared twice before the kirk session for 'carrying himself so scandalously at the late Patrickmas fair by fighting and drinking on

Saturday night till 3 o'clock in the Sabbath morning'. Campbell, who said he could not remember anything after 12 o'clock, professed his sorrow and promised to be more sober and watchful in time coming. In March, 1695, William King, also a castle soldier, was rebuked by the kirk session for offering to lift some pieces of timber lying upon the river side on the Sabbath day lest they should be carried away by the tide before Monday. In July of the same year another castle soldier, Duncan Campbell, was remitted to the presbytery after failing to appear to answer a charge of 'scandalous carriage' on the Sabbath day when, in a quarrel with Isobel Murray, a Highland woman separated from her husband, he shouted and roared abuse at her. The Dumbarton magistrates were also able to exercise jurisdiction over the castle garrison in 1696, when three men who had been imprisoned in the castle as deserters from foreign service were liberated after an appeal to the Privy Council on their behalf by Dumbarton burgesses.[108]

Castle Garrison

The muster rolls for the Dumbarton Castle garrisons which have been preserved begin in the year 1682, when the strength of the garrison stood at 35, including the Duke of Lennox as absentee captain and Major George Arnott as acting lieutenant.[109] By 1684, the garrison strength had been increased by detachments from the two foot regiments, the Regiment of Guards and the Earl of Mar's Regiment, one soldier from each of the ten companies in each regiment.[110] The strength of the garrison was again increased after the Revolution of 1689. In June, 1690, six months after he had taken over command of the garrison, Lord Neil Campbell petitioned the Privy Council for a considerable increase in the garrison strength which, he claimed, had formerly in times of trouble consisted of 100 soldiers, a number he considered to be a minimum for proper security. In addition, he requested that a preaching chaplain, a surgeon and a captain of arms be added to the establishment. The council, probably considering that the need to reinforce the garrisons in the Highlands was more pressing, limited the establishment for Dumbarton Castle to 60, one of them to be nominated captain of arms, while a surgeon was to be appointed with an allowance of 2s. sterling per day. In view of the increased number of soldiers, 30 more beds were to be provided, and the amount of money for coal and candle increased by one-third. The larger garrison was given an extra supply of muskets, ammunition and powder, and 100 hand grenades were sent for the use of the gunners, who were to be trained as grenadiers. There is no record of a 'preaching chaplain' on the garrison strength, but William Sempill appears as 'chirurgeon' on the muster roll of December, 1690.[111]

The number of soldiers in the garrison declined after the death of Lord Neil Campbell in April, 1692, and in May of that year the Privy Council recommended Sir Thomas Livingston, commander-in-chief of the king's forces in Scotland, to make inquiry about the strength of the garrison of Dumbarton Castle and ensure that there was a full complement of soldiers and officers. At the end of the year, in order to raise troops for King William's campaign in Flanders, the king sent instructions to recruit soldiers from the Scottish forces, including those in castle garrisons — from Dumbarton, 13 men; from Blackness, 11 men; from the Bass, 7 men; and from Edinburgh and Stirling, 48 men each. The names of all the soldiers in the garrisons were to be placed in hats and drawn out to obtain the number required.[112] Under Major Hugh Bontine of Kilbride, successor to Lord Neil Campbell as governor, 'the full complement required by the establishment' for Dumbarton Castle was 50 soldiers, in addition to the officers and n.c.o.s.[113]

The pay of the ordinary soldier had not varied much since the middle of the century. In 1650, he was paid 5s. Scots a day, while in 1690 he received 6d. a day sterling, the equivalent of 6s. Scots. There was by 1690 a regular deduction of one per cent for soldiers' pensions, called 'invalids' money', and another deduction of 4s. a month for 'cloaths, etc.', while there was an allocation of £15 per annum for 'coal and candle money'. The deductions left the ordinary soldier with only 10s. subsistence money a month.[114] The rates of pay in the garrisons of Stirling and Edinburgh Castles, as laid down in the establishment of 1691, were identical with those of the Dumbarton garrison. However paltry a sum the private soldier's pay might seem, it was 'all found' and, as a rule, received regularly. (An exception, noted above, occurred in the time of Major George Grant.) We learn from other sources that the wives of private soldiers actually lived in the castle and that some of them had domestic servants who can, however, have received only a pittance in wages.

The pay of officers and n.c.o.s by 1690 had improved somewhat since the period before the setting up of a military establishment, as the following figures show (the 1650 figures, in brackets, have been converted to sterling): lieutenant, 4s. (2s. 6d.) per day; sergeant, 1s. 6d. (1s.); corporal, 1s. (8d.). In addition to the above ranks, an ensign in 1690 was paid 3s. a day, a scrivener, 2s. a day, and two drummers, 1s. a day, all of them, like the private soldiers' pay, subject to a deduction of one per cent for 'invalids' money'. The surgeon appointed in 1690 was paid the same as the scrivener, 2s. a day, but did not remain long on the garrison strength.[115]

Among the names on the muster rolls of the late seventeenth century are many of local origin such as Buchanan, Colquhoun, Glen, Robison, Mitchell, MacFarlane, MacAlpine and Arroll. Six Arrolls appear in the muster rolls in the period 1682-1703. The Arrolls belonged to the parishes of Buchanan and Drymen on the eastern side of Loch Lomond and are said to have quarrelled with all their neighbours at one time or another.[116] They probably found little opportunity for expressing their belligerent tendencies in the daily routine of the castle. Two of them, Patrick and Robert Arroll, became corporals and another Patrick was the longest-serving soldier of the garrison, with a service of at least seventeen years. A new governor meant little difference in the personnel of the garrison, although after the appointment of Lieutenant Colonel John Erskine of Carnock in 1701 the names of six Erskines appear in the muster rolls.[117]

It is not from the muster rolls but from church records that we learn of the presence in the castle of women and children. In a case which came before the kirk session of Dumbarton parish church in 1703, Eupham Walker, one of the governor's servants, and Sarah Cameron, servant to Alexander MacFarlane, a private soldier in the garrison, appeared as witnesses. MacFarlane's wife, Margaret Graham, also gave evidence in the same case in regard to occurrences in the castle. In 1700, Margaret Ford, wife of Robert Gibb, a soldier in the castle, admitted having given part of a savin plant, which her husband had taken from the castle garden, to a young girl, Margaret Williamson, in order to induce an abortion. In this case the kirk session summoned, among other witnesses, the gardener of Dumbarton Castle to appear, but he was later excused because of being absent on duty. The gardener was presumably one of the soldiers of the garrison.[118]

Relations between the castle garrison and the people of the burgh of Dumbarton in peacetime were not restricted to the occasional affairs of servant girls and soldiers mentioned in the minutes of the kirk session. Reference has been made above to soldiers appearing before the kirk session for breaches of the fourth commandment in 1694 and 1695. The soldiers and their officers attended divine service in the parish church every Sabbath and were subject to church discipline and received pastoral care equally with civilians. In the diary which the parish minister, the Rev. John Anderson, kept for some months in 1705, there is mention of a visitation 'to the families in the castle garrison' and of the burial of a child of Ensign Cathcart, an officer in the garrison. Cathcart, who acted as ensign in the castle garrison from 1692 to 1706, seems to have been possessed of a conscience rather unusual in a soldier of the period. In 1700, he made a formal complaint to the presbytery of Dumbarton against the kirk session of Dumbarton parish church for their neglect in permitting Patrick Arroll, a soldier of the garrison, to cohabit with Margaret Brock before marriage without reprimand from the session. The presbytery, after investigation, absolved the kirk session of any blame in their handling of the case. The following year, Cathcart himself appeared voluntarily before the kirk session and confessed that he had several times been 'overtaken' with drink and had taken the name of God in vain, As he had made his confession voluntarily and as he was not habitually guilty of such misconduct, he was rebuked and absolved. Times had indeed changed since the keepership of Sir John Stewart of Methven, who was dismissed from his charge in 1627.[119]

One of the occasional duties of the garrison soldiers was the supervision of prisoners. Hamilton of Orbiston, a local laird imprisoned presumably because of suspected Jacobite sympathies, was given the benefit of open prison in March, 1696, being permitted to walk 'upon the rock within the castle' under the guard of two sentinels. There are records of only a few prisoners after 1690. Henry Neville Paine, an English 'trafficking Papist', who spent over ten years in prison, mainly in Edinburgh and Stirling Castles, was for a short time in Dumbarton Castle in 1693. Three alleged deserters from Flanders were detained there until liberated by order of the Privy Council in 1695; and in the following year John MacFarlane, the Greenock merchant who was arrested on suspicion of dealings with Jacobites at Inversnaid, was imprisoned in the castle for a few days. One prisoner left a record of his presence in the castle inscribed on a stone which had been a chimney piece in the Wallace Tower. The inscription was cut well and deep, according to Professor John Anderson, who saw it in 1782:

> Taken March 24 1694. Now 1704.
> Persecuted for Christ and mistaken
> Prison'd John Harlaw, not forsaken.[120]

Descriptions of the Castle

One of the earliest descriptions of Dumbarton Castle is that of an Englishman, John Hardyng, who composed a rhyming chronicle of English history in the first half of the fifteenth century. He had been employed on various missions to Scotland and had visited Dumbarton Castle, which he described as so strong that 'without hunger and cruel punishment, it cannot be taken to my judgement'. According to Hardyng, the Castle Rock was encircled twice a day at high tide 'without any fail'. It is possible that in those days, before the channel of the Clyde deepened, the river spread itself inland, particularly at spring tides, and washed the eastern side of the rock, but it is not so likely that it surrounded the rock every day. Sir James Balfour, in the seventeenth century, wrote of the eastern side of the rock being 'wholly covered with waters' at every tide, the ground on that side being muddy and boggy as a result. Before the end of the seventeenth century, however, the main entry to the castle was from the south, approached by a road which ran from the town of Dumbarton by the eastern side of the rock and which was not likely to have been subject to daily flooding at high tide.[121]

For our knowledge of the buildings on the rock we are largely dependent on chance references in the various inventories of guns, munitions, etc. drawn up by keepers on surrendering or assuming custody of the castle, and in the accounts of masters of works when repairs were carried out. Neither inventories nor accounts necessarily detail every building and one must be careful about drawing conclusions from the omission of a building from an inventory.

It is from the inventory of 1580, when Sir John Stewart of Caberston succeeded John Cunningham of Drumquhassil, that we learn that the 'Beak', up which the raiders of 1571 forced an ascent, was the eastern peak and that on the summit of the western peak was the White Tower. The other buildings mentioned in the 1580 inventory were the Wallace Tower, the Hall in the nether bailey, the Windy Hall on the level ground between the peaks, all of which were detailed in an inventory of 1510, which also mentioned St. Patrick's Chapel. There is no reference to the chapel after the Reformation, the stones presumably being used in the construction of later buildings, but the last chaplain, (Sir) John Cook, was in receipt of the chaplain's stipend from 1555 until his death in 1595. In the 1580 inventory, mention is made of a 'chalmer between the craigs', probably the 'cross chamber' of later inventories and accounts and, in modern times, called the small guardhouse at the foot of the steps leading up between the peaks. In addition, there were a kitchen, a brewhouse, a bakehouse, a peat-house, 'twa little chalmers' at the back wall (on the western side) for soldiers, 'in ilk ane of them a stand bed', a constable's 'chalmer at the yett' with 'ane stand bed and ane little house for ane dry stule'. According to the inventory, the Hall in the nether bailey had on the ground floor a great girnel with a capacity of 16 chalders of victual and on the upper floor a handmill for grinding corn.[122]

Repairs to the Wallace Tower, the Windy Hall, and the Hall in the nether bailey were carried out in 1617, 1618, 1629 and 1633, as has been mentioned earlier. The work of 1633 was left incomplete, and in 1634 the newly appointed keeper, Sir John Maxwell of Pollok, complained that the north-east corner of the Hall, which had been taken down the previous year as being 'somewhat ruinous', was not yet repaired and, as a result, the Hall was not watertight. In addition, the brewhouse, the bakehouse, the barn and the stables were 'altogether ruinous'.[123] In 1644, when John Sempill took over the keepership, his inventory of guns, munitions, etc. mentioned only the Wallace Tower, the Hall, the chamber of dais, the pantry, the 'auld larder', the brewhouse, and the armoury. The chamber of dais was the upper portion of the hall, sometimes provided with a canopy; it contained 'ane standing bed, ane laich bed, and under the same ane grit iron pot'. The armoury may have been the Windy Hall under a new name.[124]

In the 1670s, repairs were carried out during the keepership of Major George Grant. In 1674, the bakehouse was rebuilt, a new chamber was provided for the sutler at the rock foot, the walls of the Wallace Tower were repaired and new window-cases were fitted. As the result of a severe storm in November, 1675, the ammunition house, built on the summit of the eastern peak, was badly damaged and 200 deals of timber were purchased to cover the powder. At some date not long afterwards, a new ammunition house was built on to the eastern rampart but the walls of the old magazine were left standing. New windows were installed in the various buildings to replace those broken during the storm. A flagstaff, 36 feet high, was provided and presumably bore a flag, as one is shown on a mound on the eastern peak in one of the illustrations in Slezer's *Theatrum Scotiae* (published in 1693), although in 1696 it was reported that there had been neither flag nor flagstaff for a long time. On the western peak in the same illustration appears a small round tower, the White Tower of earlier inventories. A major reconstruction of the southern defences of the castle, that is, of the ramparts of the nether bailey, was carried out by Major Grant in 1677-79. 'A great fort' and a rampart were built at the entry to the nether bailey to replace the ruinous gate and entry to the turf wall in front. The reconstructed southern defences are illustrated in Slezer's *Theatrum Scotiae*, and in Slezer's plan of the castle in 1696 the southern entry is called the 'new entry' and the northern entry at the Wallace Tower 'the old entry'. Among other works carried out at that time, gardens were laid out in terraces in the nether bailey and these have been maintained as such down to modern times. Minor repairs were necessary in 1681 — the glazing of windows broken by the firing of the guns when the Duke of York, the King's brother, visited the castle.[125]

When Lord Neil Campbell took over command of the garrison in 1690, the castle was described as badly in need of repair, despite a contract made with James MacLellan, wright, in 1688, and MacLellan was instructed to complete the work specified in the contract. Among other items noted in a memorandum about the contract, there is mention of the 'loch', the water of which was 'rotten sometimes'. This was the upper of the two wells in the castle at that time and was where the covered, stone-built well is today; the lower well was situated at the top of the stairs beyond the portcullis arch.[126]

Lord Campbell's successor, Major Hugh Bontine of Kilbride (1693-96), seems to have done little to maintain the defences of the castle, for his successor, Francis Montgomerie of Giffen, son of the Earl of Eglinton, sent a lengthy list of complaints to the Privy Council. Montgomerie's appointment was an unusual one: he was a civilian, a privy councillor, but he received a commission as lieutenant to enable him to command the company of foot in the castle. Montgomerie's 'Trew Account of the Guns, Ammunitions and Conditions of the rooms and bedcloathes' in the castle of Dumbarton, dated April 9th, 1696, is the most detailed description of the castle in the seventeenth century and, supplemented by Slezer's plan of 1696 and the illustrations in his *Theatrum Scotiae*, enables us to obtain a fairly clear impression of the castle buildings before the major reconstruction of the eighteenth century.[127]

In his 'Trew Account', Montgomerie listed 12 guns, one on the rampart at the entry to the nether bailey, one on the new battery west of that rampart, two on the south-west battery, two at Buttock's Bower battery overlooking the river Leven on the west, one on the Wallace

Tower battery, two on the Bellhouse battery east of the Wallace Tower, three on the three-gun battery on the east side of the eastern peak — all of them in bad condition, their carriages ruinous or lacking, with ladle, rammer and sponge for only two of the twelve, and the ammunition kept in a magazine built inconveniently with a sloping roof to the outer wall and so much out of order that the south gable was ready to fall.[128]

The Governor's Lodging, entered from the courtyard above the south entry, had an arched pend and a stair leading to an upper court behind the house. On the ground floor of the Governor's Lodging there was on one side a room called the 'Stable', in which there were a large meal girnel and nine bedsteads, most of them 'insufficient', and on the other side a kitchen in a dilapidated condition.[129] The second floor of the Governor's Lodging was the main floor, with three bedchambers, one of which had formerly been the dining-room, and a hall in which the mantelpiece had recently fallen down. On the third floor were four little rooms, a closet, and a garret, the ceilings of all much decayed. At the north end of the Governor's Lodging were the walls of a building designed for a brewhouse and a bakehouse but never roofed, according to Montgomerie. The Cross Chamber, now called the guardhouse, had only one room and a garret. On top of the portcullis arch was a building which lacked both doors and windows and in which were kept the heavy cannonballs. The top of the portcullis arch was used as a bridge to the western peak, where there was a windmill, but the bridge was so decayed as to be 'near impassable'. On the level ground between the peaks was the lodging called the 'new chamber', first mentioned in an account of 1676. It was three storeys high — on the ground floor a quantity of old rusty guns and a sword, on the first floor two rooms with five beds, and on the second floor a quantity of match mostly spoiled, many of the windows broken and the roof in need of pointing. The Wallace Tower, which commanded the old entry from the north, was a four-storey building, on the ground floor two small rooms, beneath which were a prison and a vaulted dungeon, on the first floor one large room, on the second floor two rooms, and on the third floor two rooms also, with thirteen beds distributed among the rooms. In a supplementary note, Montgomerie stated that of the 13 bedsacks (paill-asses), 7 were 'quite gone', that all of the 47 blankets except 12 pair were 'so worn and rent that they are altogether useless', not worth 2s. Scots (2d. sterling) a pair, and that all the 34 coverings except 6 were old, torn and full of holes. At the time of Montgomerie's 'Trew

Account' there were, according to the muster-roll, 50 private soldiers, 3 officers, 4 n.c.o.s, a gunner and a drummer in the garrison.

Such was the depressing condition of the castle buildings in 1696. Dumbarton Castle was, however, of little military importance in the eyes of the government, which was more concerned with the possibility of trouble in the Highlands; one of the small garrisons maintained on the Highland border was at Drymen, only twelve miles from Dumbarton. Improvements were made at Dumbarton Castle but it was destined, as a result partly of neglect and partly of deliberate policy, to lapse into insignificance in the scheme of national defence.

5

Modern Times

The Union and After

The Union of Parliaments of 1707 did not at first make much difference to the governors and garrisons of Dumbarton Castle and the other Scottish fortresses, as their importance had already considerably declined and the royal approval for appointments in the Scottish army, even before the Union, was given on the advice of Queen Anne's English minister, Godolphin. In 1704, the commander-in-chief of the Scottish army, General George Ramsay of Carriden, wrote a letter to Godolphin, in which he informed him of army officers who were M.P.s and who had voted contrary to the queen's instructions about the succession to the throne (naming as an example the Earl of Mar, governor of Stirling Castle and colonel of a regiment of foot); and he suggested that promotion should be awarded only to those officers who supported the queen's policy. Ramsay also remarked in his letter to Godolphin that the garrisons in the castles of Edinburgh, Stirling and Dumbarton (120, 100 and 40 men respectively) were 'altogether insufficient' to deal with any civil commotion.[1] The command of a royal fortress, even with an insufficient garrison, was however still regarded as an honourable appointment, and the royal patronage was exercised by ministers in order to gain support for the queen's policy in regard to the succession and a union of parliaments. The Earl of Seafield, Lord Chancellor of Scotland, wrote in April, 1705, to Godolphin that the Earl of Glencairn and his friends would be uneasy if he did not receive the appointment of governor of Dumbarton Castle and that he had informed Glencairn that Queen Anne would give her consent but that the Duke of Argyll was insisting on his brother, Lord Archibald Campbell, being appointed. When the Duke of Argyll, persuaded by the promise of rewards, including an English peerage, arrived in Edinburgh in 1705 as the queen's commissioner to press for the Union of Parliaments, he had his brother, Lord Archibald (later Earl of Islay), appointed to the governorship of Dumbarton Castle, much to the chagrin of the Earl of Glencairn, whose father had been governor and whose own residence of Finlaystone was situated only a few miles down the Clyde from Dumbarton.[2]

It was in the period just before the Union of Parliaments that one of the frigates in the tiny Scottish navy, the *Dumbarton Castle*, earned some fame in its encounters with the French. The name may have been given to the frigate by Lord Neil Campbell, governor of the castle in the years 1690-1692. In 1689 he had proposed to Lord Melville that frigates be manned to operate on the west coast against the Jacobite clan MacLean. Like another frigate, the *Royal Mary*, on the east coast, the *Dumbarton Castle* was used to cruise after French privateers on the west coast after the English war with France began in 1702. Its commander, Captain Matthew Campbell, in both 1705 and 1706, captured a French privateer, the crews being lodged temporarily in the tolbooth of Glasgow.[3]

One of the myths which have grown up round the history of Dumbarton Castle relates to the Treaty of Union of 1707. When the War Office in the twentieth century proposed to abandon military occupation of the castle, public opinion in the west of Scotland was strongly critical; and one of the arguments used by the critics of the War Office was to the effect that, by the Treaty of Union, the Government was bound to maintain the four Scottish fortresses of Edinburgh, Stirling, Dumbarton and Blackness. Although the Treaty of Union contains no such provision, the belief has persisted down to the present day. A possible basis for such a belief may have been the preamble to an act of the Scottish parliament in 1584 regarding the revenues of the keepers of the four castles — 'Forasmeikle as the castles of Edinburgh, Dumbertane, Striviling and Blacknes, being four of the chiefe strengthes of this Realm, maist necessar to be kept'. A typical example of this misconception about the Treaty of Union is to be found in *The Memorials of the Castle of Edinburgh* (1862), by James Grant, a writer of historical romances. According to Grant, it was stipulated (in the Treaty of Union) 'that the fortress of Edinburgh, with those of Stirling, Blackness and Dumbarton, should be kept constantly garrisoned and in a state of repair and defence'.[4]

The Union of Parliaments was so unpopular in Scotland that the

Jacobites decided, early in 1708, to attempt, with the help of the French, an invasion of Scotland. This was foiled by bad weather and the British navy under Admiral Byng. The French were being fought in Spain, in the Netherlands and in France itself, Marlborough winning a series of brilliant victories; and the Earl of Islay (as Lord Archibald Campbell had become), on leaving Scotland to take up command of the 36th Regiment of Foot, was authorised to appoint a lieutenant-governor to be in charge of Dumbarton Castle in his absence. At the same time, the Duke of Argyll was ordered to raise 500 of his own men (to be paid out of government funds at the rate of 6d. per day), 300 of whom were to be put into the garrison of Fort William and 200 into that of Dumbarton. With the failure of the invasion attempt, a number of leading Jacobites were rounded up. Edinburgh and Stirling castles were soon filled to capacity, but Dumbarton Castle was so ruinous that there was no accommodation for prisoners, while Blackness was 'reckoned worse than a common gaol'.[5]

On Friday, February 25th, 1709, in a debate in the House of Lords on 'the late Scotch invasion', Lord Haversham criticised the Government for failing to take proper precautions. When information was received in Scotland about the projected French invasion, the regular forces in Scotland amounted to no more than 1,500, and popular feeling was such that the militia could not be trusted. Yet no increase was ordered until March 13th, when the danger was over, although the Scottish establishment was short by 3,600 men of the numbers voted by Parliament in 1707. Haversham described in detail the 'wretched state' of the castles. At Dumbarton Castle, he said, there were several breaches in the wall; of the twelve guns, none was mounted and all lacked carriages; there was no powder in the garrison and only a few flints, while all the lodgings were in a 'ruinous condition'.[6]

In a lengthy report dated February 28th, 1709, it was stated that the Wallace Tower was being used both as a storehouse and a magazine and was itself in need of a great deal of repair. The powder magazine was to be rebuilt up on the top of the rock, where it had been some years previously before becoming ruinous through carelessness and neglect. Whether it was worth while spending a large sum of money on Dumbarton Castle was questioned in a report submitted to the Board of Ordnance in February, 1710. Although it had the advantage, by its situation on the Clyde, of being capable of relief from the sea, if necessary, it was argued that the towns of Ayr and Kirkcudbright provided more convenient access to the west of Scotland. It is not clear what the writer had in mind in the way of relief from the sea, whether, for example, it was military aid against Jacobites entrenched in the west or against 'civil commotion', that is, a Scottish rebellion involving the Lowlands against the Union.[7]

As the war with France dragged on, the Government was less and less willing to spend money if it could be avoided, and party differences between Whigs and Tories did not help matters. The Earl of Islay, writing to the lieutenant-governor of Dumbarton Castle, William Campbell of Succoth, on August 11th, 1710, a few days after Anne dismissed the Whig minister, Godolphin, regretted that it was impossible to rectify conditions at the castle at present and until matters in England became 'composed'. Islay and his brother, the Duke of Argyll, were both associated with the Whigs in England, and the victory of the Tories at the elections of 1710 placed them in a difficult position. In 1712, all the Scottish garrisons were reduced to their former establishments, that of Dumbarton to 50 soldiers, and in April, 1714, further reduced to a mere 15. The news of the second reduction reached Campbell of Succoth at Dumbarton Castle in a letter from Lord Islay, who wrote that he could neither do nor hinder anything; indeed, when he read the letter from the War Office, he thought it was about his own dismissal. His brother, the Duke of Argyll, had already, on March 4th, 1714, been deprived of the governorship of Edinburgh Castle and the post of commander-in-chief of the army in Scotland, and Islay's dismissal followed in due course in July of that year. No sooner had his successor as governor, the Earl of Glencairn, been appointed, however, than Queen Anne died and the plans of the Tory minister, Bolingbroke, for a Jacobite restoration were forestalled by the succession of George I from Hanover. Campbell of Succoth was able to retain office long enough for a reversal in the Argyll family's fortune, which flourished again with the accession of George I, who relied on Whig support.[8]

Both Campbell and his father were writers and handled some of the legal business of the Argyll family. Much of the correspondence of William Campbell of Succoth, lieutenant-governor of Dumbarton Castle from 1708 to 1715, has been preserved.[9] From a letter sent to him by the Earl of Islay in 1709, we learn that the earl wanted to be elected provost of Dumbarton and that he intended to use every means possible to achieve that end. Although he did not succeed in his aim, many of the Argyll family in the eighteenth century became provosts of Dumbarton — absentee provosts — as part of their policy of controlling elections to Parliament. In November, 1711, Lord Blantyre, who resided at Erskine (formerly the home of Hamilton of Orbiston and, earlier still, of the Earls of Mar), complained to Campbell of Succoth about one of the soldiers of the castle garrison, William MacKeay, a native of Kilpatrick, to whom, according to Blantyre, Campbell was so kind as to dispense with his duties at the garrison, as a result of which he spent much of his time in and about Kilpatrick. There, pretending to security from arrest, he insulted and maltreated in a very audacious manner servants of Blantyre's and had been detected in various thefts. MacKeay's conduct illustrates the weakness of the control over the garrison and reflects the decline in the importance of the castle.[10]

Rebels and Rioters

The Jacobite Rebellion of 1715 began with the raising of the standard at Braemar by the Earl of Mar on September 6th and collapsed just over two months later with the defeats at Sheriffmuir near Stirling and at Preston in Lancashire. Little happened in the west of Scotland where the Duke of Argyll's influence and power prevailed. The Jacobite plans prepared by Bolingbroke had originally involved the landing of the Pretender (or James VIII and III, as he and his supporters claimed) on the west coast at Dumbarton. James himself was not enthusiastic about the place of disembarkation, preferring somewhere farther north 'much nearer my friends'. As it happened, illness and other causes delayed his departure from France and it was not until the rebellion was over that he landed at Peterhead on the north-east coast. The year after the rebellion, Colin Campbell of Glendaruel, writing to the exiled Earl of Mar, also expressed the opinion that Dumbarton was the best landing-place in the west because of its comparatively short distance from Stirling, which he looked upon as the centre of Scotland.[11] The garrison of Dumbarton Castle would have been quite ineffective if a Jacobite landing had taken place near there in 1715. The governor, the Earl of Glencairn, wrote in August of that year about his garrison of fifteen men that they were 'without one night's meal within the walls' and lacked even a single boat. Once the rebellion started, Dumbarton Town Council sent some of their militia men to reinforce the garrison which, however, was in no danger of attack throughout the short-lived rebellion.[12]

The guns of the castle were actually in action at the time of a raid by the MacGregors into the Vale of Leven. The MacGregors of Loch-lomondside and the Trossachs, led by MacGregor of Balhaldie, MacGregor of Glengyle and the notorious Rob Roy, had declared for the Jacobite cause. Under the pretext of supporting the rebellion, they took advantage of the disturbed state of the country to make a raid into the Lowlands. Over eighty of them seized boats on Loch Lomond at the end of September, 1715, and, landing near Balloch at the south end of the loch, prepared to advance southwards down the Vale of Leven. But when the bells of Bonhill Church were rung and warning salvoes fired from 'two great guns' at Dumbarton Castle, the raiders prudently withdrew to the isle of Inchmurrin in Loch Lomond, where they killed off a great number of deer, returning home laden with venison. The threat of another MacGregor raid was countered by a well-organised expedition based in Dumbarton. A guard of 120 volunteers from Paisley was stationed in the town, and over 400 volunteers from Ayrshire were sent to the district of Menteith adjacent to MacGregor country, where they were posted as garrisons at Cardross and Gartartan, and also at Drumakill near Drymen. On October 11th, a force of 100 navymen from the men-o'-war in the Firth of Clyde arrived at the quay in Dumbarton in four pinnaces and three longboats; and the next day the seven naval vessels and three Dumbarton boats were drawn up the river Leven by horses to Loch Lomond. While the navymen sailed up the loch, the men of Dumbarton and the neighbouring villages, accompanied by the gentlemen of the shire on horseback, marched up the west side of the loch. After an overnight stay at Luss, the Lochlomond expedition reached Inversnaid, where the MacGregors might have made some resistance but chose to remain in the rugged fastnesses of Ben Lomond and the Trossachs. The expeditionary force, having reconnoitred the area without finding an enemy, confiscated all the boats they could find and returned to Dumbarton, well satisfied.[13]

The part played by the governor and garrison of Dumbarton Castle during the 'Fifteen' thus amounted to very little; and in the years following the rebellion there was no move to increase the size of the garrison, which remained at fifteen soldiers. For some years, the Government's policy of containing the threats from the Highland clans continued to be one of setting up small garrisons on the Highland borders. A week after the daring kidnapping of Robert Graham, younger, of Killearn, the Duke of Montrose's factor, by Rob Roy MacGregor in November, 1716, the Duke of Montrose wrote to Viscount Townshend, one of George I's ministers, advocating the stationing of troops inside the MacGregor territory. The following year, a garrison of twenty men (under Captain John Brown) from Major-General Wightman's regiment was established at Inversnaid on the east side of Loch Lomond and only a short distance from Craigroyston, Rob Roy's home.[14] In 1721, Brigadier Preston was instructed to send detachments of thirty soldiers, each under command of a subaltern, to ten places in Jacobite territories, such as Loch Earn, Glenorchy, and Kinlochrannoch.[15] The pacification of the Highlands proceeded slowly but effectively after 1725 under General Wade, whose first task as military commander in Scotland was to deal with rioting and disorder in Glasgow.

The riots which erupted in Glasgow against the hated Malt Tax in the summer of 1725 proved too difficult for the magistrates to deal with and two companies of foot soldiers under Captain Bushell were sent from Edinburgh. Despite the presence of the troops, a mob burned down Shawfield House, the residence of the M.P. for the Clyde district of burghs, Daniel Campbell, whom they associated with the Malt Tax as he was a supporter of the Whig Government. The following day, after the soldiers opened fire on a crowd of stone-throwing women and boys and killed two innocent passers-by, the mob broke into the town's magazine and carried off arms and ammunition. So alarming was the situation that the provost advised Captain Bushell to withdraw his troops out of town. Bushell decided to march his men to Dumbarton Castle and on the way there they were harassed by some of the Glasgow rioters, two of the soldiers who had fallen behind the rest being beaten up by relatives and friends of the dead and wounded. In all, the civilian casualties amounted to 10 dead and 17 wounded, while a number of soldiers suffered injuries from stone-throwing. Captain Bushell and his men remained at Dumbarton Castle from June 25th to July 12th, but General Wade himself arrived at Glasgow on July 9th with a large body of troops, a regiment of foot, twelve troops of dragoons and one of the Highland companies under Sir Duncan Campbell of Lochnell. Dragoons constantly patrolled the streets, six of the magistrates and twenty men were arrested, and the Glasgow agitation against the Malt Tax was suppressed for good.[16]

When General Wade visited Dumbarton Castle on September 2nd after his return from a tour of the Highlands, he must have received a poor impression of the fortress on the Clyde. Not only was the garrison pitifully small but the defences on the north side were weakened by the fall of a considerable part of the rampart. In 1727, as part of a general reorganisation of the Scottish garrisons, Wade ordered the re-building of the fallen rampart and increased the establishment of the garrison from 15 to 50 soldiers, those of Edinburgh and Stirling being augmented at the same time from 60 to 100 men each. The increase in numbers did not necessarily add proportionately to the strength of the garrison. In 1746, Captain Turnbull, lieutenant-governor of the castle, complained to Lord Milton that over the nineteen years in which he had charge of the castle, the vacancies in the garrison had been filled up by 'the scums and dregs of the marching regiments'.[17]

Information received from a Jacobite agent in 1727 about plans for another Jacobite invasion indicated that it would begin with a landing at the Gareloch, a sea-loch eight or ten miles down the Clyde from Dumbarton. Nothing was to come of this projected invasion but the possibility induced Wade to order a large-scale reconstruction of the fortifications at Dumbarton Castle, which, if seized by rebels, might be used as a military and naval base. Under the direction of Captain John Romer, military engineer for Scotland, the Governor's House on the south side of the Castle Rock was built in 1735. An imposing Georgian building, it faces the visitor to the castle immediately after entering by the outer gate. In front of it is King George's Battery, also built in 1735, as an inscription on a quoin at the angle of the battery under a turret indicates, the initials accompanying the date denoting John, 8th Earl of Cassillis, the governor, and Captain Robert Turnbull, the lieutenant-governor. At the same time, the Bower Battery was reconstructed and another small battery, the Spanish Battery, added on the western side.[18]

The '45

The Jacobite rebellion of 1745 presented a much more severe threat to the British government than the two earlier rebellions of 1715 and 1719. Within a month of raising his standard at Glenfinnan in August, 1745, Prince Charles Edward had his father proclaimed James VIII in Edinburgh and then won a resounding victory over the government forces at Prestonpans. But his march south into England in November and December, although it created panic in London and elsewhere, halted at Derby, and it was a dejected army which retreated north, entering Glasgow on Christmas Day.

The west of Scotland, predominantly Presbyterian, had provided little support for the Jacobites. The Duke of Argyll and his cousin, Major-General John Campbell of Mamore, were able to establish military control over Argyll and the districts to the south of it. General Campbell, an experienced soldier, was recalled in October from Flanders to take over command of the government forces in the west highlands, and he saw to it that Dumbarton Castle which, he said, 'commands the navigation of the Clyde', was well supplied with stores and provisions. In his instructions to Captain John Noble on November 23rd, 1745, he described Dumbarton Castle as 'a place of supreme importance'; and as he knew that there were no arms there, he arranged for a supply to be sent from Stirling Castle. The lieutenant-governor of the castle, Captain Turnbull, was instructed to see that a sufficient quantity of oatmeal and other provisions should be laid in store.[19]

Prince Charles, on his retreat from Derby, followed the western route which brought his army to Glasgow, only fourteen miles from Dumbarton, and as the Jacobites remained at Glasgow over Christmas and the New Year, there was considerable alarm in all the adjacent towns and countryside. The troops stationed at Dumbarton under the command of General Campbell's son, Colonel John Campbell (M.P. for the Glasgow district of burghs), were placed on the alert. 600 Argyll men were dispatched to Dumbarton to reinforce the troops stationed there under Colonel Campbell and Captain John Noble, 'an exceeding good and careful officer'. The Jacobites left Glasgow after the New Year, making for Stirling and the north. But in case they returned, General Campbell arranged for the erection of wooden buildings in Dumbarton Castle sufficient to accommodate 100 men. The officers there were ordered to defend it 'to the last extreme' and to inform the general of any attempted assault. As there was a shortage of gunners in the castle, General Campbell borrowed from the *Greyhound*, the man-o'-war in the Firth of Clyde, two gunners and a gunner's mate; and he was able to assure General Hawley (a week before the latter's defeat at Falkirk on January 17th) that Dumbarton Castle had been put in 'a very good posture of defence'. Stationed near Dumbarton Castle were almost 1000 troops, mainly on the west side of the river Leven, with small outposts at Milton, two miles east from the castle, and between Milton and Levenside (the modern Strathleven). As the water of the Leven in early January was very low and the river fordable by cavalry, the troops were kept near the west bank. When there was a threat of mutiny by some of the Argyllshire militia at Kilchurn on Loch Awe in March, 1746, General Campbell withdrew Captain Noble and 40 of the fusiliers from Dumbarton Castle and arranged for some guns to be transported from the castle to Inveraray on the tender *Charles*. The general still maintained substantial forces at Dumbarton and Inveraray and arranged for a supply of tents to cover 1,600 men in those two places. The situation in the west remained quiet, however, and all threats vanished with the Jacobite defeat at Culloden on April 16th, 1746.[20]

During the course of the rebellion, Dumbarton Castle, like the other royal fortresses, was used for the detention of captured rebels. The first prisoner to arrive there was a young man, Robert Colquhoun, who was arrested on September 9th on suspicion, as he had been a witness of the capture of some soldiers by MacGregor of Glengyle. In the following spring, in May 1746, he was still languishing in prison, and Sir James Colquhoun of Luss wrote to a kinsman, John Grant of Elchies, an advocate in Edinburgh, asking him to plead with the Lord Justice Clerk, Lord Milton, on behalf of young Colquhoun, whom he described as innocent of any Jacobite dealings and whose father and mother and ten brothers and sisters were in dire straits on account of his imprisonment. Two months later, on July 29th, Sir James wrote direct to Lord Milton, offering to bail young Colquhoun if necessary, and a month later, on August 28th, he was at last liberated.[21] The next prisoners to be admitted to the castle were Argyllshire lairds, both of known Jacobite sympathies, Sir James Campbell of Auchinbreck, near Lochgilphead, and Duncan MacTavish, younger of Dunardry, Sir James's neighbour. Sir James, although a Campbell, had a number of links with the Jacobites — his daughter was married to Donald Cameron, the Lochiel of the Forty-five — and he had been in correspondence with the Pretender for years. Letters from MacTavish, described as 'treasonable', were found at Auchinbreck, and were regarded as sufficient evidence to warrant the apprehension of the two lairds, who were taken to Dumbarton Castle on November 26th.[22] The previous week, MacGregor of Glengyle had made a raid into Argyll but was held up on the south shores of Loch Fyne at Ardnoe nearly opposite Inveraray. Sixteen of Glengyle's regiment were taken prisoners and the following month they were transported to Dumbarton Castle on December 17th. Eight of them escaped from the castle on February 2nd, 1746 — three MacGregors, three Fergusons, Duncan MacNeil and James Cook. The rest of them were confined in a dungeon in the Wallace Tower, with no air and little food, and were so badly treated that one of them, Peter King, died on May 22nd, 1746.[23]

Prisoners continued to be brought in during the spring of 1746. On March 9th, Sir James Colquhoun of Luss and his servants captured Duncan MacLachlan, a known Jacobite, from Glen Douglas, four miles north of Luss. He was overpowered after a chase by 'a sturdy, able fellow', who wrested his dirk from him.[24] The defeat of the Jacobites at Culloden on April 16th was followed by the dispersal of the rebels in flight in all directions. Among those who chose a southward route was William Murray, Marquis of Tullibardine, hoping to find a ship to take him to the Isle of Man, which then belonged to his family. He had been 'out' in both the '15 and the '19 rebellions and had been one of the 'seven men of Moidart' who had accompanied Prince Charles to Scotland from France. Along with an Italian, Michele Vezzosi, who had been the prince's valet, and five servants, Tullibardine arrived in an exhausted condition at Ross near the present Gartocharn, on the southeastern side of Loch Lomond, at seven o'clock on Sunday morning, April 27th. It is possible that Tullibardine had deliberately sought shelter at Ross as the laird's son, William Buchanan, younger, of Drumakill and Ross, was married to Lilias Murray, daughter of Tullibardine's kinsman, John Murray of Polmaise. But Buchanan was a justice of the peace and the Jacobite fugitives were at any rate too exhausted to do anything other than surrender. Buchanan conveyed them to Dumbarton Castle, eight miles away, and delivered them to the lieutenant-governor the next day. There Tullibardine was treated as befitted his rank. Attended by a French servant, who shared his room, he also had the services of two others, who lodged in a house in Dumbarton. Orders were sent from Edinburgh to have Tullibardine transported there, and after a few days he was put on board H.M.S. *Eltham* at Leith and taken to London, where he died on July 9th, before he could be brought to trial. His companion, Michele Vezzosi, known in Scotland by the name 'Mitchell', had been a servant of the Prince and his father for nearly thirty years. When in Dumbarton Castle he was so ill from a serious 'flux' that a certificate was signed by the surgeon and the minister of Dumbarton to the effect that he could not be moved without danger to his life. He was finally released in September, 1746, after a short spell in the tolbooth of Edinburgh.[25]

No sooner had Captain Turnbull been relieved of the responsibility for such a notable prisoner as Tullibardine than he was put in charge of three lairds of the eastern Lennox, who were captured on May 8th near Largs on board a Dutch tobacco ship bound for Amsterdam. James Stirling of Keir had been 'out' in the '15 and had thereafter been in hiding for years. Although too old at sixty-seven to take part in the '45 rebellion, he had influenced two of his sons to do so. Hugh, his tenth son (he had fourteen sons), who was captured along with his father, had been engaged in the tobacco trade in Glasgow and had probably arranged with the Dutch skipper for the escape to Holland. Both Hugh and his father had associated with Prince Charles and his rebel army when in Glasgow and were said to have encouraged the Jacobites in their extortions from the inhabitants of the city. James Stirling, later 11th of Craigbarnet, was known as 'Burry', like his grandfather, both having a burr in their speech. The Stirlings of Craigbarnet (and of Glorat) had a traditional loyalty to the Stewarts, and 'Burry' had fought and been wounded in the first battle of the rebellion at Preston-pans. All three were taken from Port Glasgow to Dumbarton Castle on May 11th along with a Mr. Charles Stirling, of whom little is known although he is described in the official records as belonging to the family of Keir.[26]

Captain Turnbull, lieutenant-governor of the castle, writing to Lord Milton, the Lord Justice Clerk, on the day of the Stirlings' arrival, declared that although no Jacobite, he had compassion for every man in affliction and would treat his prisoners as human nature and common sense dictate. In accordance with these expressions of humane feeling, he allowed the Stirlings freedom to receive visits from friends and relatives. But one of the officers in the garrison, Duncan Campbell, wrote to Captain John Noble, complaining that Captain Turnbull was 'very good to the prisoners if they are men of quality', which caused hardship to the garrison. When Duncan Campbell remonstrated to Turnbull about this discrimination, the latter was 'like to burst to pieces in the vinegar of his wrath'. Bailie James Duncanson of Dumbarton was another who complained to Captain Noble about the miserable condition of the soldiers of Glengyle's Regiment, captured in November, 1745. They were not treated as human beings and Christians but kept in a dungeon with no air and little food so that one of them had died and three others were 'just going'.[27]

Captain Turnbull's kindness to the gentlemen prisoners was ill-rewarded. Following visits on Monday, May 16th, by a number of friends and relatives, the young Hugh Stirling of Keir and 'Burry' Stirling of Craigbarnet disappeared during the night. Tradition has it that they managed to escape by means of a rope-ladder brought in by Hugh's sister, Margaret, under her skirt. According to Captain Turnbull, in his report to Lord Milton, he had satisfied himself that all his prisoners were in bed by ten o'clock at night, but when he made his rounds at four o'clock next morning, two had vanished. Turnbull later complained in a letter requesting six 'honest men' to fill vacancies in the garrison that for years he had to receive into the garrison 'the scum and dregs of the marching regiments, such as native Irishmen, mutineers, pardoned deserters, thieves and common drinkers', and he added, 'Such, my Lord, are the fine men for the most pairt that I have had to assist me dureing the present cursed rebellion.' Hugh Stirling made his way first to the Isle of Man and thence to India, where he became a merchant in Calcutta; but 'Burry' Stirling of Craigbarnet remained for a long time in hiding-places near his own home and later took up the tobacco business in Glasgow, accumulating enough money to enable him in 1768 to buy back the family estate of Craigbarnet.[28]

Prisoners brought in later during the summer of 1746 included six men of Ardsheil's Regiment (five of them MacColls) captured in Appin in May, and ten men from Tiree (seven of them MacLeans) captured in August. On June 14th, there were brought in two Jacobites of standing, Aeneas and Allan MacDonald, brothers of MacDonald of Kinloch-moidart, who had surrendered to General Campbell on May 13th. Aeneas MacDonald, who had been a banker in Paris, was one of the 'seven men of Moidart' who arrived in Scotland along with Prince Charles. He was taken from Dumbarton Castle to Edinburgh Castle, then to Newgate prison in London, from which he escaped by throwing snuff in the turnkey's eyes; but as he was wearing only soft slippers he was speedily recognised and recaptured while running down Warwick Lane. After three years in prison he returned to France, where he was killed during the Revolution, as was also his brother, Allan.[29]

Many of the prisoners remained in Dumbarton Castle for over a year. In August, 1746, General Campbell, probably as a result of Captain Turnbull's letter requesting six 'honest men', decided to send two additional companies to strengthen the garrison at the castle because of the number of prisoners. By then, out of the fifty-three who had been imprisoned there at one time or another, twelve had escaped (a proportionately high figure), one had been liberated (John Broadie or Breadie on February 2nd), two had died (Peter King of Glengyle's Regiment on May 22nd and James Kerr of Crummock near Beith on June 5th), and Tullibardine had been transferred to Edinburgh before May 13th. Although some others, including the Italian Vezzosi and the banker Aeneas MacDonald, were also transferred in 1746, most of the prisoners were detained until after the general amnesty in the summer of 1747. The last to be released was Sir James Campbell of Auchinbreck. He had managed to live fairly comfortably at the castle as he had been able to enjoy the company of his wife and three sons and, at times, of neighbours and friends, while he had his own cook and four servants in attendance on him. Indeed, he had written to Lord Milton in December, 1746, asking to be allowed to remain in Dumbarton Castle' as the air of the place agreed with him and he much preferred it to any other'. He was excluded from the general amnesty but was probably released before 1748.[30]

French Wars

Throughout the eighteenth century, Britain and France were almost continuously at war, but after the '45 the duties of the garrison of Dumbarton Castle were for the most part ordinary peace-time routine. A French invasion of Britain was always a possibility but the British navy ruled the seas, and the guns of Dumbarton Castle were pointed down the Clyde, ready for an invasion fleet which never came. The governorship of the castle came to be regarded as a sinecure. Lieutenant-colonel Archibald Montgomerie, later 11th Earl of Eglinton, governor of the castle from 1764 to 1782, received the appointment as a reward for raising a regiment of Highlanders (later the 77th Foot) and commanding them successfully in Canada during the Seven Years' War. The governorship of Dumbarton Castle imposed no onerous duties on Montgomerie (it is doubtful if he ever visited the castle), and in 1766 he was given another appointment that was no less a sinecure, that of Deputy Ranger of Hyde Park and St. James's Park in London. Montgomerie, who succeeded his brother as Earl of Eglinton in 1767, resigned the governorship of Dumbarton Castle in 1782, when he was appointed governor of Edinburgh Castle. During the whole period of his governorship, the lieutenant-governor in command of the garrison was a nephew of the 4th Duke of Argyll, Captain Campbell Edmonstone, whose pay was £91. 5s. as lieutenant-governor and the same amount as lieutenant of the independent company in the castle, while that of the governor was £300.[31]

During the second half of the eighteenth century, Dumbarton Castle became a tourist attraction. In 1773, Dr. Samuel Johnson visited the castle along with Boswell, who wrote of the lexicographer ascending the 'rock with alacrity and surveying all that was to be seen'. According to Joseph Irving, writing in 1859, the learned doctor had difficulty in extricating himself from the small turret near the magazine on the summit of the eastern peak. Sheriff Neil Campbell of Barnhill, who accompanied the travellers, would have lent a helping hand but was restrained by Boswell, who knew that the doctor was sensitive about being assisted in such circumstances.[32] In 1782, John Anderson, professor of natural philosophy at Glasgow University, spent from June 27th to October 15th at Dumbarton Castle, engaged in experiments with spheroidal shot for field artillery. During his short stay, he kept a diary in which he recorded, among other things, visits by a variety of people, ranging from the Dean of Cork to a party of botanists from Dumbarton. In one week in July, the castle visitors included Lord Fitzmaurice and his tutor, Dr. Enfield of Warrington, a Mr. Maxwell, and a Mr. Charles Ross. Professor Anderson in the course of his experiments encountered various difficulties; the weather was often unfavourable and there was a lack of co-operation from the gunners. 'The gunner drinks shamefully and though there are sober men in the castle, yet it is the epidemic disease of the old soldiers, and creates much trouble and expense.'[33]

Books by celebrities, such as Dr. Johnson's on his journey to the Hebrides, created a fashion for English travellers, and Dumbarton Castle was usually included in Englishmen's tours because of its picturesque situation and historical associations. Thomas Newte, who dedicated his *Prospects and Observations on a tour in England and Scotland* to King George III, visited the castle on June 29th, 1785, when the thermometer stood at 84°F. According to Newte, the garrison then consisted of a captain, a lieutenant, an ensign and 60 privates, while the total of guns mounted on the rock was 30 (the highest number recorded). The traveller who perused Richardson's *Guide to Loch Lomond*, published before the end of the century, was informed that 'for a trifle' he could be conducted on a tour of the castle by one of the few 'invalid' (veteran) soldiers, who were generally polite and attentive. Dorothy Wordsworth, who visited the castle rock with her brother, William, and Samuel Taylor Coleridge, on August 24th, 1803, saw the soldiers' wives hanging out linen upon the rails near the barracks between the peaks. The English trio were conducted on their tour of the rock by a soldier, who imparted various items of information. On their return from the summit, they were shown in the guardroom, halfway down the rock, a large rusty weapon, called Wallace's sword, and a trout in a well close by, where they were told it had been confined for upwards of thirty years.[34]

It was in the war with Napoleon Bonaparte that Britain was in greatest danger of invasion. Although the south coast of England was the most vulnerable, there was always a possibility of a landing farther north in Scotland and a risk of damage to shipping by French privateers. In 1803, in order to protect the merchant shipping in the Firth of Clyde, where there could be as many as a hundred ships at one time, it was proposed to build small batteries on both sides of the firth, some miles down from Dumbarton, the battery on the north to be manned by a sergeant and three 'invalid artillery' men and that on the south to be manned by the volunteers of Greenock.[35] Before the battle of Trafalgar in October, 1805, which shattered French sea-power and all prospects of a French invasion, soldiers, regulars, militiamen and volunteers were on the alert all over Britain. In October, 1804, a second battalion of the 71st Highlanders was embodied at Dumbarton Castle under Lord George Beresford. The battalion remained only a short time in the castle but did not leave Britain for the first eleven years of its existence, providing drafts for the first battalion. The following summer, the 74th Highlanders (which later combined with the 71st Highlanders to form the Highland Light Infantry) returned from South Africa with a much reduced strength of 165 and were sent to Dumbarton Castle. After a few months there, the 74th traversed the Highlands on a recruiting campaign but in two years collected only 700 men, an indication of the extent to which successive governments had drained the Highlands of manpower over the previous decade.[36]

In 1811, the question of the maintenance of Dumbarton, Stirling and other Scottish fortresses was under consideration by the War Office, the Master-General of the Ordnance being of the opinion that they were kept up on political rather than on military grounds. Lieutenant-General Cathcart, commander of the forces in North Britain, argued however in favour of retaining Stirling and Dumbarton. Stirling, Cathcart maintained, was a depot for stores and ammunitions, secure from the immediate effects of insurrection and popular commotion and the breaking loose of prisoners of war in the not impossible case of invasion. As for Dumbarton Castle, although the steepness of the rock made it difficult to use as a depot for stores, it commanded in great measure the navigation of the Clyde and was the only battery and place of strength in that part of Scotland. Neither Fort William nor Fort Augustus, which were in 'considerable decay', had much to commend their continued existence.[37]

The master gunner appointed in 1810 was Romeo Drysdale, and he was to fill a unique position in the history of the castle, as he remained as master gunner (and from 1836 in charge of the castle) until his death in 1849 at 84 years of age. In 1814, he had under him two corporals, one bombardier and six gunners, all of them veterans. In addition, the castle housed a company of infantry and a number of French prisoners of war. From gravestones in Dumbarton parish churchyard (now removed) we learn that a light company of the Ayrshire Militia was stationed there in June, 1812, when William McAlla was 'cut off in the flower of his youth by a fall from the east rock in the twenty-fourth year of his age', and soldiers of the East York Militia in August, 1813, when Captain Kirkus of that unit died at the castle.[38] One of the Frenchmen lodged in a building still known as the French Prison was a general, Édouard François Simon, who had been taken prisoner at the battle of Busaco on September 27th, 1810, when Wellington defeated the French army under Masséna. During his stay on the castle rock, General Simon was allowed to walk daily to the summit of the eastern peak, guarded by two soldiers with loaded arms and fixed bayonets, and this exercise he could engage in twice a day, from 10 a.m. to 12 noon and from 4 p.m. to 6 p.m. The tradition that on his release he entertained the magistrates and other Dumbarton notables to a banquet in the town's inn is of comparatively late origin and probably derived from the imagination of some soldier guides.[39]

From 1796 to 1824, the lieutenant-governor in charge of the castle was Colonel, later Major-General, Ilay Ferrier of Belsyde, near Torphichen. Little is known of his activities in connection with the castle but the exigencies of active service during the French wars, 1793-1815, must have permitted his presence there from time to time, for his association with the castle and the town of Dumbarton was close enough for him to arrange for his burial in the parish churchyard in 1824. The office of governor continued to be a sinecure, given as a reward for services rendered. From 1782 to 1797 it was held by Sir Charles Grey, who resigned on being appointed governor of Guernsey. He became Earl Grey in 1802, and was succeeded by his son, prime minister of Britain in the 1830's. Grey's successor as governor of Dumbarton Castle was Lieutenant-General Gerard Lake, who had acted as commander-in-chief of the army in Ireland during the rebellion of 1798. He demitted office when appointed governor of Plymouth in 1807 on his return from a successful campaign in India. His successor, Lieutenant-General William Loftus, held the post of governor for only

L

three years, resigning in 1810 on his promotion to the office of Lieutenant of the Tower of London with a salary of £663. 1s. 7d., more than double that of the governor of Dumbarton Castle. It is not known whether any of the governors during the Napoleonic wars visited Dumbarton Castle, with the possible exception of General Andrew John Drummond of Strathallan, the only Scotsman to hold office during this period and the only governor to die in office. He was succeeded in 1817 by another Scotsman, General Francis Dundas, whose successor in 1824, General George Harris, although an English-man, had been colonel of a Highland regiment, the 73rd Perthshire Regiment, since 1800. After Lord Lynedoch, who had been governor of Dumbarton Castle since 1829, died at the advanced age of ninety-five years in 1843, there was no further appointment of governor in the nineteenth century.[40]

Nineteenth-Century Garrisons

The nineteenth century saw a slow decline in the military status of Dumbarton Castle. The offices of governor and lieutenant-governor disappeared; infantry units were no longer quartered in the barracks after 1865; the number of artillery veterans was whittled down until at last there was only one, who acted as caretaker; and the guns were fired only thrice during the century, on ceremonial occasions. The castle had long since lost its military importance. Its artillery had been intended to protect the Clyde against an invasion fleet, which in the nineteenth century would have been most unlikely to appear and would at any rate have been dealt with much lower down river or in the Firth of Clyde. It had been used as a depot for arms and military stores but only to a limited extent because of the steepness of the rock making transport difficult, although the impregnable character of the fortress rendered it more secure during times of civil strife as a depot for arms and ammunition. It had also long since ceased to house political prisoners apart from the aftermath of the '45.

Civil strife was still regarded as a distinct possibility in the first half of the nineteenth century, and in the days before police forces were established, troops were relied upon to quell disturbances. In the years after the Napoleonic Wars, there was indeed in the minds of the authorities a constant fear that Britain might follow the example of France and be plunged into bloody revolution. The post-war unrest broke out in demonstrations and rioting in 1819 and 1820 in the industrial areas but there was little bloodshed except for the 'Peterloo Massacre' at Manchester, where cavalry charged an orderly crowd of 80,000 and several were killed. The last political prisoner to be interned in Dumbarton Castle was a Greenock merchant, John Cameron, who was arrested in 1819 during the Radical agitation on Clydeside in that year. A man of the highest integrity, he was arrested on suspicion of sedition (which in those days could mean merely criticism of the government) and conveyed by dragoons to Dumbarton Castle, where he was kept *incommunicado* for several weeks. His case was taken up by the editor of the *Greenock Advertiser*, who wrote an article in his defence. Cameron's wife sent the newspaper cutting about her husband, in a sandwich she had prepared for him. The news helped to sustain his courage and soon afterwards he was released without being charged.

The following year, when there was talk on all sides of revolution, and a confrontation between the Radicals and the authorities seemed imminent, the Volunteers of the Napoleonic Wars were mobilised. An attempted march on Carron ironworks to seize cannon was halted at Bonnymuir by dragoons on April 4th, 1820, the two leaders, Baird and Hardie, being later executed and the others sentenced to transportation. The following day, April 5th, a threatened march on Glasgow by 10,000 Renfrewshire weavers and spinners came to naught because of a torrential downpour of rain — the 'Wet Radical Wednesday of the West'. That afternoon, the Dumbarton Volunters reported at Dumbarton Castle, preparatory to marching on Duntocher, where the Radical cotton-spinners were said to have been manufacturing pikes and other weapons. The Volunteers, resplendent in their uniforms, could not have relished the first duty assigned to them after their rendezvous at the Castle. This was to transport a load of coals, which had been left at the castle gate, into the castle, presumably to prevent the coals falling into rebel hands. The next morning at dawn, they set off, cavalry and riflemen, from the castle on their six-mile journey to Duntocher and arrested in their beds eight Radicals (four cotton-spinners and four smiths from the forge-mill), bringing them back to Dumbarton along with a few home-made pikes and a pair of bellows from the forge where the pikes had been made. On their return, the Volunteers were greeted not as conquering heroes but with derision, and the local people christened the affair 'the battle of the bellows'.

Although detachments of infantry soldiers occupied the barracks down to 1865, they performed no duties connected with the castle; nor were the veteran artillerymen actively engaged either but instead conducted visitors round the castle, expecting a gratuity in return. Mention has already been made of the master gunner, Romeo Drysdale, who was eighty-four years of age when he died in 1849, still in charge after thirty-five years on the Castle Rock. In conformity with the recommendation of the select committee on army and navy appointments in 1833 that in the case of Dumbarton Castle and similar stations, no further appointment should be made after the death, demission or promotion of the governor or lieutenant-governor, there was no lieutenant-governor at Dumbarton Castle after Major-General Vincent was appointed colonel of the 69th Foot in 1836 and, similarly, no governor after the death of Lord Lynedoch at the age of ninety-five in 1843. Master Gunner Drysdale and his successors as master gunners were thus nominally in charge for the rest of the century.[41]

It is not likely, however, that the master gunner would have had any authority over the infantry detachments (usually from Glasgow or Paisley) garrisoned at the castle; and apart from the infantry officers, there was also a barrack-master on the strength of the garrison.[42] Among the infantry units stationed at the castle in the 1850s were detachments from the 93rd Highlanders in 1851, from the 33rd Foot and the 82nd Foot in 1852 (the 33rd soldiers were taken down to London to attend the funeral of the Duke of Wellington, whose first command had been the 33rd), from the 77th Foot in 1853, from the Fifeshire Militia in 1855, and from the 21st North British Fusiliers in 1858. On November 14th, 1858, there was a disastrous fire at Ship Terrace, off the High Street, Dumbarton, and a fire-engine arrived from the castle to assist in controlling the blaze. Under the command of Captain Smelt, the soldiers of the 21st formed a chain down Brewery Lane to the river Leven, passing buckets from man to man. A hundred men of the Edinburgh City Militia occupied the castle barracks in 1859, and the last infantry to be stationed there was a company of the 59th Foot in 1865, although a detachment of eighteen artillerymen was transferred from Woolwich Arsenal to Dumbarton Castle for a brief period at the time of an Irish Fenian scare in 1867. Before the infantry detachments left the castle for good, there was a school on the rock, said to have been attended by as many as eighty children.[43]

The great event in the history of the castle in the nineteenth century in the eyes of the local people was the visit of Queen Victoria in 1847, the first by a royal personage since that of James, Duke of York (later

James VII and II) in 1681. The visit was made during a cruise on the royal yacht, the *Fairy*. The royal party landed at a wharf specially constructed on the north side of the castle at the Castlegreen shipyard of Denny and Rankin (later known as the Victoria yard); and from there the queen drove round in a carriage to the main entrance on the south. An untoward incident occurred when the welcoming salvo from the castle guns caused the horses of the royal carriage to take fright. Fortunately, Dr. Richard, a local medical practitioner, had sufficient presence of mind to seize the bridle of the leading horse. At the entrance to the castle, a loyal address was presented to the queen by Earl Grey on behalf of the magistrates and town council of Dumbarton; and the royal party, which included the Prince Consort and the young Prince of Wales, then proceeded up the steep stairway between the peaks to the Argyll Battery. There, the Glasgow magistrates, who had taken the trouble to contact Earl Grey a few days earlier at Loch Ryan, were permitted to present their loyal address personally to the queen, much to the chagrin of the Dumbarton councillors, always jealous of their wealthy and powerful neighbours up the river Clyde.[44]

When the guns were being fired in 1847 in honour of Queen Victoria, the masonry of the emplacement showed signs of giving way and the guns were drawn further back on the battery. The defect was presumably corrected by 1849, when the guns of the Argyll Battery were fired on the occasion of a brief visit by the Prince Consort to Dumbarton. The castle guns were silent thereafter except for a salvo in May, 1874, when the pier at the Clyde in front of the castle was declared open by Provost Bennett. After the death of Queen Victoria in 1901, eighty-one minute guns were fired, one for every year of her age, to add gloom to the public mourning on the day of her funeral.

Long before that, the castle garrison had virtually disappeared. In 1881, Master Gunner Thomas Irwin had 5 men under him. He had been at the castle since 1866, when the garrison strength was as low as 7, and had served as schoolmaster for ten years until 1877, when he succeeded Thomas Wiggins as Master Gunner. Irwin was the last master gunner permanently stationed on the castle rock, and the garrison was gradually reduced by the retirement or death of the veteran gunners. Latterly, the War Office appointed old soldiers as caretakers, the last being a Corporal Steele, who occupied the post from 1901 to 1908, when the War Office gave up responsibility for the castle, and again, under the Office of Works, from 1909 to 1937, when he died a few days before the visit of King George VI and Queen

Elizabeth to the castle.[45]

One incident which provoked the ire of Dumbarton people towards the end of the century was the removal of the Wallace sword to the Abbey Craig at Stirling in 1888. As far back as 1825, the sword had been examined by the most eminent authority of the day, Dr (later Sir) Samuel Maybrick, whose considered opinion it was that the sword was not older than the fifteenth century. At the laying of the foundation of the Wallace Monument at Stirling on June 24th, 1861, the sword was nevertheless borne in the procession by Master Gunner Murdoch from Dumbarton Castle in front of the Dumbarton magistrates and councillors. One of the prime movers in the campaign to have the Wallace Monument erected was Sir Charles Rogers, who, after the monument was completed in 1869, turned his attention to securing the sword for the monument. In 1872, when he approached the War Office on behalf of the Grampian Club to have the sword removed from Dumbarton Castle to the Wallace Monument, he was refused on the ground that the official view, based on Meyrick's investigation of 1825, was that the sword was not that of Wallace. In addition, it was intimated to Dr Rogers that 'directions will be sent to Dumbarton Castle to refrain from exhibiting it as such in future'. Years later, however, the assiduous Dr Rogers was rewarded for his perseverance when the War Office agreed to its transfer from Dumbarton Castle to the Wallace Monument in 1888. At a ceremony in Stirling Castle, Colonel Nightingale, commander of the garrison there, handed it over to Dr. Rogers, who in an emotional speech declared that by the delivery of this sword he had had conferred upon him 'the highest honour it was possible for the British Government to bestow on any native of our northern kingdom'. Dr. Rogers and probably most Scotsmen of his day were in no doubt about the authenticity of the claim that it was Wallace's sword and felt that it was unpatriotic to say otherwise. The triumph of Dr. Rogers was almost too much for the people of Dumbarton to bear and there was bitter comment in the local press, which described the sword's removal as an act of spoliation. Dumbarton folks felt that the last relic of the castle's historic past had been filched from them, although the castle had never come under the burgh's jurisdiction. No longer would the bands on steamers passing down the river Clyde strike up 'Scots wha hae' as they passed the Castle Rock. The garrison had been reduced to one man as custodian and now, they complained, there was little or nothing left for him to protect.[46]

An Ancient Monument

In July, 1894, in the debate on the Army Estimates, A. C. Morton, Liberal M.P. for Peterborough, raised the question of the maintenance of Dumbarton Castle, which, he claimed, threatened to fall into ruin and for which nothing was provided in the vote. Morton referred to the Treaty of Union, which, he declared, imposed an obligation on the government to maintain Dumbarton Castle and three other Scottish fortresses, and he expressed the hope that with a Scottish Secretary for War, who represented a Scottish constituency (Henry Campbell-Bannerman, M.P. for Stirling Burghs), something would at last be done about Dumbarton Castle. Campbell-Bannerman, in his reply, stated that Dumbarton Castle 'could hardly be called a military position at all' and, although nominally under the charge of the War Office, was 'no use to the army'. Then he continued, in what must have been an unpremeditated addition to the offical reply, 'If my honourable friend and his friends would join in taking charge of Dumbarton Castle and restore the buildings, I should be glad to see it, but I am unable to spend any money upon it.'

To have the ancient Scottish fortress given away to an Englishman provoked an outcry in the west of Scotland, and the Dumbarton weekly, the *Lennox Herald,* carried an editorial headed, 'Poor Old Dumbarton Castle'. Morton, who took the statement of the War Secretary at its face value, was sensible enough not to propose to undertake personal charge but suggested that the castle should be entrusted to some local body such as Glasgow Corporation or the Clyde Trust. This suggestion added fuel to the fire so far as Dumbarton Town Council was concerned, and at a meeting summoned during the annual Fair Holiday the councillors decided to inform Morton that Dumbarton Town Council was a much more appropriate body to take charge of the castle than Glasgow Corporation or the Clyde Trust. The members of the County Council for Dumbartonshire, which had only come into being in 1890, were not at all pleased at the prospect of Dumbarton Town Council being given charge of the historic fortress, and at a meeting of the Western District Committee of the Council, it was claimed by one member, J. W. Burns, the shipowner, that 'the Government had managed Dumbarton Castle badly enough and Dumbarton Burgh would manage it worse'. One of the county councillors, Francis C. Buchanan of Rhu (then called Row), went further still and sent off a telegram to A. C. Morton — 'Don't give

Dumbarton Rock to the burgh. It was placed there by Providence to enable the County to keep an eye on the burgh. Give it to the County Council. They will use it for a hospital site, county buildings or road metal'. The controversy raged for some weeks and various suggestions were put forward, the *Glasgow Herald* favouring the establishment of a school for boy soldiers on the Castle Rock. But at length the argument died down after Campbell-Bannerman announced that the War Office had no plans to surrender the castle to anyone.[47]

At the end of the Boer War in 1901, following rumours that the castle was to be totally displenished and the sole remaining soldier removed, the provost of Dumbarton, Robert MacFarlan, got in touch with the War Office. Statements which appeared in the press that the War Office was intending to hand over custody of the castle to Dumbarton Town Council moved the Office of Woods (the title then used for the department responsible for the maintenance of the hereditary possessions of the crown) to inform the War Office that if the castle was no longer to be used for military purposes, control must revert to the Office of Woods. The question of whether the Treaty of Union imposed an obligation upon the War Office to maintain a garrison there was again raised and was investigated by the Scottish agent to the Treasury solicitor, an Edinburgh lawyer, George Inglis. In a memorandum, he gave details of the relevant Scottish acts of 1584, 1641, 1661 and 1707 and also suggested that the source of the widely accepted belief about the Treaty of Union was to be found in a book about Edinburgh Castle, published in 1862. The War Office took the view that there was no obligation to maintain any of the four Scottish fortresses but was reluctant to abandon control. It was pointed out that in wartime there would be a probable military occupation of the castle in connection with the defence of the local shipyards engaged in naval construction and also that the local Volunteers regularly made use of the magazine in the castle. In the end, the decision taken was to retain the *status quo*, and Corporal J. W. Steele, who had served in the army since 1877 when he enlisted as a boy soldier, was appointed caretaker.[48]

The continual dilapidation of the castle buildings, most of them, except the Governor's House, of a jerry-built construction, made the War Office in 1906 once again consider handing over custody of the castle to the Office of Works (as the Office of Woods had become). The Office of Works, which had already in 1905 made an approach to the War Office, considered the possibility of letting the Castle Rock to

Dumbarton Town Council under strict conditions, similar to those laid down when Scarborough Castle was let as a 'showplace' to Scarborough Town Council, the Office of Works undertaking the necessary repairs. The proposals in 1907 to form a new Territorial Army caused the Army Council, however, to delay a decision. When the transfer by the War Office was being considered on this occasion, Dumbarton Town Council and Dumbartonshire County Council, alarmed that the military status of the castle was to be abandoned, joined forces and formed a small joint committee, to which was added the chairman of the newly formed county Territorial Association, the shipbuilder John M. Denny, who had been the local M.P. from 1895 to 1906. Various other bodies such as the Scottish Patriotic Association lent their support to the campaign to retain the military status of the castle; but the War Office, in response to the representations of the joint committee, stated that while recognising 'the firm hold which this castle has on the affections of the Scottish people', the Secretary for War regretted that 'the retention of the ancient military status was impracticable'.

The Dumbarton Castle Committee in its submission to the War Office included as a recommendation which would ensure a military occupation a proposal for a military convalescent home. But the committee had other recommendations — that the castle be recognised as a saluting station; that on special occasions salutes should be made from the castle; that the flag should continue to fly as on bygone days; that the bugle be systematically sounded from the castle rampart; that soldiers on the active list, even if limited in numbers, be regularly stationed at the castle; that a guard be regularly maintained at the castle gate; that where possible, articles of historic interest removed from the castle be returned or replaced; that accommodation be provided on request for the territorial forces of the county. Discussions about the proposed convalescent home or sanatorium went on for some time but foundered on practical details. The custody of the castle was formally taken over from the War Office on June 29th, 1909 by the Office of Works, which arranged for the army flag to be kept flying as formerly, i.e. on Sundays and special occasions; and Corporal Steele, who had acted as caretaker under the army authorities, was re-appointed to the post. The Office of Works specifically undertook 'the charge of the Castle and Rock for the purpose of maintaining this ancient fortress as a place of historic interest'. Since 1909, the castle has remained in the care of the Office of Works (which became the

Ministry of Public Building and Works and, later, part of the Department of the Environment) and Dumbarton Castle, as a scheduled ancient monument, has been better maintained than in the centuries that went before.[49]

Two World Wars

Between 1909, when control of the castle was surrendered by the War Office, and 1914, when the First World War began, little seems to have been done in the way of restoration or maintenance of the castle buildings by the Office of Works. According to John Irving, the twentieth-century historian of Dumbartonshire, 'ruin and decay were fast overtaking all buildings, no attention being given to any local protest' when war broke out on August 4th, 1914. Perhaps it was because of the dilapidated condition of the castle buildings that the programme of the royal visit to Dumbarton in July, 1914, did not include the Castle Rock. The official reception for George V and Queen Mary was held in Knoxland Square, about a quarter of a mile from the castle; and although the royal couple thereafter proceeded to Castle Road, it was not in order to visit the castle but the nearby shipyard of William Denny & Brothers.[50]

In November, 1914, the War Office decided to resume occupation of the castle in order to provide accommodation for soldiers of the 9th (Reserve) Battalion of the Argyll and Sutherland Highlanders, the Dumbartonshire territorial battalion. The decision of the War Office to use the castle as a barracks gave great satisfaction to the local people as 'once more the ancient Rock, where armed men have stood continuously on guard throughout the whole period of recorded Scottish history, again re-echoed to the sentry's challenge and the bugle call'. The seventeen wooden huts which were erected on the Castle Rock were occupied from January to November, 1915, during which time recruits arrived and, after training, departed first for England, and then for France or Flanders.[51]

In the week of the evacuation of the barracks by the reserve battalion, Lord Inverclyde convened a meeting to consider the holding of a fête at the castle in the following June. The fête was organised by a committee which consisted almost entirely of the members of the sub-committee formed in 1908 to advocate the retention of the military status of the castle — Lord Inverclyde, the lord lieutenant of

Dumbartonshire, Francis C. Buchanan, convener of the county council, John Buchanan, provost of Dumbarton, and William Craig, the county clerk. The object of the fête was to raise funds to assist war-wounded soldiers and sailors, and the fête proved a tremendous success, the total sum obtained exceeding £20,000. Among the numerous attractions was an exhibition of historical relics, including the Wallace sword, which had been removed from the castle in 1888.[52] For Lord Inverclyde and his colleagues, the military occupation of the castle in 1915 and the success of the fête in 1916 must have provided compensation in some degree for the failure of their efforts in 1908-1910 to preserve the military status of the castle. But on the coming of peace the castle once more became merely an ancient monument, with no sentry to give his challenge and no bugle call to be heard, and the sole custodian of the castle the veteran gunner, Sergeant Steele.

It was not long before another attempt was made to restore the military status of the castle. In July, 1920, Captain D. J. Dunbar, secretary of the Dumbartonshire Territorial Force Association, applied to the Office of Works for the use of the castle as headquarters for the county battalion, the 9th Argyll and Sutherland Highlanders. In support of this request, Captain Dunbar pointed out that such a headquarters would assist recruitment, which had been started in May but with disappointing results. The initial reaction of officials in Edinburgh was unfavourable and, under the impression that the intention was to use the castle as a barracks, officials expressed alarm at the prospect of 'recruits wandering all over the place', as 'they were perhaps the worst offenders in damaging old buildings'. General Davies, G.O.C., Scottish Command, supported the application however and pointed out that 'the question of sentiment is very strong and Dumbartonshire people are immensely proud of their castle'. While negotiations were in progress, the castle was actually occupied, in April, 1921, by soldiers of the 9th Argyll and Sutherland Highlanders Defence Force, as a temporary measure because of an impending miners' strike. But the county territorial association began to have second thoughts when informed of the expenditure likely to be incurred and, after a long delay, Captain Dunbar, in September, 1922, informed the Office of Works that the association could not take advantage of the offer of accommodation in the castle. Two years later, however, in December, 1924, a new application was made by Captain Dunbar for limited accommodation, proposing to occupy only the two lower floors of the Governor's House. The application was successful and in

July, 1925, the headquarters of the local territorial battalion became Dumbarton Castle (one of the rooms in the Governor's House being used as an officers' mess), and this part-time military occupation continued until war broke out again in September, 1939.[53]

Between the wars, the temporary buildings which had been erected were removed and also some of the ramshackle structures of the nineteenth century, leaving the Governor's House, the Guard House over the stairs, and the French Prison, all of which received much-needed care and attention to prevent their deterioration. With the removal of the barracks in front of the French Prison, it was possible to uncover the remains of the Wallace Tower. The result of the remedial and maintenance work carried out was to enhance the attractiveness of the buildings in their picturesque setting, so that the few tourists who chanced to visit the castle were agreeably surprised, after the drab approach down Castle Road, to find the Castle Rock beside the Clyde so rewarding. Much of the improvement in the interior of the Governor's House was due to Sir George Stirling, Bart., of Glorat, who was appointed keeper of the castle in 1927. This was an honorary but highly prized distinction and it was appropriately awarded to one whose ancestors had been in charge of the castle in the sixteenth century. Both Sir George Stirling and his successors as keepers, Major-General Alexander Telfer-Smollett (1948-55) and Admiral Sir Angus Cunninghame Graham (1955 to date), were men with distinguished records of war service and family associations with the Lennox over many centuries. They successively built up in the Governor's House an attractive collection of pictures, books, weapons, uniforms and other relics, which help the visitor to reconstruct and visualise the past history of the castle.

For the first half of this century, the castle buildings were looked after by a caretaker, Sergeant Steele, from 1901 to 1937 (when he died only a few days before the royal visit in July of that year), and thereafter by his daughter, Miss Rose Ann Steele, who had spent most of her life on the Castle Rock. It was during Sir George Stirling's keepership that the ceremony of handing over the keys to the reigning monarch was revived. The first occasion when this colourful ceremony was held was on July 9th, 1937, when King George VI and Queen Elizabeth visited Dumbarton. A similar ceremony took place on April 16th, 1953, when Queen Elizabeth and the Duke of Edinburgh made an official visit to the castle on a day of steady rain and a strong south-west wind, the kind of weather most unsuitable for a visit to

Dumbarton Castle in its exposed situation.[54]

When war broke out in 1939, the local territorial battalion had ceased to be an infantry battalion but had become the 54th Light Anti-Aircraft Regiment of the Royal Artillery in November, 1938. Soon after the outbreak of war, the officers of the 58th Light Anti-Aircraft Regiment (a duplicate unit of the 54th) established an officers' mess in the Governor's House in the Castle, vacating it after two weeks for the 139th Light Anti-Aircraft Battery of the Royal Artillery under Major Alastair M. Stewart and Captain L. R. Craddock, M.C. The second military occupation of the twentieth century had begun.[55]

The initial period of the war — the 'phoney war' as it was called — ended with the battle of France in May-June, 1940, and in the course of the next year the air-raid sirens sounded on forty nights in Dumbarton district, but the anti-aircraft battery on the Castle Rock went into action on only a few occasions. It was in the spring of 1941 that Clydeside was visited in three successive months by the German Luftwaffe. In each month, the raids were carried out under the light of the moon, the 'bombers' moon'. On March 13-14 and 14-15, Clydebank was devastated by air attacks, while Dumbarton received a few high-explosive bombs and parachute mines, one of the latter landing near the castle in the canteen of Denny's shipyard; failing to explode, it was immobilised by a naval bomb disposal squad. On May 5-6, 1941 — the first of two successive nights of heavy bombing — over a hundred German bombers took part in a raid on Dumbarton and district, 82 high-explosive bombs and 4 parachute mines being dropped in the area of Dumbarton burgh. Fortunately, a decoy site on the hills above Dumbarton attracted even more of the enemy bombs.

Four high-explosive bombs landed on Dumbarton Rock. They were almost certainly aimed either at the Blackburn aircraft factory immediately to the north-east of the Rock or at the naval ships in the fitting-out basin of Denny's shipyard immediately to the north of the Rock. There were no casualties and comparatively little serious damage was done. One bomb carried away part of the rampart, 70 feet long, between the Argyll Battery and the look-out tower on the north-eastern side of the Rock. The magazine building (no longer used as a magazine) on the summit of the eastern peak received a direct hit, and the north-east corner of the outer wall was demolished. A third bomb, which struck the rock behind and above the Governor's House, brought down the ceilings and broke the windows in the upper rooms and also damaged the men's duty hut. The fourth bomb, which failed to explode, landed in the lilac tree near the wall to the west side of the Governor's House. This raid, the first enemy attack on the castle for nearly three hundred years, was almost the last effort of the German air force in Scotland and little more than a month later it turned its attention from Britain to Russia.[56]

Since the end of the war, as already mentioned, there have been the royal visit of 1953 and the archaeological excavations of 1974 and 1975, but otherwise there has been little to record about the castle. In contrast to the busy scenes at Edinburgh and Stirling Castles, Dumbarton Castle remains a sequestered spot, with a comparatively small number of visitors, considering its accessibility. Few have come and gone away, however, without feeling their visit to the castle worth while. The buildings left standing fit in well to the impressive physical background and are evocative of the past history of the castle. The ascent by steps to the western summit is perhaps most rewarding. The Castle Rock commands a view of the river Clyde from the Glasgow conurbation down to the Tail of the Bank and the Holy Loch. To the south, beyond the Clyde, Renfrewshire presents a rural scene not greatly changed in modern times. The view northwards, however, has been transformed by the development of the burgh of Dumbarton. A century ago, there were several shipyards occupying sites on both banks of the river Leven. The largest firm of its kind in the burgh, William Denny and Brothers, had moved in 1867 from the Woodyard on the west bank across the river to the Victoria Yard, which was gradually extended right to the Castle Rock, Castlegreen House and the old road to the castle disappearing in the process. Only two shipyards survived into the twentieth century, Denny's and Macmillan's. Macmillan's closed down during the economic depression between the wars, their yard and dock being acquired in 1937 by the Canadian firm, Hiram Walker and Sons, Ltd., which built on the site of the yard the largest and most modern distillery of the period in Europe. The end of shipbuilding in Dumbarton came with the closure of Denny's in 1963, the dock immediately below the castle being taken over by a timber firm. Beyond the town and the Vale of Leven rise the hills of Lochlomondside, dominated by Ben Lomond, and in the distance the mountains of Perthshire and Argyll.

Notes

Chapter 1

EARLIEST TIMES

1. *Transactions of the Geological Society of Glasgow,* XX, Part 1 (1940), 121.

2. Euan W. MacKie, *Scotland: An Archaeological Guide* (1975), 113; R. W. Feachem, *A Guide to Prehistoric Scotland* (1963), 181; A. L. F. Rivet, ed., *The Iron Age in Northern Britain* (1966), 80, 83; Leslie Alcock, 'Civitas Brettonum Munitissima; Excavations at Castle Rock, Dumbarton' in *Glasgow University Gazette,* no. 79 (1975), 2-3.

3. Anne S. Robertson, *The Antonine Wall* (1973), 90.

4. Joseph Irving, *History of Dumbartonshire* (1860), 16-17. The exposure of Bertram's forgery was made independently by two scholars, B. H. Woodward in *Gentlemen's Magazine* (1866) and Professor Mayor in the introduction to his edition of the works of Richard of Cirencester (1868-69). The *Encyclopaedia Britannica* repeated Bertram's statement about the fictitious Theodosia in successive editions down to 1945.

5. Magnus MacLean, *The Literature of the Highlands* (1925), 88; D. S. Thomson, *The Gaelic Sources of Macpherson's 'Ossian'* (1952), 49.

6. George Chalmers, *Caledonia* (1807), I, 245; Leslie Alcock, *Arthur's Britain* (1971), 66; W. F. Skene, *Celtic Scotland* (1876), I, 116; J. R. N. Macphail, ed., *Highland Papers,* II (1910), 69-71; W. D. H. Sellar, 'The Earliest Campbells' in *Scottish Studies,* vol. 17 (1973), 109-123.

7. *A.P.S.,* I, 85; *E.R.,* II, 211. A memorandum drawn up in preparation for an English invasion of Scotland in 1542, containing details of distances between towns, mentioned 'the strongest castle in Scotland called Dumbretton; here St Patrick was born and by his petition there should never be horse dung in it' (*L. and P., Henry VIII,* XVIII, 585).

8. J. B. Bury, *St Patrick* (1905), 322-325; T. F. O'Rahilly, *The Two Patricks* (1942), 33; Père Grosjean, 'Notes d'hagiographie celtique' and 'Les Pictes

apostates dans l'Épître de S. Patrice' in *Analecta Bollandiana*, lxiii (1945), 65-130 and lxxvi (1958), 534-578; R. P. C. Hanson, *St Patrick* (1968), 113-116. That the birthplace of St Patrick was in Strathclyde has been the opinion of some Scottish historians in recent years — W. Douglas Simpson, *St Ninian and the Origins of the Christian Church in Scotland* (1940), 21; J. Bulloch, *The Life of the Celtic Church* (1963), 43-44; A. A. M. Duncan, *Scotland — The Making of the Kingdom* (1975), 38.

9. Skene, *Chronicles*, 405; Anderson, *Early Sources*, I, 302.

10. Anderson, *op. cit.*, I, 139.

11. W. J. Watson, *History of the Celtic Place-names of Scotland* (1926), 15, 208.

12. Skene, *op. cit.*, 73, 354; Anderson, *op. cit.*, I, 208, 213. There are at least four places called Lurg on possible routes of the Scots army advancing towards Alclut in 711 — one a mile south of Rowardennan, a second a mile north of the head of Glen Fruin, a third a mile north of Balloch, and a fourth near Mains, north of Milngavie (Will Edgar, A New Map of Loch Lomund, 1743, in British Museum; Sir William Fraser, *Lennox*, II, 148; H. Campbell, *Argyll Sasines*, 244). Watson suggested (*op. cit.*, 387) that Minuirc may have been Clach nam Breatuinn in Glen Falloch.

13. Anderson, *op cit.*, I, 237, 238, 239; Anderson, *Scottish Annals from English Sources* (1908), 57. Ovania, the place of the Angles' defeat in 756, may have been at or near Strathaven, which was on the route of their homeward march.

14. Skene, *op. cit.*, 385, 405; Anderson, *Early Sources*, I, 249; Alcock, *op. cit.*, 3-4. Irish annals also record the burning of fortresses without mentioning an enemy, presumably due to accidental causes — Dunolly in 698 and Tarbert in 712 (J. Bannerman, *Studies in the History of Dalriada* (1974), 16.

15. Anderson, *op. cit.*, I, 301-303; Skene, *op. cit.*, 15, 124, 361, 405; A. P. Smyth, *Scandinavian York and Dublin*, I (1975), 18; Duncan, *op. cit.*, 95. According to Smyth, the Vikings may have come through to the west of Scotland and Ireland by sailing up the Forth in their shallow-draught ships and drawing them overland to the Clyde. Smyth actually postulates a twenty-mile haul but the distance from the Forth to the river Endrick (a route suggested by Professor Alcock) would be much shorter.

16. Alcock, *op. cit.*, 3-4; Alcock, 'A multi-disciplinary chronology for Alt Clut, Castle Rock, Dumbarton' in *Proceedings of the Society of Antiquaries of Scotland*, 107 (1978), 103-113.

Chapter 2

THE MIDDLE AGES

1. Irving, *History*, 45.

2. P. McNeill and R. Nicholson, *Historical Atlas of Scotland c. 400-c. 1600* (1975).

3. *Lennox Cartularium*, 1.

4. Dickinson, *New History of Scotland*, I, 101; Barrow, *Regesta*, II, 41; *Historical Atlas*, 30.

5. Dickinson, *Sheriff Court Book of Fife*, xix, 347.

6. Duncan, *op. cit.*, 475-476.

7. I. M. M. MacPhail, 'Families of the Lennox' in *Scottish Genealogist*, XXII (1975), 40.

8. Fraser, *Lennox*, I, 26-32. The earldom of Lennox was more or less co-extensive with the sheriffdom of Dumbarton in the early Middle Ages but contained in addition the parishes of Killearn and Baldernock. The deanery of Lennox in the medieval Roman Catholic church contained the parishes of the medieval sheriffdom and also the parish of Kilsyth.

9. *Paisley Registrum*, I, 218.

10. *Ibid.*, 214.

11. *E.R.*, I, 140.

12. Anderson, *Early Sources*, II, 625-626; James Fergusson, *Alexander III*, 95; Duncan, *op. cit.*, 581.

13. Fraser, *Menteith*, I, 67; *Paisley Registrum*, 191; *E.R.*, I, 30, 48.

14. A. A. M. Duncan, 'The community of the realm of Scotland and Robert Bruce: a review' in *S.H.R.*, xlv, 192.

15. *E.R.*, I, 38. Robert I granted (1315x1320) to William Fleming of Dumbarton remission for the term of his life of the annual payment of 10 marks for the lands of Kirkmichael lying within the liberty of the burgh of Dumbarton (Robertson's *Index*, no. 82). Kirkmichael Fleming is now called Strathleven.

16. *A.P.S.*, I, 102; *Paisley Registrum*, 191; Fraser, *Menteith*, I, 67.

17. Barrow, *op. cit.*, 55.

18. Duncan, *op. cit.*, 192.

19. *Cal. Docs. Scot.*, II, 133, 137, 140.

20. Barrow, *Bruce*, 90.

21. *Cal. Docs. Scot.*, II, 224; *Rot. Scot.*, I, 30.

22. *Rot. Scot.*, I, 36.

23. Barrow, *Kingdom of the Scots*, 374, 383.

24. Barrow, *Bruce*, 114; Nicholson, *Later Middle Ages*, 53.

25. Barrow, *op. cit.*, 125, 130; *Cal. Docs. Scot.*, IV, 381.

26. Rogers, *Book of Wallace*, II, 135.

27. *Cal. Docs. Scot.*, IV, 381.

28. Fraser, *Menteith*, I, 443.

29. Henry the Minstrel, *Wallace* (1889), Book VIII, 1376-1470.

30. *Complete Peerage*, VII, 593 *et seq.*

31. *Cal. Docs. Scot.*, V, no. 492.

32. Stevenson, *Wallace Documents*, 67-73, 103-129.

33. *Chron. Wyntoun*, IV, 370.

M

34. Henry the Minstrel, *op. cit.*, 948-1044.

35. Palgrave, *Documents*, I, 295; Barrow, *Bruce*, 193.

36. Fraser, *Menteith*, I, 449.

37. Stones, *Documents*, 133.

38. Fraser, *Menteith*, I, 443; Palgrave, *op. cit.*, II, 470.

39. *Cal. Docs. Scot.*, V, nos. 471 and 492.

40. Barrow, *op. cit.*, 264-265.

41. Fraser, *Menteith*, I, 452.

42. Fordun, *Scotichronicon* (ed. Goodall), II, 243.

43. *Hamilton MSS* (H.M.C.), 202; Buchanan, *History*, I. 230. The 'Roland, a certain carpenter' of Bower's tale may have been the father of the Oliver Carpentar of Robert I's charter, or the substitution of a Roland for an Oliver may have resulted from a natural *lapsus pennae* of the chronicler. Carpentar-Carpenter was already established as a surname by the time of the War of Independence, although this fact does not preclude the possibility of members of the family pursuing the hereditary occupation (Black, *Surnames of Scotland, s.v.*, Carpenter).

44. Barrow, *Bruce*, 439-441.

45. Barrow, *loc. cit;* Eunice Murray, *The Church of Cardross*, 6-8. In the Exchequer Rolls of the fourteenth and fifteenth centuries there appears on four occasions, among the payments of various blench-fermes to the sheriff of Dumbarton, that of Arthur's Castle, identified by some older historians as Dumbarton Castle, for which however no blench-ferme was payable (*A.P.S.*, I, 170; *E.R.*, VI, 84, 154; *ibid.*, VIII, 9). Near the present Castlehill beside Cardross Road, Dumbarton, is a mound which has the appearance of a medieval motte and is named 'Arthur's Seat' on the large-scale Ordnance Survey map. The conjunction of the names, Arthur's Seat and Castlehill, provides grounds for the suggestion that this is the location of the Arthur's Castle of the Exchequer Rolls. Why it was so named is a question still to be resolved but one that is not unique for students of Arthurian lore.

46. Gray, *Scalacronica*, 59.

47. *Chron. Lanercost*, 223; Barbour, *Bruce*, 267.

48. Nicholson, *Later Middle Ages*, 97.

49. Gray, *Scalacronica, loc. cit.*

50. *Lennox Cart.*, 1-2; Fraser, *Lennox*, II, 21-22.

51. *E.R.*, I, 115, 250, 257, 259; Rogers, *Book of Wallace*, I, 13-14.

52. *R.M.S.*, I. App. I., no. 112.

53. Nicholson, *Edward III and the Scots*, 96-97.

54. *Chron. Wyntoun*, II, 404; *Scotichronicon*, II, 311.

55. *Scots Peerage*, VIII, 520; Fraser, *Lennox*, 27-28; *R.M.S.*, I, no. 81.

56. Nicholson, *Early Middle Ages*, 130, 143.

57. *Chron. Wyntoun*, II, 408, 414-415.

58. Nicholson, *Edward III and the Scots*, 169.

59. Dennistoun MSS (in N.L.S.), II, 305 *et seq.*

60. *Chron. Bower*, II, 365.

61. *E.R.*, II, 124, 195, 221, 259, 295; *Chron. Wyntoun*, II, 304; Crawfurd, *Officers of State*, 297.

62. Nicholson, *Early Middle Ages*, 238-239.

63. *Chron. Wyntoun*, II, 399.

64. *E.R.*, IV, lxxxii, 365.

65. Balfour-Melville, *James I*, 121.

66. *Chron. Bower*, II, 482-483; *Chron. Pluscarden*, I, 372.

67. *Chron. Bower*, *loc. cit.*

68. The personal names of the early Colquhouns were Humphrey, Ingelram and Robert, whose ancestors may have come from Flanders or some part of France other than Normandy.

69. Fraser, *Lennox*, I, 262; *ibid.*, II, 58-60; Fraser, *Colquhoun*, I, 32.

70. Moncreiffe, *Highland Clans*, 205; Fraser, *op. cit.*, II, 7.

71. Nicholson, *op. cit.*, 289.

72. Barbé, *Margaret of Scotland*, 53-54; Balfour-Melville, *op. cit.*, 218. The previous winter had been one of the severest ever recorded in the west of Scotland. A frost started on Martinmas Day (November 11) and lasted until late February, when people could walk across the river Leven at Dumbarton (*Extracta e variis cronicis* [Abbotsford Club, 1842], 250).

73. Barbé, *op. cit.*, 67-68.

74. Lesley, *History*, 14. Lindsay of Pitscottie and the Auchinleck Chronicle both give the name of Murdoch Gibson for Murdoch MacDonald (which appears as MacConnel, a phonetic rendering of the Gaelic pronunciation, in Lesley's *History*). The name Gibson, which is foreign to the Highlands and Islands, may be a copyist's mistake for Gillean, a name sometimes given to those of the clan MacLean.

75. *Scot Peerage*, V, 601-602.

76. *A.P.S.*, II, 55-56.

77. *Scots Peerage*, *loc. cit*; W. Douglas Simpson, *The Earldom of Mar* (1969), 65.

78. On January 13, 1439, Sir Thomas Erskine, son of Lord Erskine, had sworn before witnesses on the sands at the north side of Dumbarton Castle to protect his cousin and esquire, Patrick Galbraith, during his lifetime (*Mar and Kellie MSS* [H.M.C.], II, 17).

79. Pitscottie, *Historie*, I, 49; *Chron. Auchinleck*, 4-5, 35-36.

80. Pitscottie, *loc. cit.*

81. *E.R.*, V, 146.

82. *Mar and Kellie MSS* (H.M.C.), II, 17.

83. Annie I. Dunlop, *Life and Times of James Kennedy* (1950), 110; Nicholson, *Early Middle Ages*, 349-350.

84. *E.R.*, VI, 209.

85. *E.R.*, VI, 84, 154, 231; *ibid.*, VII, 291; *ibid.*, VIII, 8-9; Crawfurd, *Officers of State*, 314.

86. Fraser, *Colquhoun*, I, 33-44.

87. Nicholson, *op. cit.*, 536-538; Fraser, *Lennox*, I, 84-95.

88. Irving, *Dumbartonshire*, 427; Bruce, *West Kilpatrick*, 202-204.

89. *T.A.*, I, xciv, xcv and *passim*.

90. Nicholson, *loc. cit.*

91. Buchanan, *History*, II, 70.

92. *A.P.S.*, II, 223. In the list of remissions are the names of 19 Stewarts, 8 Lindsays, 6 Colquhouns, 5 Galbraiths, 4 MacFarlanes — all Lennox names.

93. *E.R.*, XI, 341. On July 26, 1501, he received payment of his fees for the preceding five years.

94. Nicholson, *op. cit.*, 543.

95. *T.A.*, I, 242.

96. Nicholson, *loc. cit.*

97. *T.A.*, III, xvii.

98. *T.A.*, I, 383, 385.

99. *T.A.*, III, *passim*.

100. *E.R.*, I, 257, 508.

101. *E.R.*, II, *passim; ibid.*, VII, 59, 393.

102. *E.R.*, III, *passim; ibid.*, IV, *passim*.

103. *E.R.*, IV, *passim*.

104. *A.P.S.*, II, 42.

105. *E.R.*, VI, 84, 155.

106. Crawfurd, *Officers of State*, 319.

107. Bruce, *West Kilpatrick*, 93-99. Sir William Fraser, in *Chiefs of Colquhoun*, I, 64, revealed his ignorance of both Latin and Scots by translating *farina* as 'corn-mill' and *wache mele* as 'walk-mill'. The first mention of the watchmeal of Kilpatrick is in 1348, when Robert the Steward, acting as *locum tenens* for his nephew, David II, and as sheriff of Dumbarton, stipulated that the tenants of Paisley Abbey lands should be free of any exactions other than 'a certain amount of oatmeal for the custodians of Dumbarton Castle'. In 1363 David himself sent letters to Malcolm Fleming, keeper of the castle and sheriff of Dumbarton, warning him against constraining or molesting those tenants from whom were due only 5 chalders of oatmeal for the garrison of Dumbarton Castle. In a charter of 1381, confirming Paisley Abbey in the church lands of Kilpatrick, the *reddendo* is given as '5 chalders of oatmeal as was wont to be paid for the sustenance of those who were for the time being watchmen in the castle of Dumbarton' (*Paisley Registrum*, 177, 206-209). The payment of watchmeal continued down to modern times. In 1706, the Duke of Montrose, who had acquired the estates and revenues of the duchy of Lennox, obtained a decreet for the enforcement of the payment in kind against the lairds and tenants of Kilpatrick. The Kil-

patrick men, who for many years had been accustomed to make a cash payment, argued that the watchmeal had been intended not for the soldiers of the garrison but for dogs kept at the castle for the purpose of hunting down wolves and other ravenous beasts. By the end of the nineteenth century, the watchmeal tax had been redeemed by the proprietors with the exception of the duty on Lord Blantyre's lands, which was purchased by Dr David Murray of Cardross (Bruce, *op. cit.*, 96-99). The collection of local books donated by Dr Murray to Dumbarton Public Library is called the Watchmeal Collection, the small revenue of about £5 from the watchmeal duty being used (up to 1975) to provide additions to the collection.

108. *E.R.*, VII, 291; *ibid.*, IX, X, *passim.*

109. Crawfurd, *op. cit.*, 296; *E.R.*, II, 344, 364, 393.

110. *R.M.S.*, I, no. 802.

111. *R.M.S.*, I. App. 1, no. 112; *E.R.*, I, 259; *ibid.*, II, 79; *ibid.*, III, 311, 344, 356, 427; *ibid.*, V, 422.

112. Fraser, *Keir*, 293. I. MacIvor, in the official guide to the castle (1958), p. 8, surprisingly dates the Wallace Tower from 1617. The Wallace Tower was standing for more than a century before 1617.

Chapter 3

THE SIXTEENTH CENTURY

1. For a full account of his career, see Marie W. Stuart, *The Scot who was a Frenchman* (1940).

2. Lesley, *History*, 101.

3. *R.S.S.*, I, no. 2225.

4. Lesley, *loc. cit.*

5. Fraser, *Keir*, 301-302.

6. Buchanan, *History*, II, 268.

7. Fraser, *Lennox*, I, 346, 364.

8. *L. and P., Henry VIII*, II(2), 811; Donaldson, *James I to James VII*, 35.

9. In 1524 Stewart appointed William Fullarton as his proxy to receive 350 ducats of gold from David Balfour, a servant of Lord D'Aubigny and formerly a man-at-arms under Stewart in the castle of Milan. Balfour had been entrusted by the Bishop of Ventimiglia with the money, which was in payment of Stewart's services as 'keeper of the castle rock of Milan' (*L. and P., Henry VIII*, IV(2), 26).

10. *Ibid.*, III(2), 1421, 1429; *ibid.*, XVIII(1), 288.

11. *Ibid.*, III(2), 1518; *ibid.*, IV(1), 26.

12. Fraser, *Keir*, 324.

13. Fraser, *Lennox*, I, 357.

14. Pitscottie, *History*, II, 327.

15. *A.D.C.P.*, 355; Fraser, *Lennox*, II, 236-242.

16. J. Guthrie Smith, *Strathblane* (1886), 130.

17. Chalmers, *Caledonia*, III, 878; *T.A.*, III, xxviii, 318.

18. J. Bain, *Stirlings of Craigbernard and Glorat* (1885), 79-83; *E.R.*, XII, 462.

19. Fraser, *Keir*, 293.

20. Bain, *op. cit.*, 89; Fraser, *op. cit.*, 329.

21. Fraser, *op. cit.*, 138.

22. *E.R.*, XIV, 192.

23. Fraser, *Lennox*, I, 90.

24. Fraser, *Keir*, 139, 352; Pitcairn, *Trials*, I, 170.

25. *L. and P.*, *Henry VIII*, XVII, 658; *Hamilton Papers*, I, 635.

26. A. I. Cameron, *Scottish Correspondence of Mary of Lorraine*, 4, 11, 31.

27. Fraser, *Lennox*, II, 240-242.

28. *Hamilton Papers*, I, 511.

29. *Ibid.*, I, 534.

30. *L. and P.*, *Henry VIII*, XVIII (1), 323; Bain, *op. cit.*, 92.

31. *Hamilton Papers*, II, 8.

32. R. K. Hannay, 'Letters of the Papal Legate in Scotland' in *S.H.R.*, XI (1916), 2, 5, 17; G. Dickinson, *Brosse Missions*, 9, 31

33. *Ibid.*, 10.

34. Hannay, *op. cit.*, 15; Cameron, *op. cit.*, 49.

35. *Brosse Missions*, 39; *L. and P.*, *Henry VIII*, XVIII (2), 364.

36. *L. and P.*, *Henry VIII*, XVIII (2), 156.

37. *Ibid.*, 169.

38. Lesley, *History*, 177.

39. Pitscottie, *History*, II, 25.

40. *L. and P.*, *Henry VIII*, XIX (1), 324, 475.

41. *Ibid.*, XIX (1), 475, 629.

42. Lesley, *History*, 186; *Hamilton Papers*, II, 108.

43. Lesley, *loc. cit.*

44. D. Gregory, *History of the Western Highlands and Isles of Scotland* (1881), 166.

45. *R.S.S.*, III, nos. 1107, 1121, 1149; Bain, *op. cit.*, 97-98; M. Wood, *Balcarres Papers*, 125.

46. *Diurnal of Occurrents*, 88. Four days later, according to the *Diurnal*, the Bishop of Glasgow forcefully protested against Cardinal Beaton's claim to bear his cross in the cathedral of Glasgow. The crosses of both bishop and cardinal were broken in the ensuing altercation.

47. Gregory, *op. cit.*, 174-175. Gregory compressed the events of 1545 and 1546 into one year.

48. *T.A.*, VIII, 400.

49. Pitscottie, *History*, II, 84; Fraser, *Keir*, 383; J. Guthrie Smith, *op. cit.*,

127. Stirling's father had been given a feu of the kirklands of Strathblane in 1519.

50. *L. and P., Henry VIII*, XXI (2), 6. Professor Donaldson errs in assuming that 'Lennox and his brother the Bishop of Caithness . . . seized Dumbarton Castle' (*James I to James VII*, 75). Lennox had sent his brother north, intending to follow, but the developments at Dumbarton prevented him from doing so.

51. *T.A.*, VIII, 465, 468. The boys were each paid 3 shillings.

52. *Public Affairs*, 553; *R.S.S.*, III, no. 1831.

53. *L. and P., Henry VIII*, XXI (2), 6; Bain, *op. cit.*, 100. Of the twelve lairds, George Buchanan of Buchanan, John Brisbane of Bishopton, Alexander Douglas of Mains, James Galbraith of Culcreuch, Robert Dennistoun of Colgrain, Alexander MacAulay of Ardincaple, John Bontine of Ardoch, John Napier of Kilmahew, John Stirling of Craigbarnet, John Lindsay of Bonhill, John Colquhoun of Luss, Walter Stirling of Ballagan, only the last four could sign their names without assistance from the clerk.

54. *L. and P., Henry VIII*, XXI (2), 6.

55. Bain, *op. cit.*, 98; Lesley, *History*, 190; *Diurnal of Occurrents*, 42.

56. *T.A.*, IX, 102, 442.

57. *R.P.C.*, I, 66. During the disturbed period of his keepership, Stirling, unable to collect the revenues due to him and in order to maintain his large garrison, had recourse to plundering lands near Dumbarton. Sometimes his associates went farther afield. In June 1546, Alexander Hamilton, Abbot of Kilwinning, made complaint to the Lords of Council that a band of Cunninghams, including three sons of the Earl of Glencairn, one of them the bishop-elect of Argyll, had seized him in 'the hie gait aboun the kirk of Stewarton at the Foulshaw' and taken him to Dumbarton Castle, robbing him of goods and money. The abbot seems to have incurred the displeasure of the Cunninghams by his appointment in October, 1544, as bailie of the abbey lands, of Hugh Montgomerie, Earl of Eglinton, an inveterate enemy of the Cunninghams (*Public Affairs*, 550; Crawfurd, *Renfrewshire*, 251).

58. Pitscottie, *History*, II, 190.

59. *Public Affairs*, 553-554; Watt, *Fasti* (2nd ed.), 61, 353.

60. *R.S.S.*, III, nos. 2505, 2574, 2697, 3033.

61. Donaldson, *James I to James VII*, 87; *T.A.*, IX, 50, 73. A statute prohibiting the 'annual frolic' of Little John and Robin Hood on May Day was passed in 1555 but the frolic continued for some years afterwards (*A.P.S.*, II, 500; P. Hume Brown, *Scotland in the Time of Queen Mary* (1916), 166).

62. J. Bruce, *West Kilpatrick*, 87, 89. Hamilton received numerous grants of land during his keepership — in 1549 the lands of Bothkennar near Falkirk and Kilmardinny in Kilpatrick parish; in 1550 a tenement of land in Dundee on the north side of Market Street; in 1552 (when the lands of Kilmardinny were restored to John Colquhoun) the neighbouring lands of Baljaffray and also the tolls and petty customs of the burgh of Dumbarton (*R.S.S.*, IV, nos. 264, 265,

493, 674, 1571, 1572).

63. *T.A.,* IX, 441, 444. The expenditure in 1546-47 on Dunbar Castle, which controlled the eastern sea route from England and France, was also considerable, amounting to more than £3,000.

64. Pitcairn, *Trials,* I, 451.

65. Bruce, *op. cit.,* 275.

66. Donaldson, *op. cit.,* 76; *Historical Atlas of Scotland,* 84; Lesley, *History,* 310; D. H. Fleming, *Mary, Queen of Scots* (1910), 192.

67. *T.A.,* IX, 127, 134; Knox, *History,* I, 97.

68. *C.S.P. Scot.,* I, 55.

69. Donaldson, *op. cit.,* 78.

70. *Historical Atlas of Scotland,* 84.

71. *C.S.P. Scot.,* I, 80; *T.A.,* IX, 177.

72. *Cal. State Papers* (Thorpe), I, 83; *C.S.P. Scot.,* I, 97; Beague, *History of the Campagnes 1548 and 1549* (1707), 24; Donaldson, *loc. cit.*

73. *Source-Book of Scottish History,* II, 144-145.

74. W. C. Dickinson, *New History of Scotland,* I, 321.

75. Beague, op. cit., 25; *Hamilton Papers,* II, 603, 617; *Cal. State Papers* (Thorpe), I, 93.

76. *C.S.P. Scot.,* I, 157; Antonia Fraser, *Mary, Queen of Scots* (1970), 55-57. It was at Roscoff that, two centuries later, Prince Charles Edward arrived from Scotland after the collapse of the Jacobite Rebellion of 1745-46.

77. *C.S.P. Scot.,* I, 320.

78. Donaldson, *op. cit.,* 79.

79. *C.S.P. Scot.,* I, 568-569.

80. *Ibid.,* 609.

81. *S.H.R.,* XXV, 13-19.

82. *C.S.P. Scot.,* II, 174; Crawfurd, *Officers,* 327.

83. Keith, *History,* II, 807-810.

84. *C.S.P. Scot.,* II, 441, 448.

85. *Hamilton MSS* (supp.), 4; *Pepys MSS* (H.M.C.), 125.

86. Goodall, *Casket Letters,* II, 360; *C.S.P. Scot.,* II, 454.

87. *C.S.P. Scot.,* II, 516, 621.

88. *Ibid.,* 670.

89. *R.P.C.,* II, 11-12, 20-21.

90. *C.S.P. Scot.,* III, 28.

91. *Diurnal of Occurrents,* 155.

92. Donaldson, *op. cit.,* 164.

93. *Diurnal of Occurrents,* 156.

94. *C.S.P. Scot.,* III, 383, 485.

95. *Diurnal of Occurrents,* 168; *C.S.P. Scot.,* III, 102, 105, 113.

96. *Warrender Papers,* I, 82-85, 88, 93; *C.S.P. Scot.,* III, 343; Bannatyne, *Journal,* 38.

97. *C.S.P. Scot.*, III, 438; Bannatyne, *Transactions*, 519. The 'white kye' were said to be descended from cattle introduced by the Romans. Three herds of this breed survived in Britain from the Middle Ages — at Chillingham (Northumberland), Cadzow (Lanarkshire) and Vaynol (North Wales).

98. *C.S.P. Scot.*, III, 250; Irving, *History*, 587-589.

99. Calderwood, *History*, III, 54; *C.S.P. Scot.*, III, 316.

100. Buchanan, *History*, II, 592; Donaldson, *op. cit.*, 164.

101. Calderwood, *History*, III, 54.

102. The story of the events leading to the capture of the castle in 1571 is based on the accounts of Buchanan, Calderwood (who follows Buchanan), Bannatyne, and Captain Crawfurd's letter to John Knox.

103. *R.P.C.*, I, 626.

104. Cunningham's son, Cuthbert, was presented while still a minor to the provostry of the well-endowed St. Mary's Collegiate Church of Dumbarton by Regent Lennox in October, 1570, and six months later, in March, 1571, granted in feu to his father Ladyton in Bonhill and other lands belonging to the Collegiate Church of Dumbarton. (J. Guthrie Smith, *Strathblane*, 188-190).

105. The argument in John Irving's *History of Dumbartonshire* (1917), 115-116, in favour of locating the ascent by the west peak has been conclusively refuted by A. F. Galbraith in an article in the *Lennox Herald*, March 1st, 1936.

106. Fraser, *Lennox*, I, 106.

107. D. H. Fleming, *op. cit.*, 459-460.

108. Elizabeth also asked that the Englishman, John Hall, who was suspected of being a Catholic agent, be delivered to Sir William Drury, Marshal of Berwick. It transpired later that he was involved in a plot by Sir Thomas Gerard and other English Catholics to rescue Mary, Queen of Scots, from Chatsworth and convey her to Dumbarton Castle (*C.S.P. Scot.*, III, 552; *Cecil MSS* (H.M.C.), I, 501, 503, 508, 533; *ibid.*, II, 548; Antonia Fraser, *op. cit.*, 499-500).

109. There is a facsimile reproduction of the letter in Fraser, *Lennox*, II, 354.

110. Fraser, *op. cit.*, I, 106-108.

111. *C.S.P. Scot.*, IV, 195, 220, 513.

112. *R.S.S.*, VI, nos. 1177, 1520, 1769; *C.S.P. Scot.*, IV, 519. In 1575 Cunningham received the gift of the escheat of a tack or lease given by the Abbot of Kilwinning of half of the teinds and fruits of the parish church of Dumbarton, which was appropriated to Kilwinning Abbey (*R.S.S.*, VII, no. 2801).

113. *C.S.P. Scot.*, V, 3; Sir James Melville, *Memoirs* (1827), 262.

114. Melville, *op. cit.*, 261; *C.S.P. Scot.*, V, 38; *R.P.C.*, III, 5, 22, 162. As the documents of the earldom of Lennox were kept in a coffer in Stirling Castle and the key had been sent to the Countess of Lennox or her brother-in-law, both recently deceased, the Privy Council ordered the coffer to be broken open

(*R.P.C.*, III, 162; *C.S.P. Scot.*, VI, 466).

115. Calderwood, *History*, III, 528.

116. *C.S.P. Scot.*, V, 393, 428, 490; *R.S.S.*, VI, no. 2436; *R.P.C.*, III, 319-320.

117. *King James the Sext* (1827), 209; Pitcairn, *Trials*, IV, 332, 352; David Moysie, *Memoirs*, 1577-1603 (1830), 52.

118. *C.S.P. Scot.*, V, 617, 660.

119. Fraser, *Douglas*, II, 319, 335; *King James the Sext*, 181; *C.S.P. Scot.*, V, 663, 667, 671.

120. Donaldson, *op. cit.*, 175, 178-180.

121. *C.S.P. Scot.*, VI, 155.

122. *Ibid.*, VI, 168, 222-224; James Melville, *Diary*, 96.

123. *C.S.P. Scot.*, III, 577.

124. Andrew Lang, *History of Scotland*, III, 355.

125. *C.S.P. Scot.*, X, 615, 631-633, 648. Smollett, 'a person of greater cunning and practice than of credit and sound dealing' according to Bowes, the English ambassador (*C.S.P. Scot.*, X, 819), led a life of adventure and intrigue. In 1583 he visited London and had audiences with Queen Elizabeth on behalf of the Duke of Lennox, whose death brought the negotiations to a sudden halt. He was associated with MacLean of Duart in various affairs, notably the blowing up of the Spanish galleon, the *Florida*, in Tobermory Bay in November, 1588. He narrowly escaped execution for complicity in Bothwell's plots but died in his bed in 1603, the year in which his cousin, Tobias Smollett, was killed by MacGregors at the battle of Glen Fruin (*C.S.P. Scot.*, VI, 304, 309, 328, 450-451, 461, 464, 473, 497, 534, 566; *ibid.*, IX, 629, 632-633).

126. Donaldson, *op. cit.*, 189, 190; *C.S.P. Scot.*, XI, 234.

127. *C.S.P. Scot.*, VII, 599-609; *ibid.*, XI, 77, 507; *C.S.P. Spanish, 1587-1603*, 742.

128. *C.S.P. Scot.*, 216.

129. *Ibid.*, XI, 77.

130. D. Gregory, *op. cit.*, 264 *et seq.*

131. F. Roberts and I. M. M. MacPhail, *Dumbarton Common Goods Accounts, 1614-1660* (1972), 18.

132. Fraser, *Lennox*, II, 19-22.

133. Fraser, *Colquhoun Cartulary*, 419, 270.

134. *A.P.S.*, III, 153; *E.R.*, XIX, 505; *R.P.C.*, V, 373, 421; *ibid.*, IV, 535.

135. *R.S.S.*, V, no. 2150; *ibid.*, VI, no. 1194; *ibid.*, VII, no. 2436; *A.P.S.* III, 352, 403.

136. *T.A.*, X, 131, 212, 213.

137. *R.S.S.*, V, no. 3423; *ibid.*, VI, no. 921. A chalder contained 10 bolls and a boll in Dumbartonshire was equal to 4.768 Winchester bushels. Of the lands detailed in the grant to Lord Fleming in 1567, all are, as might be expected, in the parish of Cardross except Cunningpark (the coney or rabbit

park), which is on the east side of the river Leven, more or less opposite Mains of Cardross, the site of Bruce's residence.

138. *R.M.S.*, III, no. 2630; *ibid.*, V, no. 1868; *ibid.*, VIII, no. 325. Archibald Campbell had been custumar of Dumbarton from 1538 to 1540 (*E.R.*, XVII, 183, 301).

139. *E.R.*, VI, 84, 154; *R.P.C.*, VIII, 241; *R.M.S.*, V, no. 3423.

140. Bruce, *West Kilpatrick*, 96-99.

141. *T.A.*, X, 294; *E.R.*, III, 378.

142. *E.R.*, XII, 267; *ibid.*, XVIII, 337; *ibid.*, XXIII, 182. A dacre is a set of ten; a last of herrings was equal to 12 barrels.

143. *R.S.S.*, VI, no. 1194.

144. *E.R.*, XVII, 183, 301, 391, 459; *ibid.*, XVIII, 104, 116, 148, 172, 196, 221, 256, 284, 337; *ibid.*, XIX, 39, 170.

145. Roberts and MacPhail, *op. cit.*, 268. The Dumbarton Register of Ship Entries, 1595-1658, is preserved in Dumbarton Public Library.

146. Balcarres Papers in N.L.S. In 1577, a complaint was also made against the keeper of Dumbarton Castle, Cunningham of Drumquhassil, for attempting to levy the duty of assize herring from Dumbarton fishing boats, contrary to a charter of David II granting them exemption, and a letter was sent to the keeper of the castle ordering him to refrain from demanding the assize herring (Dumbarton Burgh Charters, no. 28, in Dumbarton Public Library).

147. *R.P.C.*, V, 10, 87.

Chapter 4

THE SEVENTEENTH CENTURY

1. *R.P.C.*, X, 200, 259.

2. Irving, *History*, 397-398. Lennox was created Duke of Richmond in 1623.

3. Roberts and MacPhail, *Dumbarton Common Good Accounts, 1614-1660*, 55; Irving, *D.B.R.*, 50.

4. Irving, *op. cit.*, 86-87; D.T.C.M., Aug. 9, Oct. 4, 1662.

5. *C.S.P. Dom., Charles II, 1672-75*, 127-128; *ibid., 1680-81*, 354.

6. *A.P.S.*, XI, 135.

7. *C.S.P. Dom., William and Mary, 1693*, 450.

8. Fraser, *Pollok*, II, 250-252.

9. *Mar and Kellie MSS* (H.M.C.), I, 114, 130; *A.P.S.*, VI, 720.

10. *A.P.S.*, VI, 508. Sempill died in May, 1653, and in the inventory of his goods the Estates of Scotland were listed as owing him at his death for his expenses as keeper of the castle of Dumbarton the sum of £15,988 with interest due from Lammas, 1649 (Pont, *Cunningham*, 215).

11. Treasury Vouchers, S.R.O., E 28/425/1/7.

12. *M.W.*, II, 32; Masters of Works Accounts, S.R.O., E67/14/2/2, 14.

13. *R.P.C.*, VII.

14. Roberts and MacPhail, *op. cit.*, 279; Irving, *D.B.R.*, 28, 38.

15. *Ibid.*, 39.

16. *R.P.C.*, 3rd ser., I, 100-101, 654.

17. *Ibid.*, 533-535; *ibid.*, VIII, 311, 505; *ibid.*, IX, 86; *Argyll Papers* (H.M.C.), 311-313. Dumbarton Town Council in 1744 considered the question of possible legislation, proposed by 'gentlemen in Argyleshire' who dealt in the cattle trade, to have the burgh's impost on all cattle that passed the water of Leven declared illegal. The council, claiming that the custom had been levied for over a century without protest from the Argyllshire gentlemen, expressed the hope that the proposed legislation did not have the support of the Duke of Argyll and decided to send a copy of the council minute to their provost, General John Campbell of Mamore, M.P. for Dumbartonshire (D.T.C.M., Dec. 31, 1744).

18. Irving, *History*, 157.

19. *R.P.C.*, VI, 31, 803.

20. *Ibid.*, VII, 735-737. On January 18, 1605, one of the Dundee burgesses, Andrew Flesher, was released from ward in Dumbarton Castle to go to Edinburgh and remain there until he had 'convalesced of his present disease', after which he was to return to ward in Dumbarton.

21. *R.P.C.*, VII, 61.

22. *Ibid.*, VII, 242-247.

23. *Ibid.*, VII, 129; Calderwood, *History*, VI, 292.

24. *R.P.C.*, VII, 283-284, 509, 515, 747; Pirie-Gordon, Captains and Keepers (Sir William Stewart of Heildon).

25. *R.P.C.*, VIII, 175, 524, 569, 747.

26. *Ibid.*, VIII, 176, 186, 189, 190, 532-533; Calderwood, *History*, VI, 819. The earthquake was attributed to the effects of the extraordinary drought in the preceding summer and winter.

27. *R.P.C.*, IX, 89. The murderer whose name is given was John, son of Malcolm, son of Andrew MacFarlane.

28. *Ibid.*, XI, 405.

29. J. Storer Clouston, *A History of Orkney* (1932), 299-318.

30. The story of Earl Patrick's imprisonment in Dumbarton Castle is recounted in detail in Pitcairn's *Ancient Criminal Trials of Scotland*, III, 272-307.

31. *R.P.C.*, X, 200, 259.

32. Shortly after Earl Patrick was removed to Edinburgh, Middlemist received into Dumbarton Castle several persons who had been apprehended on charges of having heard mass in Glasgow from Father John Ogilvie, the Jesuit who was recently canonised (Bellesheim, *Catholic Church of Scotland*,

III, 444; Calderwood, *History*, VII, 193).

33. Calderwood, *op. cit.*, 194.

34. *R.P.C.*, XI, 208-209.

35. Fraser, *Pollok*, II, 253.

36. *R.P.C.*, 2nd ser., I, 202, 337, 372, 417.

37. *A.P.S.*, IV, 587.

38. *R.P.C.*, XI, 545, 546; Calderwood, *History*, VII, 471; Scott, *Fasti Ecclesiae Scoticanae*, II, 158; *ibid.*, V, 192.

39. *R.P.C.*, XIII, 725.

40. *R.P.C.*, 2nd ser., I, 416-418.

41. *Ibid.*, 192, 358, 378, 380.

42. *R.P.C.*, 2nd ser., II, 131, 133, 150-153, 156-158.

43. *Ibid.*, 252. In 1622, 'on suspicion and slander', William Young, servant in Dumbarton Castle, was inhibited the company of Isobel Beaton, 'in any suspicious place or manner hereafter', by the kirk session of Dumbarton parish church. Isobel Beaton, who was named in 1626 as the mother of one of Stewart of Methven's illegitimate children, had been, along with Isobel Scot, because of their evil and scandalous behaviour, inhibited in 1623 by the kirk session 'the suspicious bearing of company to any men whatsoever' (D.K.S.R., in *Dumbarton Argus* (1833), 77, 323).

44. *R.P.C.*, 2nd ser., II, 236; Pirie-Gordon, Captains and Keepers (Sir John Stewart of Methven).

45. *M.W.*, I, 32-45, 112-116.

46. Roberts and MacPhail, *op. cit.*, iii, v, ix. Thomas Fallisdaill was seven times elected provost of Dumbarton. He was of a quarrelsome nature: in November, 1627, he was, by order of the provost and bailies, placed in ward along with William Colquhoun, a former bailie, because of evil words having passed between them and the likelihood of further trouble, and in November, 1629, he was fined £5 for striking William Mackie, a fellow councillor, in church.

47. *M.W.*, *passim*.

48. *Ibid.*

49. *R.P.C.*, 2nd ser., II, 133.

50. *Mar and Kellie MSS* (H.M.C.), II, 244.

51. Charles Rogers, *The Earl of Stirling's Register of Royal Letters* (1885), I, 334.

52. *M.W.*, II, *passim*. Fallisdaill, overseer in 1617, 1618 and later in 1633, was not available for the castle work as he was engaged in a similar duty at the town's water-work on the river Leven (Irving, *D.B.R.*, 31).

53. *M.W.* II, *passim*. The leading mason in 1618, Matthew Fulton, who had also worked at Edinburgh Castle in 1616, was paid £4. 6s. 8d. a week, and the other masons, three of whom were Fultons, only £3 a week. Matthew, William and Allan Fulton were paid £51. 19s. in 1628 for hewing and building the new

mercat cross in Dumbarton and 'mending the brig' at the east end of the town (Roberts and MacPhail, *op. cit.*, 56).

54. *M.W.*, II, *passim*.

55. *R.P.C.*, 2nd ser., II, 145; Fraser, *Pollok*, II, 252-253.

56. S. R. Gardiner, *Hamilton Papers* (1880), 17.

57. D. Stevenson, *The Scottish Revolution*, 1637-44 (1972), 140-141.

58. Irving, *D.B.R.*, 56, 57.

59. Spalding, *Memorialls*, I, 110-111; Balfour, *Annals*, I, 322; Breadalbane Muniments, S.R.O., GD112/39.

60. Gardiner, *op. cit.*, 68.

61. Roberts and MacPhail, *op. cit.*, 107; Argyll MSS (copy) in Strathclyde Regional Archives, TD40/2; Irving, *D.B.R.*, 60.

62. *C.S.P. Dom.*, *Charles I, 1639-40*, 504-505; *ibid.*, *1640*, 198, 362; *ibid.*, *1640-41*, 118; Argyll MSS *ut supra*, TD 40/20.

63. The poem is printed in Irving, *History*, 590-592.

64. Irving, *D.B.R.*, 61; Roberts and MacPhail, *op. cit.*, 117. The magistrates entertained Major Maxwell and his fellow officers on September 15th, 1640, when 5 pints of wine, 10 ounces of sugar and some pears were consumed by the fifteen persons present (*ibid.*, 118).

65. *A.P.S.*, V, 433; *ibid.*, VI, 84-85.

66. According to Sempill's inventory, dated May 31st, 1644, there was in the Wallace Tower 'an auld twa handed sward without a scabbard', the weapon later (but probably wrongly) identified as Wallace's sword (Irving, *History*, 195-196).

67. Roberts and MacPhail, *op. cit.*, 140, 141, 145; *Transactions of the Gaelic Society of Inverness*, XLVIII (1976), 226.

68. Dumbarton Presbytery Records, S.R.O., October 14th, 1645.

69. *Erskine Papers* (H.M.C.), 519; Fraser, *Lennox*, I, 116-117.

70. Dennistoun MSS, N.L.S., I, 483, 485; *A.P.S.*, VI, 508; Edmonstone Papers in *Various Collections* (H.M.C.), V, 176. Provost Dick of Edinburgh ruined himself and his family by his war contributions, amounting to £500,000, most of which was never repaid (Donaldson, *op. cit.*, 323).

71. C. H. Firth, *Scotland and the Commonwealth* (1895), 24.

72. Erskine Murray Papers, N.L.S., 5070; Dennistoun MSS., N.L.S., I, 487.

73. Roberts and MacPhail, *op. cit.*, 175, 180, 184.

74. *C.S.P. Dom.*, *1651-52*, 6, 82; J. Nicoll, *Diary of Public Transactions, 1650-67* (1836), 71, 73, 79.

75. Erskine Murray Papers, N.L.S., 5693; *C.S.P. Dom.*, *1651-52*, 178. There were in Dumbarton Castle in 1652 1 demi-cannon of eight, 2 demi-cannons of seven, 2 demi-culverins, 4 sackers and 1 minion, while in 1708 there were 12 cannon, all brass — 1 demi-culverin (bore, $4\frac{1}{2}$ ins; length, 10 ft.), 4 sackers (bore, $3\frac{3}{4}$ ins; lengths from 8 ft. $6\frac{1}{4}$ ins. to 10 ft.), 6 minions (bore, 3 ins; lengths from 8 ft. 3 ins. to 9 ft. 4 ins.), 1 falconet (bore, 2 ins; length, 7 ft.)

(Account of Ordnance and Stores at Dumbarton, 1708, House of Lords Record Office).

76. Donaldson, *op. cit.*, 343-344; C. S. Terry, *Cromwellian Union* (1902), 50, 154; Firth, *op. cit.*, 39.

77. Firth, *op. cit.*, 240, 242, 276; Nicoll, *op. cit.*, 112-114.

78. 'Account of Glencairn's Expedition' by John Graham of Duchray in *Miscellanea Scotica,* IV, 28-79; *C.S.P. Dom., 1654,* 339; *ibid., 1655,* 270.

79. Firth, *op. cit.*, 367-369.

80. Roberts and MacPhail, *op. cit.*, 212, 223, 263; Irving, *D.B.R.*, 77; D.T.C.M., Aug. 25th, 1660.

81. *Ibid.*, April 23rd, 1661; Nicoll, *op. cit.*, 323.

82. Fraser, *Grant*, III, 467.

83. D. Crawford, ed., *Lauder of Fountainhall's Journal*, 184.

84. D.K.S.R., S.R.O., 1667, 1669, *passim;* Dumbarton Presbytery Records, S.R.O., 1674, 1675, *passim.* Major Grant's bequest of £333 was one of the many listed on the old Bequests Board of the parish church (Andrew Mair, *Dumbarton Castle* (1916), 33).

85. Charles Dalton, *The Scots Army, 1661-1688* (1909), 84-94.

86. *R.P.C.*, 3rd ser., II, 589.

87. *Ibid.*, 3rd ser., V, xxvi, 1-2, 101-102.

88. *Ibid.*, 3rd ser., V, 135, 154, 277, 546, 551-552.

89. *Ibid.*, 3rd ser., II, 268, 272-274; *ibid.*, 3rd ser., V, 353, 366, 510, 538.

90. Treasury Vouchers, S.R.O., E67/14/2/19.

91. *C.S.P. Dom., Charles II, 1671,* 153.

92. *R.P.C.*, 3rd ser., II, 384; *ibid.*, 3rd ser., III, 131, 385, 422, 581; *ibid.*, 3rd ser., IV, 15; A. McKerral, *Kintyre in the Seventeenth Century* (1948), 113-117.

93. *R.P.C.*, 3rd ser., IV, 286, 322, 363, 546; *ibid.*, 3rd ser., VI, 2, 8, 87; *C.S.P. Dom., Charles II, 1678,* 393. General Drummond was made an honorary burgess of Dumbarton not long after his release (D.T.C.M., March 23rd, 1676).

94. William Buchanan of Auchmar, *History of the Ancient Surname of Buchanan* (1793), 29-32.

95. Treasury Vouchers, S.R.O., E28/243/1; D.T.C.M., April 3, June 19, 1680.

96. *C.S.P. Dom., Charles II, 1680-81,* 510.

97. Dumbarton Garrison Muster Books, S.R.O., E100/39/3/1; *R.P.C.*, 3rd ser., VIII, 311; Blair Drummond Papers in *H.M.C., 10th Report*, Pt. 1, 136-137.

98. Irving, *History*, 212-213; Wodrow, *Church History*, IV, 188.

99. J. Willcock, *A Scots Earl* (1907), 387 *et seq;* D.T.C.M., June 27th, August 8th, 1685. Archibald Lamont of that ilk was made an honorary burgess of Dumbarton on June 27th, 1685, for his good services to the burgh in helping to persuade the Duke of Gordon in his camp at the Gooseholm not to let any

of his soldiers have free quarters in the town.

100. *R.P.C.*, 3rd ser., XIII, 219. In May, 1685, James Smith, overseer of H.M. Works, was instructed to order girnels to be erected at Stirling, Dumbarton and Edinburgh Castles, large enough to store 15,000, 5,000 and 5,000 bolls respectively (*Laing MSS* (H.M.C.), I, 441).

101. Balfour-Melville, *op. cit.*, I, 51. The two frigates saw service in the Irish Sea, capturing a number of Irish merchant ships, but were themselves captured by three French men-o'-war, both captains being killed. The frigates had originally belonged to Provost Gibson of Glasgow (*ibid.*, I, 60, 166, 168, 180).

102. Irving, *D.B.R.*, 88.

103. *R.P.C.*, 3rd ser., XIII, 491, 563; *A.P.S.*, IX, App. 30a.

104. *Leven and Melville Papers* (1843), I, 353-354.

105. Hamilton of Barns and Cochno Papers in *H.M.C., 8th Report*, 161 et seq; *Downshire MSS* (H.M.C.), I, part 1, 222; Balfour-Melville, *op. cit.*, II, 69; D.T.C.M., April 6, Dec. 6, 1689; July 4, 1690.

106. Hamilton of Cochno Papers, Bundle XXIV; R.P.C., S.R.O., PC1/50, April 4, April 5, May 7, July 2, 1696.

107. *R.P.C.*, 3rd ser., XV, 311; Irving, *D.B.R.*, 100.

108. D.K.S.R., S.R.O., March 29, April 2, April 9, 1694; March 7, June 20, July 4, 1695; Dumbarton Burgh Court Book, 1690-1743 (D.P.L.), March 8, 1695; R.P.C., S.R.O., PC1/50, Feb. 18, 1695.

109. Dumbarton Garrison Muster Books, S.R.O., E 100/39/3. The name of the Duke of Lennox remained on the muster roll until 1690, when it was replaced by that of Lord Neil Campbell; but the castle revenues during this period were paid to the Dowager Duchess of Lennox (*C.S.P. Dom., Charles II, 1673-75*, 127-128; *ibid., 1680-81*, 354). There is extant an earlier muster roll for Dumbarton Castle, dated February 12th, 1650, in the Erskine Murray Papers, N.L.S., 5071.

110. *Mar and Kellie MSS* (H.M.C.), I, 214; *C.S.P. Dom., Charles II, 1683-84*, 114.

111. *R.P.C.*, 3rd ser., XV, 255, 275-276, 306; Dumbarton Garrison Muster Books, S.R.O., E100/39/3/16.

112. *R.P.C.*, S.R.O. PC1/47, May 19, 1692, Dec. 22, 1692. Major Hugh Bontine of Kilbride, who had been muster-master of the army in 1689, had only a remote connection, if any, with the Bontines of Ardoch near Dumbarton, his family having lived for generations at Kilwinning. He himself later sat in Parliament as commissioner for Ayrshire (*C.S.P. Dom., William and Mary, 1690-95*, 431; *R.M.S., 1660-68*, 396; *A.P.S.*, X, *passim*).

113. Dumbarton Garrison Muster Books, S.R.O., E100/39/3/22.

114. Treasury Vouchers, S.R.O., E28/425/1/7. Payment of pension was not guaranteed. In 1690, George Scot, 'ane distressed old soldier, decrepit and infirm', aged sixty-nine, petitioned the Privy Council for 'invalid money', as he

had served many years as a sentinel in the castles of Edinburgh and and Dumbarton and had paid 'invalid money' and was 'superannuat' (senile). The council granted his petition to be enrolled as an invalid, and Dr. Adam Frier, 'intendant of the invalids', was to give him a share of the invalid money at the next distribution (*R.P.C.*, 3rd ser., XV, 228).

115. Treasury Vouchers, S.R.O., E28/425/1; Dumbarton Garrison Muster Books, S.R.O., E100/39/3/12.

116. According to Buchanan of Auchmar, the Arrolls were of such a perverse and insolent disposition that anyone hearing a report of a quarrel or fight in the district ordinarily asked, 'Who beside the Arrolls?' (Wm. Buchanan of Auchmar, *op. cit.*, 109).

117. Dumbarton Garrison Muster Books, S.R.O., E100/29/3/46.

118. D.K.S.R., S.R.O., April 1, April 15, May 13, 1703; Sept. 26, Oct. 30, 1700. The savin was a variety of juniper and, according to witnesses, was boiled before being administered. The gardeners of Erskine and Kirkmichael (now Strathleven) estates had also been approached by the girl's mother and were summoned to attend before the kirk session.

119. *Papers of the Rev. John Anderson* (1914), 90, 99; D.K.S.R., S.R.O., Nov. 16, 1700; Sept. 7, 1701.

120. R.P.C., S.R.O., PC1/49, June 28, 1693; PC1/50, Feb. 28, 1695, March 11, 1696; Professor John Anderson, Dumbarton Castle Diary, 1782 (Strathclyde University Library). Hamilton of Orbiston, whose seat was at Erskine, owned lands in Kilpatrick parish and was one of several Lennox lairds who had a meeting 'hard by Dumbarton' in May, 1692 and were said to have sent their horses to 'some place in the Highlands' and to have had 'designs on the Castle of Dumbarton' (R.P.C., S.R.O., PC1/48, May 26, 1692).

121. P. Hume Brown, *Early Travellers in Scotland* (1891), 21; Dennistoun MSS, N.L.S., I, 471. Even in the nineteenth century an exceptional high tide could submerge Dumbarton quay on the Leven by as much as five feet (Roberts and MacPhail, *op. cit.*, iii).

122. *R.P.C.*, III, 319-320; *E.R.*, XX, XXI, XXII, *passim; ibid.*, 83.

123. Fraser, *Pollok*, II, 252-253.

124. Irving, *History*, 195-196.

125. Treasury Vouchers, S.R.O., E28/243/1, 2; J. Slezer, Plan of Dumbarton Castle, 1696, P.R.O., MP F.244.

126. J. R. N. Macphail, *Fraser Papers* (1924), 268-270; J. Slezer, Plan of Dumbarton Castle, 1696, P.R.O., MP F.244. Up until about 1874, when a supply of water was laid on from the town of Dumbarton, the castle garrison depended on pumping water up from the well (the 'loch' of the seventeenth-century accounts and plan) between the peaks, which according to Pennant was fourteen feet deep. There was another well a short distance above and to the right of the path leading from the present Duke of Argyll's Battery to the summit of the eastern peak, but it is said to have dried up when the dock of the

Leven shipyard was constructed at the base of the rock in 1884 (Mair, *Dumbarton Castle*, 42, 67, 71).

127. Montgomerie's 'Trew Account' in Tweeddale Papers was published by C. Cleland Harvey in *Lennox Herald*, Sept. 26th, 1914. In addition to Slezer's plan of 1696 in the Public Record Office, there is a similar one, dated 1708, of which a copy is kept in the Scottish Record Office (RHP 6523/2). Captain John Abraham Slezer, either a German or a Dutchman, was H.M. Engineer for Scotland in 1675, when he reported on mistakes made in cutting timber for the gun carriages at Dumbarton Castle (Treasury Vouchers, S.R.O., E67/14/2/17). He was sent to the Low Countries in 1681 to enlist gunners. A clever engraver on copper, he brought out his celebrated *Theatrum Scotiae* in 1693. Reprinted in 1874, it has proved of considerable value to historians. As he was several times in Dumbarton Castle, his three views of the castle are of special interest — one from the south, one from the north-west and one from Kilpatrick in the east.

128. Buttock's or Buttocks Bower was the name applied facetiously to the area on the west side of the castle rock, where there were no buildings. In modern times, the more polite 'Bower Battery' referred only to the end of the western rampart. Bellhouse Battery was modified about 1790 and re-named Duke of Argyll's Battery (I. MacIvor, *Dumbarton Castle* (1958), 13).

129. According to the inventory of 1580, there was a girnel in the same room, but the girnel was probably that which was installed by order of the Treasury in 1685, referred to in note 100 above.

Chapter 5

MODERN TIMES

1. P. Hume Brown, *Letters Relating to Scotland in the Reign of Queen Anne* (1915), 149-150.

2. *Ibid.*, 23; *Mar and Kellie MSS* (H.M.C.), I, 238-239; W. Ferguson, *Scotland, 1689 to the Present* (1968), 45-46.

3. *Leven and Melville Papers* (1843), 353-354; R.P.C., S.R.O., PC1/53, July 13, July 16, Sept. 20, 1703; March 7, July 11, 1706; March 8, 1707. The Scottish navy in the reign of Queen Anne before the Union of Parliaments comprised only the *Dumbarton Castle*, the *Royal Mary* and the *Royal William*. After the Union, the *Dumbarton Castle* was placed on the establishment of the Royal Navy. It was captured on April 26, 1708 near Waterford by a French privateer, Captain Matthew Campbell being taken prisoner along with 92 men and boys (J. Grant, *The Old Scots Navy from 1689 to 1707* (1914), 376, 383).

4. *A.P.S.*, III, 352; J. Grant, *Memorials of the Castle of Edinburgh* (1862), 155. A similar statement appears in the Rev. David Ure's *General View of the*

Agriculture of the County of Dumbarton (1794), 9; Robert Belsches' *General View of the Agriculture of the County of Stirling* (1796); and Sir John Sinclair's *Statistical Account of Scotland*, I, 100.

5. *House of Lords MSS*, New Series, VIII (H.M.C.), 122, 136.

6. *Ibid.*, xiv; *An Account of the late Scotch Invasion* (1709), 19, 27.

7. Reports on Castles of Edinburgh, Stirling, Fort William and Dumbarton, 1709-1710, P.R.O., WO 55/319/111, 112.

8. Campbell of Succoth Papers, Strathclyde Regional Archives, TD 219/3/17, 23, 28; Instructions to Duke of Argyll for reducing the garrisons of North Britain, July 30, 1712, P.R.O., WO 26/14; War Office Report Book, 1711-1714, P.R.O., WO 30/89.

9. *Scots Peerage*, I, 372; Campbell of Succoth Papers, TD 219/3/12. Campbell's grandfather had been provost of Dumbarton during the Cromwellian occupation. The estate of Succoth was a small one in the parish of Cardross near Dumbarton, acquired by Robert Campbell, a Dumbarton merchant, in 1616; but in 1687 the estate of Garscube near Glasgow was purchased from Sir James Colquhoun of Luss by Captain Archibald Campbell, 4th of Succoth. Although Garscube became the principal residence, the family has been known as Campbell of Succoth down to modern times.

10. Campbell of Succoth Papers, TD 219/3, 12, 20.

11. *Stuart Papers* (H.M.C.), I, 426, 453; *ibid.*, IV, 84, 85.

12. W. Ferguson, *op. cit.*, 65 (n); D.T.C.M., Dec. 5, 1730.

13. A detailed account of the Loch Lomond expedition of 1715 is to be found in Irving, *History*, 231-240.

14. Accompt of money payd for work, furniture, fireing and other necessarys for the detachment of the Honble. Brigadeer Wightman's regmt. now lying at Innersnait, which went thither upon the 19 of July, 1717 (State Papers, George I, P.R.O., SP 54/13).

15. Troops for opposing Raids of Highlanders in Scotland, 1721, P.R.O., WO 6/23.

16. J. F. S. Gordon, *Glasghu Facies* (1886), II, 958-975; Report on the Highlands, 1725, Wade Papers, B.M., Add. 23671, King's 102. William Ferguson, by his reference to 'ineffective intervention by part of the garrison of Dumbarton' (*op. cit.*, 142), seems to have been unaware of the dispatch of two companies from Edinburgh.

17. Report of 18th October, 1727, Wade Papers, B.M., Add. 23671, King's 103; Fraser, *Lennox*, I, 140. Not all the soldiers in Dumbarton Castle were so useless as Turnbull made out. In 1742, there was published by R. Smith, at the Gilt Bible, opposite to Gibson's Land, Saltmarket, Glasgow, a pamphlet entitled 'Satan's Ape Detected or Some Observations on a Scandalous Pamphlet against Mr. Whitefield and the Clergy of his Church, to disparage the work .at Cambuslang, and written by Mr. Adam Gib, minister of the Associate Congregation at Edinburgh'. The author of 'Satan's Ape Detected'

was Andrew Waddell, soldier in Dumbarton Castle (Dr. David Murray, Notebook VI, 148, in Templeton Library, Helensburgh).

18. I. MacIvor, *Dumbarton Castle* (1958), 9, 10; A. Mair, *Dumbarton Castle* (1916), 39.

19. Campbell of Mamore Papers, N.L.S., MS 3733/nos. 2, 26. General Campbell's spelling of the lieutenant-governor's name as 'Trumble' represents a pronunciation still heard in rural Scotland.

20. *Ibid.*, nos. 67, 74, 79; James Fergusson, *Argyll in the Forty-five* (1951), 139, 140, 167. Colonel John Campbell was elected M.P. for the Glasgow district of burghs, which comprised Glasgow, Dumbarton, Renfrew and Rutherglen, in 1744, while his father had been M.P. for Dumbartonshire since 1727. General Campbell became 4th Duke of Argyll in 1761 and his son, the colonel of 1745, succeeded as 5th Duke in 1770 (*Scots Peerage*, I, 383-386).

21. Fraser, *Colquhoun*, I, 353-356.

22. Fergusson, *op. cit.*, 43; Fraser, *Lennox*, I, 142-143; Campbell of Stonefield Papers, S.R.O., GD14/57.

23. Sir Bruce Gordon Seton, *Prisoners of the '45* (1929), II, III, *passim*; Noble of Ardmore Papers, Bundle No. 36, App. II, no. 14.

24. Fraser, *Colquhoun*, I, 352. The authors of *Prisoners of the '45* give the correct date, March 9, 1746, for MacLachlan's capture, but state that he escaped on February 2, five weeks earlier.

25. Fraser, *Lennox*, I, 131-137; Campbell of Mamore Papers, N.L.S., 3733/326, 388; *Letters and Papers (Scotland)*, P.R.O., SP 54/30. A letter to General Campbell from Tullibardine, who signs himself 'Atholl' (a title he had forfeited for his part in the '15 rebellion, his brother James being known in 1745 as the Duke of Atholl), is reproduced in this volume. In it he expresses his satisfaction with the treatment he is receiving in Dumbarton Castle from the governor, Captain Turnbull and 'everybody else'. The claim that Tullibardine was 'basely betrayed' by Buchanan (*Lyon in Mourning*, I, 281) is not borne out by the evidence of the correspondence of the parties concerned. Michele Vezzosi, in his account of the rebellion in *Young Juba* (1748), briefly states that Tullibardine 'surrendered himself' to Buchanan. But Buchanan's neighbours held it against him, and his premature death and the ill fortunes that befell his family thereafter were seen as the consequence of his treatment of Tullibardine. Full details of the Buchanan troubles are to be found in Mrs. Thomson's *Memoirs of the Jacobites* (1845).

26. J. Guthrie Smith, *Strathblane* (1886), 135-139.

27. Fraser, *Lennox*, I, 138; Noble of Ardmore Papers, Bundle 36, App. II, no. 14.

28. Fraser, *op. cit.*, I, 139-141; J. Guthrie Smith, *op. cit.*, 138.

29. *Prisoners of the '45*, *passim*.

30. Fraser, *op. cit.*, 141-143.

31. H. Pirie-Gordon, Captains and Keepers of Dumbarton Castle (Archi-

bald Montgomerie, Earl of Eglinton).

32. J. Boswell, *Tour to the Hebrides* (ed. 1930), 363; Irving, *History,* 262 (note).

33. Professor John Anderson, Dumbarton Castle Diary, 1782 (MS), Strathclyde University Library.

34. T. Newte, *Prospects and Observations on a Tour of England and Scotland* (1789), 78; T. Richardson, *Guide to Loch Lomond,* etc. (2nd ed., 1799), 39; Dorothy Wordsworth, *Recollections of a Tour Made in Scotland, A.D. 1803* (ed., 1874), 58. The *Glasgow Courier* of September 29, 1804, records the death in the previous week of the black sea-trout kept in a lead cistern at Dumbarton Castle.

35. Papers relating to Defence, 1796-1812, P.R.O., WO 30/66, 315.

36. Richard Cannon, *Historical Records of the 71st Regiment (Highlanders)* (1850), 44; *Regimental Records of the 1st Battalion Highland Light Infantry* (1906), 36; L. B. Oatts, *Proud Heritage* (1952), 51, 66; L. B. Oatts, *The Highland Light Infantry* (1969), 13, 15, 16. The 2nd battalion of the 71st Regiment of Foot was largely recruited from Glasgow and district, and by order of the War Office in June, 1808, was given the designation of the Glasgow Highland Regiment, afterwards changed to the Glasgow Highland Light Infantry (A. F. Galbraith, *Dumbartonshire Military Forces, 1793-1816* (1940), 15).

37. Report as to further need of Fortresses in Scotland, 1811, P.R.O., HO 50/420.

38. Muster Rolls and Pay Lists, Dumbarton Castle, P.R.O., WO 10/1005; A. Mair, *Dumbarton Castle* (1916), 45-47. One of the officers stationed at the castle in 1813, Captain James Laskey, of the 21st Militia Regiment, produced a catalogue of the natural history and medical specimens in the Hunterian Museum of Glasgow University (Dr. David Murray, Notebook V, 242, Templeton Library, Helensburgh).

39. H. Pirie-Gordon, *op. cit.,* (The Last Important Prisoner). The tale of the French general's banquet did not appear in print until the second edition of Donald MacLeod's *Castle and Town of Dumbarton* in 1881.

40. H. Pirie-Gordon, *op. cit.* (Major-General Vincent, Lord Lynedoch); Mair, *op. cit.,* 46-47.

41. J. Glen, *History of the Town and Castle of Dumbarton* (1847), 109-111; I. M. M. MacPhail, *Short History of Dumbartonshire* (1962), 77-78; *Edinburgh Weekly Journal,* April 12, 1820; *Glasgow Courier,* April 8, 1820.

42. The *Edinburgh and Western Almanac* listed annually the names of the governor, lieutenant-governor, barrack-master, storekeeper and master gunner. According to the inscription on his tombstone, John Alexander, barrack-master from 1814 to 1833, held the rank of Major and was proprietor of Knoxland House, half a mile distant from the castle (Mair, *op. cit.,* 44).

43. Mair, *op. cit.,* 48-49; Robert MacFarlan, *Town and Castle of Dumbarton* (1909), 27; *Lennox Herald,* Nov. 16, 1858.

44. Irving, *History*, 290-292; *Scots Pictorial*, Oct. 24, 1908.

45. Mair, *op. cit.*, 47, 50; *Lennox Herald*, March 1, 1924; information about Corporal (later Sergeant) Steele from his daughter, Mrs. S. Moore, Dumbarton. Master Gunner Irwin and Corporal Samuel Fee both had families of ten, all resident in the castle in 1881 (Census Returns, Dumbarton, 1881).

46. C. Rogers, *Book of Wallace* (1889), I, 297-303; John Irving, *History of Dumbartonshire* (1917-1924), I, 109-114. John Irving, whose history of the county was more or less a new edition of his father's history of 1860, dealt effectively with Dr. Roger's arguments in favour of assigning the Wallace sword to Wallace.

47. *Lennox Herald*, July 14, 21, 28, 1894. Alphaeus Cleophas Morton was a London architect, educated in Canada, and with strong Scottish sympathies. He lost his seat at Peterborough the year after his campaign for Dumbarton Castle but he returned to the House of Commons in 1906 as M.P. for Sutherland, holding the seat until 1918, when he was knighted. (Alphaeus was father of the apostle James (the Less), and Cleophas was one of the two disciples who met Jesus on the road to Emmaus.)

48. Correspondence between War Office and Office of Woods, *re* Dumbarton Castle, 1901, P.R.O., WO 32/7202-7205; *Lennox Herald*, Feb. 16, March 16, 1901. Of the four other Scottish fortresses of the seventeenth century, Edinburgh and Stirling Castles were in 1901 fully maintained with garrisons of regular soldiers, the Bass had its fortifications dismantled in 1701, following the Jacobite occupation of 1691-94, and Blackness Castle, after a period with a one-man garrison like Dumbarton Castle, was in 1870-74 transformed into the central ammunition depot of Scotland.

49. Transfer to Ministry of Works of Crown Property, 1908-1910, S.R.O., MW1/1229; Sub-Committee on Dumbarton Castle, 1908-1910, D. McIntosh, Dumbarton, Papers, S.R.O., GD260/6/14.

50. John Irving, *History of Dumbartonshire* (1917-1924), 94; *Lennox Herald*, July 11, 1914.

51. John Irving, *Dumbarton Castle Fête — Book of the Fête* (1916), 47; *Lennox Herald*, Nov. 13, 1915.

52. *Lennox Herald*, June 10, 1916.

53. Occupation of Dumbarton Castle by Territorial Army, 1920-40, S.R.O., MW 1/1041.

54. *Lennox Herald*, July 17, 1937; April 18, 1953.

55. Dumbarton Castle Visitors' Book.

56. Report on Bombs dropped on Castle Rock, Dumbarton, May 6, 1941, S.R.O., MW/1/1200; Dumbarton Castle Visitors' Book; information from Mrs. S. Moore, Dumbarton.

Bibliography

ABBREVIATIONS

A.D.C.P. — *Acts of the Lords of Council in Public Affairs, 1501-1554*
A.P.S. — *Acts of the Parliaments of Scotland*
B.M. — British Museum (now British Library)
Cal. Docs. Scot. — *Calendar of Documents relating to Scotland*, ed. J. Bain
C.S.P. Dom. — *Calendar of State Papers, Domestic*
C.S.P. Scot. — *Calendar of State Papers relating to Scotland*
D.B.R. — *Dumbarton Burgh Records*, ed. Joseph Irving
D.K.S.R. — Dumbarton Parish Church Kirk Session Records
D.P.L. — Dumbarton Public Library
D.T.C.M. — Dumbarton Town Council Minutes
E.R. — *Exchequer Rolls of Scotland*
H.M.C. — Historical Manuscripts Commission
L. and P., Henry VIII — *Letters and Papers, Henry VIII*
M.W. — *Accounts of Masters of Works*
N.L.S. — National Library of Scotland
P.R.O. — Public Record Office
R.M.S. — *Registrum Magni Sigilli Regum Scotorum*
R.P.C. — *Register of the Privy Council of Scotland*
R.S.S. — *Registrum Secreti Sigilli Regum Scotorum*
S.H.R. — *Scottish Historical Review*
S.H.S. — Scottish History Society
S.R.O. — Scottish Record Office
T.A. — *Accounts of the Lord High Treasurers of Scotland*
(For shortened titles, see the article, 'Abbreviated Titles', *S.H.R.*, 54, 1963.)

191

UNPUBLISHED SOURCES

Scottish Record Office
Accounts of Masters of Works
Breadalbane Muniments
Campbell of Stonefield Papers
Cunninghame Graham Muniments
Dumbarton Parish Kirk Session Records
Dumbarton Presbytery Records
Glencairn Muniments
D. McIntosh (Dumbarton) Papers
Ministry of Public Building and Works Files
Muster Rolls, Dumbarton Garrison
Register of the Privy Council of Scotland
Treasury Vouchers

National Library of Scotland
Balcarres Papers
Campbell of Mamore Papers
Dennistoun MSS
Erskine Papers
Erskine Murray Papers
Tweeddale Papers
Wodrow Papers

Public Record Office
Home Office Records (Military)
State Papers (Scotland)
War Office Papers

House of Lords Record Office
Account of Ordnance and Stores at Dumbarton, 1708

British Museum
Wade Papers

Strathclyde Regional Archives
Argyll MSS (copies)
Campbell of Succoth Papers

Strathclyde University Library
Professor John Anderson, Dumbarton Castle Diary

Dumbarton Public Library
Dumbarton Burgh Charters
Dumbarton Court Book
Dumbarton Register of Ship Entries, 1595-1658
Dumbarton Town Council Minutes

Templeton Library, Helensburgh
Dr David Murray (Cardross), Notebooks

Mackenzie, Roberton & Co., Glasgow
Hamilton of Cochno Papers

Sir Marc Noble, Knockholt, Kent
Noble of Ardmore Papers

PUBLISHED SOURCES
Public Records
Accounts of the Lord High Treasurers of Scotland, 1473-1580, 13 vols. (1877-1977)
Accounts of the Masters of Works, 2 vols. (1957, 1976)
Acts of the Lords of Council in Civil Causes, 1487-1501, 2 vols. (1839, 1918)
Acts of the Lords of Council in Public Affairs, 1501-54 (1932)
Acts of the Parliaments of Scotland, 12 vols. (1814-75)
Calendar of Documents relating to Scotland, 1108-1509, ed. J. Bain, 4 vols. (1881-88).
Calendar of Scottish Papers, 1547-1603, 13 vols. (1898-1969)
Calendar of State Papers relating to Scotland, 1509-89, ed. M. J. Thorpe (1858)
Calendar of State Papers, Domestic Series, 1639-1703, 30 vols. (1873-1924)
Exchequer Rolls of Scotland, 1264-1600, 23 vols. (1878-1908)
Letters and Papers, Foreign and Domestic, Henry VIII, vols. 3-21 (1867-1908)
Regesta Regum Scotorum, 2 vols. (1968, 1971)
Register of the Privy Council of Scotland, 1545-1691, 36 vols. (1877-1970)
Registrum Magni Sigilli Regum Scotorum, 1306-1618, 11 vols. (1882-1914)
Registrum Secreti Sigilli Regum Scotorum, 1488-1577, 7 vols. (1913-66)
Rotuli Scotiae, 2 vols. (1814, 1819)

Historical Manuscripts Commission Publications
Argyll Papers (4th Report, 1876)
Blair Drummond Papers (10th Report, 1885)
Cecil MSS, I (1883), II(1888), III(1889), XIII(1915), XXII(1971)
Downshire MSS, I, Part 1 (1926)
Edmonstone Papers in *Various Collections*, V (1909)
Erskine Papers (4th Report, 1876)
Hamilton Papers (1890, 1892)
Hamilton MSS (1932)
Hamilton of Barns and Cochno MSS (8th Report, 1881)
Hastings MSS, II (1930)
House of Lords MSS, New Series, VIII (1966)

Laing MSS (1914, 1925)
Mar and Kellie MSS (1904, 1930)
Ormonde MSS: II (1899)
Pepys MSS (1911)
Portland MSS, X (1931)
Stuart Papers, IV (1910)
Traquair House MSS (9th Report, 1884)

Scottish History Society Publications
Balfour-Melville, E. W. M., *Proceedings of the Estates in Scotland, 1689-91*
    (1954, 1955)
Brown, P. Hume, *Letters relating to Scotland in the Reign of Queen Anne*
    (1915)
Cameron, Annie I., *Scottish Correspondence of Mary of Lorraine* (1927)
Cameron, Annie I. and Rait, R. S., *Warrender Papers* (1931, 1932)
Clark, J. T., *Macfarlane's Genealogical Collections* (1900)
Crawford, D., *Journal of Lauder of Fountainhall, 1665-76* (1900)
Dickinson, W. Croft, *Sheriff Court Book of Fife, 1513-23* (1928)
Dickinson, G., *Two Missions of Jacques de la Brosse, 1543 and 1560* (1942)
Dickson, W. K., *Warrender Letters, 1715* (1935)
Firth, C. H., *Scotland and the Commonwealth* (1895)
Firth, C. H., *Scotland and the Protectorate* (1899)
Fotheringham, J. G., *Montereul Correspondence, 1645-48* (1898)
MacKay, Wm., *Chronicles of the Frasers* (1905)
Macphail, J. R. N., *Fraser Papers* (1924)
Macphail, J. R. N., *Highland Papers,* II (1920)
Miscellany, IX (1958)
Mitchell, Sir Arthur, *Macfarlane's Geographical Collections* (1907)
Mitchell, A. F. and Christie, J., *General Assembly Records, 1648-49* (1896)
Paton, Henry, *The Lyon in Mourning* (1895-96)
Paul, G. M. and others, *Wariston's Diary and Other Papers* (1896)
Pollen, J. H., *Queen Mary's Letter to the Duke of Guise, 1562* (1904)
Seton, Sir Bruce and Arnot, J. G., *Prisoners of the '45* (1928-29)
Terry, C. S., *The Cromwellian Union, 1651-52* (1902)
Wood, Marguerite, *Balcarres Papers* (1925)

Other Published Sources
Anderson, A. O., *Early Sources of Scottish History* (1922)
Anderson, A. O., *Scottish Annals from English Chronicles* (1908)
Anderson, A. W., *Papers of Rev. John Anderson* (1914)
Brown, P. Hume, *Early Descriptions of Scotland* (1893)
Brown, P. Hume, *Early Travellers in Scotland* (1890)
Dennistoun, James, *Cartularium de Levenax* (1833)
Dickinson, W. Croft, Donaldson, Gordon and Milne, Isabel A., *A Source*

Book of Scottish History (1958)

Fraser, Sir William, *Colquhoun Cartulary* (1873)

Gardiner, S. R., *Hamilton Papers* (1880)

Innes, Cosmo, *Registrum Monasterii de Passelet* (1832)

Irving, Joseph, *Dumbarton Burgh Records* (1860)

Melville, W. L., *Leven and Melville Papers* (1843)

Pitcairn, R., *Criminal Trials in Scotland, 1488-1624* (1833)

Roberts, Fergus and MacPhail, I. M. M., *Dumbarton Common Good Accounts, 1614-60* (1972)

Rogers, Charles, *Estimate of the Scottish Nobility in the Reign of James VI* (1873)

Rogers, Charles, *The Earl of Stirling's Register of Royal Letters* (1885)

Skene, W. F., *Chronicles of the Picts and Scots* (1867)

Stevenson, Joseph, *Documents Illustrative of Wallace* (1841)

Stones, E. L. G., *Anglo-Scottish Relations, 1174-1329* (1970)

Wodrow, Robert, *Analecta* (1842, 1843)

Chronicles, Memoirs, etc.

Auchinleck Chronicle (1877)

Balfour, Sir James, *Annals* (1824)

Bannatyne, Richard, *Journals of the Transactions in Scotland, 1570-73* (1806)

Barbour, John, *Bruce* (1909)

Beague, Mons., *History of the Campagnes, 1548, 1549* (tr. 1707)

Birrel, Robert, *Diary, 1552-1605* (1798)

Bower, Walter, *Scotichronicon* (ed. Walter Goodall, 1759)

Buchanan, George, *History of Scotland* (tr. 1827)

Crawfurd, David, *Memoirs of the Affairs of Scotland* (1706)

Chronicon de Lanercost (1839)

Diurnal of Remarkable Occurrents, 1513-75 (1833)

Haversham, Lord, *An Account of the late Scotch Invasion* (1709)

Henry the Minstrel, *Schir William Wallace* (ed. 1889)

Fordun, John of, *Chronica Gentis Scotorum* (1871, 1872)

Gray, Thomas, *Scalacronica* (ed. 1907)

Historie and Life of James the Sext (1827)

Knox, John, *History of the Reformation in Scotland* (ed. 1949)

Lesley, John, *History of Scotland* (1830)

Liber Pluscardiensis (1877, 1880)

Lindsay, Robert, of Pitscottie, *Historie and Cronicles of Scotland* (1899-1911)

Melville, Sir James, *Memoirs* (1827)

Melville, James, *Diary* (1829)

Moysie, David, *Memoirs of the Affairs of Scotland, 1577-1603* (1830)

Nicoll, John, *Diary of Public Transactions, 1650-57* (1836)

Spalding, John, *Memorialls of the Troubles in Scotland and in England, 1624-45* (1828, 1829)

Vezzosi, Michele, *The Young Juba* (1748)
Wyntoun, Andrew of, *Orygynale Cronykil of Scotland* (1872-79)

SECONDARY WORKS

Alcock, Leslie, *Arthur's Britain* (1971)
Anderson, Marjorie, *Kings and Kingship in Early Scotland* (1973)
Ashe, Geoffrey, *Quest for Arthur's Britain* (1968)
Bain, J., *Stirlings of Craigbernard and Glorat* (1885)
Balfour-Melville, E. W. M., *James I, King of Scots* (1936)
Bannerman, John, *Studies in the History of Dalriada* (1974)
Barbé, Louis, *Margaret of Scotland* (1917)
Barrow, G. W. S., *Robert Bruce* (1965)
Bellesheim, A., *History of the Catholic Church in Scotland* (1882)
Bruce, John, *History of the Parish of West or Old Kilpatrick* (1893)
Buchanan, Wm., of Auchmar, *History of the Ancient Surname of Buchanan*
       (1793)
Bury, J. B., *St. Patrick* (1905)
Calderwood, David, *History of the Kirk of Scotland* (1843)
Chadwick, N. K., *Celtic Britain* (1963)
Chadwick, N. K., ed., *Studies in Early British History* (1954)
Chalmers, George, *Caledonia* (1810-24)
Clouston, J. S., *A History of Orkney* (1932)
Cowan, I. B. and Easson, D. E., *Medieval Religious Houses in Scotland* (1976)
Crawfurd, George, *Officers of State* (1726)
Dalton, Charles, *The Scots Army, 1661-88* (1909)
Dickinson, W. Croft, *A New History of Scotland*, I (1961)
Donaldson, Gordon, *Scotland — James V to James VII* (1963)
Duncan, A. A. M., *Scotland — The Making of the Kingdom* (1975)
Dunlop, Annie I., *Life and Times of James Kennedy* (1950)
Elder, J. K., *Highland Host of 1678* (1914)
Feachem, R. W., *A Guide to Prehistoric Scotland* (1963)
Ferguson, William, *Scotland — 1689 to the Present* (1968)
Fergusson, Sir James, *Alexander III* (1937)
Fergusson, Sir James, *Argyll in the Forty-five* (1951)
Fergusson, Sir James, *William Wallace* (1938)
Fleming, D. H., *The Reformation in Scotland* (1910)
Fraser, Antonia, *Mary, Queen of Scots* (1970)
Fraser, Sir William, *Memoirs of the Maxwells of Pollok* (1863)
Fraser, Sir William, *The Chiefs of Colquhoun* (1869)
Fraser, Sir William, *The Chiefs of Grant* (1883)
Fraser, Sir William, *The Lennox* (1884)

Fraser, Sir William, *The Red Book of Menteith* (1880)

Fraser, Sir William, *The Stirlings of Keir* (1858)

Galbraith A. F., *Dumbartonshire Military Forces, 1793-1816* (1940)

Galbraith, A. F., *The Captains, Keepers and Constables of Dumbarton Castle* (1928)

Glen, John, *History of the Town and Castle of Dumbarton* (1847)

Goodall, Walter, *Examination of the Letters said to be written by Mary, Queen of Scots, to James, Earl of Bothwell* (1754)

Gordon, J. F. S., *Glaschu Facies* (1886)

Hanson, R. P. C., *St. Patrick* (1968)

Hunter, Wm. *Biggar and the House of Fleming* (1867)

Irving, John, *History of Dumbartonshire* (1917-24)

Irving, Joseph, *History of Dumbartonshire* (1860) (abbreviated title — Irving, *History*)

Keith, Robert, *History of the Affairs of the Kirk of Scotland* (1845)

MacFarlan, Robert, *Town and Castle of Dumbarton* (1909)

MacIvor, I., *Dumbarton Castle* (1958)

MacKenzie, W. C., *The Highlands and Isles of Scotland* (1937)

MacKerral, Andrew, *Kintyre in the Seventeenth Century* (1948)

MacKie, E. W., *Scotland: An Archaeological Guide* (1975)

Mackie, R. L., *King James IV of Scotland* (1958)

MacLean, Magnus, *The Literature of the Highlands* (1925)

MacLeod, Donald, *Castle and Town of Dumbarton* (1881)

McNeill, Peter, and Nicholson, Ranald, *Historical Atlas of Scotland, c. 400 — c. 1600* (1975)

Maidment, J., *Analecta Scotica* (1834)

Mair, Andrew, *Dumbarton Castle* (1916)

Murray, Eunice, *The Church of Cardross* (1935)

Moncreiffe, Sir Iain, *The Highland Clans* (1967)

Nicholson, Ranald, *Edward III and the Scots* (1965)

Nicholson, Ranald, *Scotland — The Early Middle Ages* (1974)

Oatts, L. B., *The Highland Light Infantry* (1969)

O'Rahilly, T. F., *The Two Patricks* (1942)

Paul, Sir James Balfour, *Scots Peerage* (1904-16)

Prestwich, M., *War, Politics and Finance under Edward I* (1972)

Rivet, A. L. F., ed., *The Iron Age in Northern Britain* (1960)

Robertson, Anne S., *The Antonine Wall* (1973)

Rogers, Charles, *Book of Wallace* (1889)

Scott, Hew, *Fasti Ecclesiae Scoticanae* (1915-50)

Shelley, H. C., *Story of Dumbarton Castle* (1901)

Simpson, W. Douglas, *St Ninian and the Origins of the Christian Church in Scotland* (1940)

Skene, W. F., *Celtic Scotland* (1876)

Smith, J. Guthrie, *Strathblane* (1886)

Smyth, A. P., *Scandinavian York and Dublin*, I (1975)

Stuart, Marie, *The Scot who was a Frenchman* (1940)

Thomson, D. S., *The Gaelic Sources of Macpherson's 'Ossian'* (1952)

Waddell, P. Hately, *Ossian and the Clyde* (1875)

Watson, W. J., *History of the Celtic Place-names of Scotland* (1926)

Watt, D. E. R., *Biographical Dictionary of Scottish Graduates to A.D. 1410* (1977)

Watt, D. E. R., *Fasti Ecclesiae Scoticanae Medii Aevi* (1969)

Willock, John, *A Scots Earl* (1907)

Wodrow, Robert, *History of the Sufferings of the Church of Scotland* (1828-30)

ARTICLES

Alcock, Leslie, 'Civitas Brettonum Munitissima: Excavations at Castle Rock, Dumbarton' in *Glasgow University Gazette*, no. 79 (1975)

Alcock, Leslie, 'A multi-disciplinary chronology for Alt Clut, Castle Rock, Dumbarton' in *Proceedings of the Society of Antiquaries of Scotland*, 107 (1978)

Black, Ronald, 'Colla Ciotach' in *Transactions of the Gaelic Society of Inverness*, XLIX (1977)

Duncan, A. A. M., 'The community of the realm of Scotland and Robert Bruce: a review' in *S.H.R.*, 1966

Firth, C. H., 'Order for Edinburgh Garrison, 1650' in *S.H.R.*, 1927

Galbraith, A. F., 'Crawfurd's Escalade' in *Lennox Herald*, March 1, 1936

Grosjean, Père, 'Les Pictes apostates dans l'Épître de S. Patrice' in *Analecta Bollandiana*, lxxvi (1958)

Grosjean, Père, 'Notes d'hagiographie celtique' in *Analecta Bollandiana*, lxiii (1945)

Hannay, R. K., 'Letters of the Papal Legate in Scotland' in *S.H.R.*, 1916

Harvey, Cleland, 'Military Papers of the Time of Charles II' in *S.H.R.*, 1916

Pirie-Gordon, H. F., 'Succession in Strathclyde' in *The Armorial* (v.d.)

Sellar, W. D. H., 'The Earliest Campbells' in *Scottish Studies*, vol. 17 (1973)

Small, T. D., 'Queen Mary in Dumbarton and Argyll' in *S.H.R.*, 1927

FLEMINGS AND DENNISTOUNS

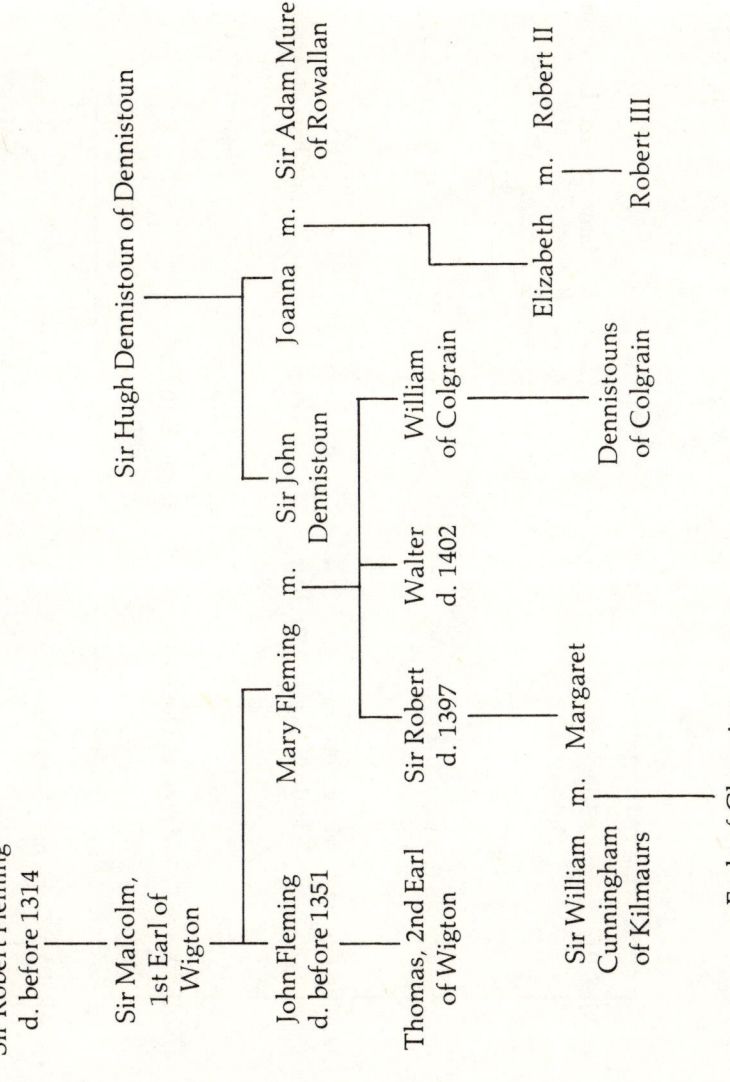

ROYAL SUCCESSION

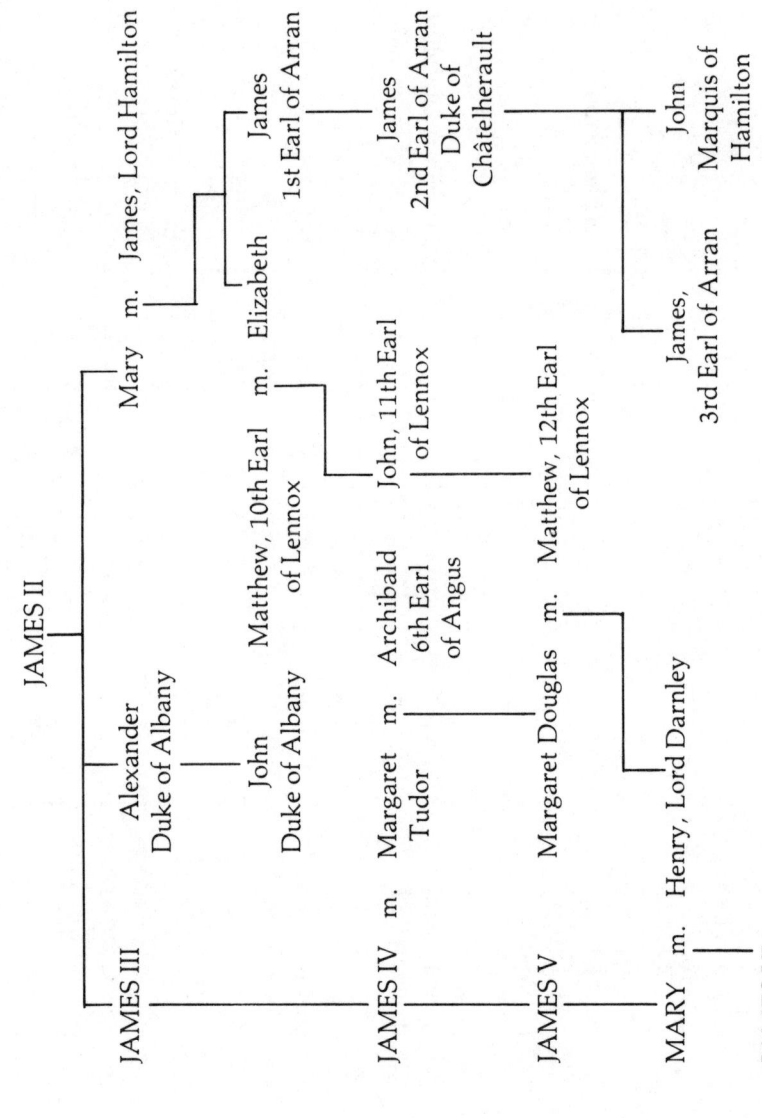

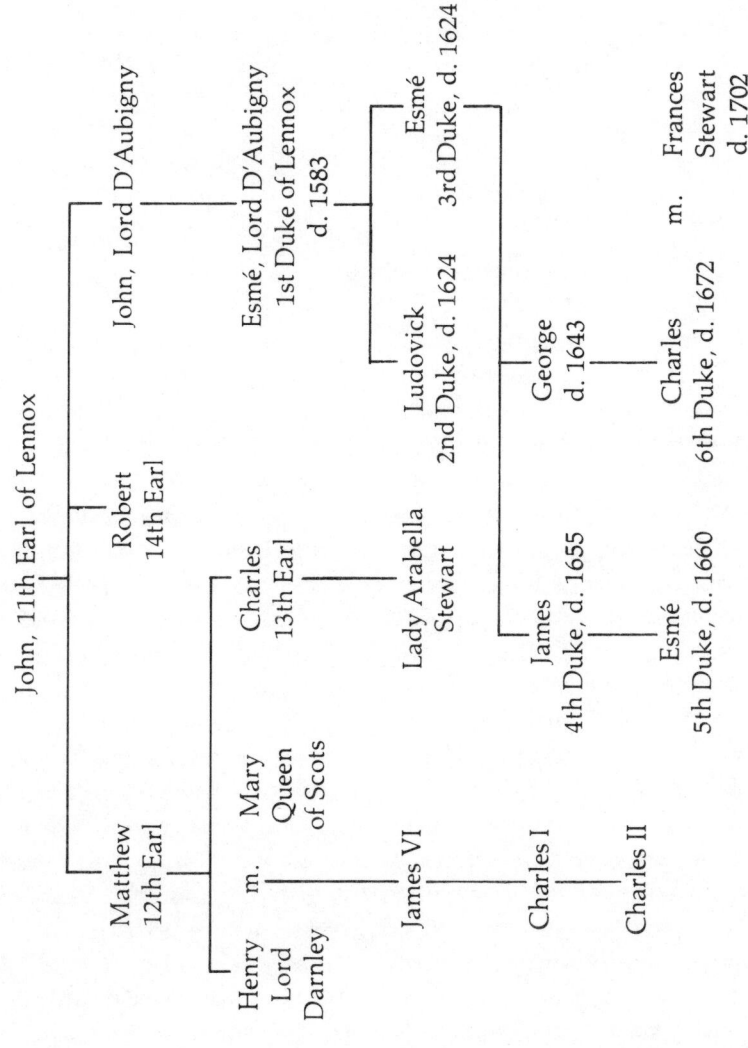

EARLS AND DUKES OF LENNOX

Appendix

Dumbarton/Dunbartonshire

The spelling of the burgh's name as 'Dumbarton' and the county's name as 'Dunbartonshire' has puzzled many people, even those who live within the county. The difference in spelling is a modern innovation but the reason for the anomaly is to be found in the history of past centuries.

The earliest recorded forms of the burgh's name, 'Dunbritan' and 'Dunbretane', represent phonetic renderings of the Gaelic *Dun Breatann*, 'fortress of the Britons'. Even before the end of the thirteenth century the first syllable appears as 'Dum', and it is 'Dumbartane' which is given as the burgh's name in the royal charter of confirmation of 1609. From the middle of the seventeenth century until 1716, the town clerks of Dumbarton however actually wrote 'Dunbritan', presumably basing their spelling on that of early charters, which were frequently produced in disputes with Glasgow over trading privileges. By the middle of the eighteenth century, 'Dumbarton' and 'Dumbartonshire' were the forms in official and everyday use, but at times there appeared variants such as 'Dunbritton' and 'Dunbarton'. Such variants tended to be preferred by the county gentry, who probably prided themselves on knowing the derivation of the name. They made no distinction however between the burgh and shire names; and indeed as there was only an inchoate county administration, the form 'Dunbarton' is found mainly in reference to the burgh or the castle. From the county gentry were appointed the commissioners of supply, whose clerks in recording their deliberations used the 'Dun' spelling, and the turnpike trustees, who set up milestones, still to be seen, with 'Dunbarton Cross' on them.

In the nineteenth century, the 'Dum' form was standard for both burgh and shire names but the commissioners of supply continued to use the 'Dun' form for both burgh and shire. The county council, which was set up by an act of parliament in 1889 for 'Dumbartonshire' and which inherited not only some of the functions of the commissioners of supply but also their spelling idiosyncrasy, at first began to spell both burgh and shire names with 'Dun'. After a few years, however, they illogically restricted the 'Dun' spelling to the county name. In the 1930s, the county clerk managed to persuade the Ordnance Survey to change the spelling of the county name on their maps to 'Dunbartonshire', and as the Ordnance Survey spelling is regarded as authoritative, the 'Dun' form for the county slowly won acceptance except in the burgh itself. It was not until the 1960s that the Post Office and newspapers in the west of Scotland adopted the new spelling. For the sheriffdom, the presbytery and the register of sasines (in which all transactions in landed property are recorded) the old 'Dum' form is still in use and it has been retained in this volume.

Index